OSPREY AIRCRAFT OF THE ACES®• 18

Hurricane Aces
1939-40

SERIES EDITOR: TONY HOLMES

OSPREY AIRCRAFT OF THE ACES • 18

Hurricane Aces 1939-40

Tony Holmes

OSPREY
AEROSPACE

Front cover
In the early evening of Saturday, 20 July 1940, eight No 32 Sqn Hurricanes were in the process of completing their standing patrol over the convoy BOSOM when they were vectored onto a large raiding force of Ju 87B-1s from II./StG 1, escorted by 50+ Bf 109Es and Bf 110Cs. The convoy was steamimg eastward towards Dover when the Luftwaffe struck, and although it initially appeared that the merchantmen were totally defenceless, the Stukas' escorts had failed to spot the mixed force of nineteen Hurricanes (from Nos 32 and 615 Sqns) and nine Spitfires (of No 610 Sqn) patrolling at altitude to the west of BOSOM. The defending fighters bounced the Germans out of the glare of the evening sun, No 32 Sqn's OC, Sqn Ldr John 'Baron' Worrall, powering his unit through the scattering ranks of the Emils into the now vulnerable Stuka formation below. In the ensuing melee, which lasted for almost an hour, No 32 Sqn downed two Ju 87Bs and crippled four more, whilst 'B' Flight commander, Flt Lt Pete Brothers, was also credited with the dest-ruction of a Bf 109E from I./JG 51.

This specially commissioned cover artwork by Iain Wyllie shows Brothers closing on two of the defending Emils, which the No 32 Sqn ace vividly remembers had yellow noses (a more widespread application of yellow identification markings on noses and wingtips came into force within the Jagdwaffe from mid-August onwards). After a series of high-G turns that saw him actually manoeuvring inside a circle of Bf 109Es whilst a solitary Emil hung grimly onto his tail hoping for an opportunity to open fire, Brothers finally managed to shake off his Messerschmitt 'shadow' and close in behind one of the German fighters which had been separated from its schwarm. Taking careful aim, Brothers fired a series of short bursts into the Emil, and the aircraft quickly caught fire and crashed into the Channel some ten miles off the Dover coast. This victory was Pete Brothers second Bf 109E kill in two days, and his fourth in total – by the end of the Battle of Britain he had increased his tally to 12

First published in Great Britain in 1998 by Osprey Publishing, Midland House, West Way, Botley, Oxford OX2 0PH, UK
443 Park Avenue South, New York, NY 10016, USA
www.ospreypublishing.com

ISBN 1 85532 597 7

Written and edited by Tony Holmes
Page design by TT Designs, T & S Truscott
Cover Artwork by Iain Wyllie
Aircraft Profiles by Keith Fretwell
Figure Artwork by Mike Chappell
Scale Drawings by Mark Styling

Printed in China through Bookbuilders
06 07 08 09 10   14 13 12 11 10 9 8 7 6 5

ACKNOWLEDGEMENTS

The author would like to thank the following organisations/individuals for the provision of photographs/information; *Aeroplane Monthly*, Aerospace Publishing, RAF Museum, S Fochuk, N Franks, R Gretzyngier, D Healey, P Jarrett, Dr J P Koniarek, F Mason, W Matusiak, M Mirkovic, Dr A Price, B Robertson, J Scutts, M Sheppard, A Thomas, T Vickeridge and J Weal.

Air Commodore Peter Brothers CBE, DSO, DFC* and Group Captain Dennis David CBE, DFC*, AFC were also very generous with their time in inviting me into their homes to be interviewed on their exploits of 1940. Thank you also to Geoff Nutkins at The Shoreham Aircraft Museum for granting me access to the cockpit door of Hurricane L1630, and Justin Sawyer for supplying details pertaining to a number of the profiles.

I acknowledge the use of brief extracts from the following essential reference works; *One of the Few* by Gp Capt J A Kent DFC and Bar, AFC; *The Hardest Day* by Dr Alfred Price, *Their Finest Hour* edited by Allan Michie and Walter Graebner; *Duel of Eagles* by Peter Townsend; *Combat Report* by Hector Bolitho; *Fighter Pilot* by George Barclay; *Fighter Pilot* by Paul Richey, *Hurricane Combat* by Wg Cdr K W Mackenzie DFC, AFC; *Arise to Conquer* by Ian Gleed; *Fly For Your Life* by Larry Forrester; *Scramble* by Norman Gelb; *Fighter Leader* by Norman Franks; *The Air Battle of Dunkirk* by Norman Franks; *Fighter Pilots of the RAF 1939-45* by Chaz Bowyer; *The History of 73 Squadron Part 1* by Don Minterne; *Adolf Galland* by David Baker; *The Blitz Then and Now Volume 1* edited by Winston Ramsey; *43 Squadron* by J Beedle; *Fighters over the Desert* by C Shores and H Ring; *Twelve Days in May* by B Cull, B Lander and H Weiss; and *Fighter Squadron at War* by A J Brookes.

CONTENTS

THE FIRST ACE

The last of the three Hurricanes gently bumped down on the grass strip at Rouvres and the pilot throttled back and rolled out in the direction of his dispersal. Watching this activity from their cockpits, a further trio of No 73 Sqn pilots continued their preparations for the next patrol over the Franco-German border.

Word quickly filtered through to them that the returned section had engaged the enemy, with some success. This hastened the heartbeat and moistened the palms of two of the pilots, who were yet to encounter the Luftwaffe. Fortunately for them, however, their section leader had already left his mark on the enemy by destroying two Do 17 bombers and a single Bf 109E in previous skirmishes. Despite being their junior in terms of age, Flg Off Edgar James 'Cobber' Kain was the best pilot in the squadron, and the most combat experienced.

Keen to see if more German aircraft were aloft in the vicinity of the Saar River (barely 30 miles from Rouvres), New Zealander Kain signalled to his groundcrew to switch on the starter trolley connected to his aircraft (possibly L1766). With electricity pouring into the power unit, the pilot flicked on the main magneto switches and the starter magneto and the Merlin II turned over, the propeller spun and the engine fired into action. This procedure was replicated in the remaining two Hurricane Is, and within a minute all three fighters had barked into life. After a quick confirmation by the section leader that his two pilots were happy with their aircraft, Kain waved the starter trolleys and wheel chocks away and led his charges out from the dispersal.

The take-off was completed with little fuss, and Green Section of 'B' Flight closed up into the standard RAF fighter vic formation and climbed in an easterly direction towards the German border town of

A number of Hurricane Is issued to No 1 Sqn were eventually passed to No 73 Sqn as the former unit received newer aircraft fitted with variable pitch (vp) propellers in late 1939. N2358 was one such aircraft, although as this photograph shows it already boasted a de Havilland vp prop! Coded 'Z' by No 1 Sqn soon after its arrival at Vassincourt in November 1939, following brief service with No 43 Sqn at Acklington, the fighter retained this marking when it was passed on to No 73 Sqn at Rouvres early in the New Year. During N2358's brief spell with the latter unit, it is likely that it was flown by Flg Off 'Cobber' Kain on at least two or three occasions. Parked in No 1 Sqn's muddy dispersal area on the edge of Vassincourt airfield, the fighter is being refuelled from the unit's Albion three-point bowser whilst its fitter tinkers with the engine. N2358 was one of twelve Hurricanes hastily plucked out of the frontline, or from maintenance units, and sent to Glosters for refurbishment, prior to being shipped to Finland in late February 1940 to serve with the Finnish air force (*via Phil Jarrett*)

Saarbrücken. Their patrol height on this Tuesday afternoon was to be 20,000 ft, and the formation levelled off at this height barely eight minutes after departing Rouvres.

Kain knew exactly where the German border was, having already gained a reputation amongst RAF fighter pilots within the Advanced Air Striking Force (AASF) for patrolling deep into enemy territory, as this description from fellow AASF pilot, and future Hurricane ace, Paul Richey, attests to;

'"Cobber" Kain was 73's most split-arse pilot. He often led a section 40 miles or more into Germany, regardless of the fact that it was against orders to cross the frontier.'

On this occasion Green Section had barely crossed the 'Siegfried Line' when Kain spotted nine Bf 109Es of III./JG 53 'Pik As' cruising in a wide vic at 26,000 ft. Despite being outnumbered, the Kiwi pilot skilfully manoeuvred his flight into an advantageous position then made his move. Initially only two enemy fighters responded to the attack, Kain's gunsight quickly filling with the grey-green shape of the leading *Emil*. He pressed the gun button on his spade-grip control column at a range of less than 250 yards, and the Hurricane shuddered as all eight .303-in Colt Brownings spewed forth a deadly hail of bullets. The tracer rounds arced across the sky and hit their target with telling effect.

The Bf 109E fell away trailing smoke and flame, and Kain wheeled around in search of further targets. Following their leader into the fray, Flg Off J G 'Tub' Perry (who was tragically killed in a landing accident just three days later) and Sgt T B G 'Titch' Pyne (lost on 14 May 1940, one of three No 73 Sqn pilots killed in combat with Bf 109Es on this date) had also chosen targets on this opening pass as more enemy fighters committed to the engagement. Both pilots quickly expended all their ammunition in the excitement of their first combat,

Plt Off 'Cobber' Kain leans on *PADDY III*, which he flew during the autumn and winter of 1939/40. Although just 21 when this shot was taken in October 1939, Kain's pre-war prowess at the controls of a Hurricane had already earned him the reputation of being No 73 Sqn's most gifted pilot (*via Andy Thomas*)

Standing up in his cockpit, No 73 Sqn's Sgt T B G 'Titch' Pyne keeps a weather eye on the two armourers loading a belt of .303-in ammunition into the starboard wing magazine of his aircraft. It usually took a two-man team 30 minutes to rearm a Hurricane (*via Mark Shepard*)

Perry later being credited with a Bf 109E destroyed, whilst Pyne's claim was rated as only a probable.

A second *schwarm* (comprising four aircraft) of 'Pik As' *Emils* then entered the fray from a higher altitude, much to Kain's consternation – he had thought that the battle was over. As the only pilot left with any ammunition in his magazines, Kain immediately latched onto one of the overshooting Bf 109Es and fired a burst into it. Having been surprised by the second enemy formation, he had not been best placed from a tactical standpoint when it came to engaging these 'late-comers'. As Kain attempted to manoeuvre 'up sun' of the fleeing Messerschmitts, he had the canopy of his Hurricane blown clean off by a well-aimed burst of cannon fire.

Feldwebel Weigelt had been flying towards the rear of the second *schwarm*, and had shadowed the solitary Hurricane as its pilot had attempted to achieve a better angle of deflection on the Bf 109Es out ahead of him. He pumped further rounds into Kain's mortally wounded fighter, which erupted in flames when spilt fuel from the punctured reserve, or gravity, tank ahead of the cockpit was ignited by tracer. The German pilot could see his RAF counterpart hunched down in the now exposed cockpit, which was all but engulfed by the conflagration. Half-dazed, Kain fumbled around blindly to his left in an attempt to shut off the fuel cock, and thus hopefully stop the fire.

At this point Weigelt hit the Hurricane with a third burst, which drove no less than 21 shell splinters into Kain's left calf. Realising he was fighting a lost cause, and in some pain from both shrapnel wounds and burns to his right hand, the Kiwi pilot gingerly undid his straps, rolled his blazing Hurricane onto its back and fell away from the stricken machine. He quickly pulled the ripcord of his parachute upon entering a cloud, before passing out from physical exhaustion. Kain came to minutes later in cloud, and landed in a field near the small French border village of Ritzing – just half-a-mile west of Germany!

His two colleagues returned to Rouvres unscathed, and quickly reported their engagement to No 73 Sqn's adjutant, Plt Off 'Henry' Hall. A search party was sent out to retrieve 'Cobber' Kain, and he was soon located and conveyed back to his unit in a French Army staff car. The wounded pilot was debriefed from his bed, and his two claims for Bf 109Es destroyed officially recorded – postwar Luftwaffe records for 26 March 1940 note the force-landing of three Bf 109Es at Trier airfield in the aftermath of this action.

As the first RAF ace of World War 2, the tall, rangy, 21-year-old New Zealander celebrated 'ace-dom' that evening in true air force fashion – horizontally on a stretcher in the sergeant's mess!

Fighter Command's first two aces of World War 2 both hailed from No 73 Sqn – Flg Offs Newell 'Fanny' Orton (left) and Edgar James 'Cobber' Kain (right). The latter had achieved ace status following his dual Bf 109E claims on 26 March 1940, whilst Orton passed the magical five mark on 21 April. Both would also receive the first Distinguished Flying Crosses (DFC) presented to pilots of No 73 Sqn, Kain being awarded his on 14 January and Orton on 3 May – the distinctive purple and white ribbon of the DFC can be clearly seen immediately below Kain's wings. The bulge in Orton's right tunic pocket denotes the presence of his service revolver, which he always carried with him into battle. The cord lanyard for said weapon can be seen positioned around his neck and trailing down to his pocket. This photograph was taken at Rouvres in the first week of May 1940 (*via Jerry Scutts*)

'PHONEY WAR'

1928

The Hawker Hurricane did not enjoy a good start to World War 2 thanks primarily to its brother-in-arms, the Vickers-Supermarine Spitfire. Britain had been at war with Germany for less than 72 hours when searchlight batteries on the Essex coast reported to their local Sector Operations Control at RAF North Weald that they had heard the engine noise of aircraft flying over, or near, them at around 0615 – no visual identification could be made because of coastal mist and thick cloud. A force of six He 111Hs from I./KG 26 had indeed been sent to perform the Luftwaffe's first armed reconnaissance of the Thames Estuary, but they had returned to base with their bombs due to the adverse weather.

Whether these aircraft were ever detected by the RAF's Radio Direction Finding (RDF – later abbreviated simply to Radar) Chain Home system is still open to conjecture, but on the strength of the reports from the searchlight batteries, North Weald scrambled two flights (12 aircraft in total) of Hurricanes from No 56 Sqn – although only a single flight had actually been instructed to launch. These aircraft were ordered to patrol between Harwich and Colchester, but as they approached the coast 'B' Flight was told to keep station further south over Essex itself. A further two pilots from No 56 Sqn had also scrambled in reserve aircraft minutes after their unit had departed, Plt Offs M L Hulton-Harrop and F C Rose heading off in search of their squadron-mates, despite being ordered to patrol over North Weald. Their late departure would soon prove their undoing.

The RDF Station at Canewdon, on the Essex coast, now picked up the scrambled Hurricanes, and because of a sensing failure that trans-

A clutch of No 56 Sqn pilots mill around Hawker-built Mk I N2479 at North Weald in March 1940. At least two of the men in this view went on to achieve ace status in the Hurricane – the pilot on the extreme left is Flg Off 'Gus' Holden (7 destroyed, 1 and 1 shared probable and 3 damaged), who had been with No 56 Sqn since April 1937, but who saw all his action with No 501 Sqn after being posted to France from North Weald in May 1940. The second ace is Flt Sgt 'Taffy' Higginson (12 destroyed, 1 probable and 2 damaged), seen here wearing a pre-war white flying overall. He too had joined No 56 Sqn in 1937, and unlike Holden, he stayed with the unit until mid-1943! Although issued new to No 56 Sqn in March 1940, N2479 only remained at North Weald until 13 May, when it disappeared out of the frontline before turning up with No 213 Sqn at Exeter on 17 August 1940. Its stay with the latter unit was again brief, the fighter being posted to No 6 OTU just eight days later. Converted into a Mk IIA in 1941, N2479 was re-serialled BV168 and sent out to No 208 Sqn in North Africa (*via Phil Jarrett*)

posed the plots, No 56 Sqn looked like it was flying westward towards the Thames Estuary, rather than eastward out to sea. Worse still, the two trailing Hurricanes then took on the appearance of the scrambled intercepting force on the plotters' scopes.

Thanks to these spurious contacts, the Sector Controller at North Weald was suddenly faced with a much larger 'raid' than initially reported. He acted immediately by ordering a full squadron scramble for No 151 Sqn from North Weald, their 12 Hurricanes being joined by both flights of Spitfires from No 74 Sqn and single flights from Nos 54 and 65 Sqns – the latter three units were all based at Hornchurch.

Future ace Sqn Ldr E M 'Teddy' Donaldson (5 and 1 shared destroyed, 3 unconfirmed destroyed and 1 damaged) was leading No 151 Sqn on this fateful morning, and he described what happened next in *The Blitz - Then and Now* (After the Battle Publications, 1987);

'On September 6th when we took off we were ordered to climb to the east, dead into the rising sun, to intercept the enemy coming up the Thames. I was leader. I spotted a large number of aircraft coming but they were difficult to identify, so I gave the warning over the radio, "Bandits ahead. 12 o'clock. I believe they are friendly. Do not shoot unless positive identification".'

Just as Donaldson made this call, the 'Tally-Ho' was given by 'A' Flight of No 74 Sqn, who had spotted the loose 'vic' of North Weald Hurricanes between Gravesend and Ipswich and assumed that they were the enemy due to the direction in which they were flying, their loose vic formation and large numbers. A positive identification was, however, impossible because of the angle of the sun – they couldn't even tell if they were single- or twin-engined aircraft. 'A' Flight also spotted the two No 56 Sqn Hurricanes trailing below and behind, and as these were definitely single-engined types, the Spitfire pilots felt confident that they were a pair of escorting Bf 109s. A section of three aircraft duly broke off and engaged the 'enemy', as Donaldson explained;

'I saw two of the Spitfires turn in on two of the Hurricanes and open fire. I yelled over the R/T "Do not retaliate. They are friendly!" A frantic mêlée ensued but not one of the North Weald wing fired, although there was frantic manoeuvring by almost everyone. The Hurricanes fired at got split up. Hulton-Harrop must have been hit by gun-fire for his aircraft did not seem to be damaged substantially. It glided down in a left turn until it struck the ground apparently quite gently.

'I managed to get the wing reformed and we landed back at North Weald very angry at the terrible mess-up where our controllers had so irresponsibly vectored two wings onto each other, guns loaded and pilots warned for combat.'

Realising what had happened, the Spitfires broke away from the larger Hurricane force and returned promptly to Hornchurch. However, the damage had already been done as Plt Off Hulton-Harrop had been fatally wounded by a well-aimed burst of fire from one of the attacking trio of Spitfires. His bullet-ridden Hurricane (L1985) crashed at Manor Farm, in Suffolk, whilst the second machine (L1980) was successfully forced landed by Plt Off Rose in a sugar beet field near Wherstead, again in Suffolk. The aircraft's cooling system had been hit three times, but its pilot had escaped from the ordeal unscathed – the Hurricane was quickly repaired but was later lost when HMS *Glorious* was sunk on 10 June 1940, the fighter having served with No 46 Sqn in the ill-fated Norwegian campaign.

Only as the various scrambled squadrons began to run low on fuel and return to base was the erroneous signalling by the Canewdon RDF Station detected. The repercussions of this disastrous morning, which was eventually dubbed the 'Battle of Barking Creek', were felt almost immediately. The Sector Controller, Grp Capt D F Lucking, was sacked by Air Officer Commanding No 11 Group, AVM Keith Park, and the two Spitfire pilots identified as having shot down the Hurricanes (only Flg Off V Byrne and Plt Off J Freeborn had actually fired their guns) were court-martialled. However, once all the facts became clear, Lucking received a cursory punishment and went on to gain further promotion later in the war, whilst the two pilots were exonerated and returned to frontline flying.

Failures in Fighter Command's fighter tactics, control system, radar and Observer Corps reporting and plotting had all been exposed on the morning of 6 September 1939, with ultimately tragic results. The RAF moved swiftly to reduce the risks of further fratricide by introducing new plotting directives and better methods of communication within Fighter Command organisations, whilst the Observer Corps also improved their aircraft recognition training.

That the death of 26-year-old PltOff Montagu Leslie Hulton-Harrop was not totally in vain can be judged by the fact that losses attributed directly to 'friendly fire' were few and far between in 'Hell-Fire Corner' – as south-east England became known during the summer of 1940 – from this point onwards.

TENTATIVE BEGINNINGS

Two days after Fighter Command had suffered its first casualty of World War 2, the Hurricane finally got to fire its guns in anger, although on this occasion the target was again a 'friendly' – an errant barrage balloon that had broken free from its moorings over Portsmouth harbour and had headed inland to Farnborough. Its trailing steel cable was deemed to pose a possible threat to both life and property, so a No 43 Sqn Hurricane was scrambled from RAF Tangmere, and its pilot, Irishman Flg Off J I 'Killy' Kilmartin (who survived the war with a score of 12 or 13 destroyed, 2 shared destroyed and 1 damaged, all in Hurricanes), duly despatched the balloon with 1200 rounds.

Up until 21 October, the humble barrage balloon proved to be the Hurricane's only aerial opposition, Nos 32 and 79 Sqns joining No 43 Sqn in downing over a dozen wayward blimps – the one day record was actually set by the RAF's premier Hurricane unit, No 111 Sqn, whose pilots downed 11 on 4 October alone flying from their Northolt base!

In the days leading up to the Hurricane's 'baptism of fire' against the Luftwaffe in October 1939, Spitfires of Nos 602 and 603 Sqns had drawn first blood for Fighter Command over the Firth of Forth on the 16th of the month, followed by Spitfires of No 41 Sqn over Scapa Flow (see *Osprey Aircraft of the Aces 12 - Spitfire Mark I/II Aces 1939-*

Flg Off 'Killy' Kilmartin's first 'kill' of World War 2 was an escaped barrage balloon that had slipped its moorings over Portsmouth harbour on 8 September 1939. He was a pilot with No 43 Sqn at the time, a unit he had joined upon completing his flying training in late 1937. Kilmartin secured a 'plum posting' with No 1 Sqn in France in November 1939, and within weeks of his arrival he had shared in the destruction of Do 17P. He scored a further two kills during the 'Phoney War', before claiming 9 and 1 shared destroyed in the first week of the *Blitzkrieg*. Sent to No 5 OTU to instruct fledgling fighter pilots upon his return from France in late May, Kilmartin rejoined an embattled No 43 Sqn at Tangmere as a flight commander on 4 September. He immediately added a further two kills to his tally, but the unit was posted north to No 13 Group just four days later after losing two COs and two flight commanders in barely a week. Although he rose in rank to wing commander by war's end, and flew a vast number of sorties over Europe between 1941-45, Kilmartin failed to add any further kills to his 1940 tally of 12 or 13 and 2 shared destroyed and 1 damaged (*via Norman Franks*)

41 for further details) and a trio of Gladiators from No 607 Sqn off Northumberland just 24 hours later. On the 21st it was at last the turn of the Hurricane, No 46 Sqn's 'A' Flight, which had been sent off to patrol the Wash from its forward satellite field at North Coates on the Lincolnshire coast, being vectored onto a formation of nine He 115B floatplanes from 1./KüFlGr 906 that had been searching for merchant ships in the North Sea.

The Heinkels had initially been engaged by two patrolling No 72 Sqn Spitfires, whose pilots had inflicted telling damage on the float-planes before running out of ammunition. The six Hurricanes waded into the fleeing He 115s, which had broken formation and descended to wave-top height in an effort to avoid interception. Four were quick-ly despatched (as confirmed by Luftwaffe records), although upon returning to base the No 46 Sqn pilots were credited with five kills – a further two victories were claimed by No 72 Sqn. One of the success-ful No 46 Sqn pilots on 21 October was Plt Off P W 'Pip' Lefevre, who went on to score 5 and 5 shared destroyed, 1 shared probable and 1 damaged. He was eventually killed in action on 6 February 1944 fly-ing a Typhoon IB whilst commanding No 266 Sqn.

With the declaration of war on 3 September, a long-standing agree-ment between Britain and France that would see the former rapidly despatch a substantial armed force to the continent, was invoked. Known as the British Expeditionary Force (BEF), it was comprised of two distinctive elements from an RAF standpoint. The first of these was the Advanced Air Striking Force (AASF), made up of Fairey Battle III medium bombers from Bomber Command's No 1 Group and, eventually, Blenheim IVs from No 2 Group. These squadrons were tasked primarily with strategic bombing operations, and initially had no dedicated fighter cover from Fighter Command – the French *Armée de l'Air* was responsible for protecting AASF assets.

The second element, which was to operate closely with the ground forces of the BEF, was comprised of the whole of No 22 (Army Co-operation) Group, plus a quartet of Hurricane I squadrons and two ex-No 1 Group Blenheim I units. Emphasising their close-support mis-sion, the bulk of No 22 Group's squadrons were equipped with Lysander IIs.

The four Hurricane units sent across the Channel were Nos 1, 73, 85 and 87 Sqns, and upon their arrival between 9 and 15 September, they became part of No 60 (Fighter) Wing. Amongst the first pilots to leave for the continent on 9 September was Flg Off Paul Richey, who described the build up to No 1 Sqn's departure in his autobiography *Fighter Pilot* (Jane's edition, 1980);

'That first week of war at Tangmere was tense. There was no more news of our impending departure for France, and our time was spent standing-by our Hurricanes and scrambling at each alarm. We expect-ed to be bombed at any moment, but no bombers came and the ten-sion gave way to a feeling of unreality. It was difficult to realise that we were really at war, and that men were dying in their thousands on the Polish frontier while all was peaceful here. The sun shone just the same, the fields and woods and country lanes were just the same. But we were stalked by a feeling of melancholy that resolved into the fact:

we are at war. At last, on 7 September, we were ordered to France.

'We took off in sections of three, joining up, after a brief individual beat-up, into flights of six in sections-astern, then went into aircraft line-astern. Down to Beachy Head for a last look at the cliffs of England, then we turned out across the sea. As we did so Peter Townsend's voice came over the R/T from Tangmere: "Good-bye and good luck from No 43 Sqn".

'There was not a cloud in the sky, scarcely a breath of wind on the sea, and the heat in the cockpits was almost unbearable, as we had on all our gear – full uniform, overalls, web equipment, revolver, gas mask slung, and Mae West. Only the almost complete absence of shipping in the Channel brought home to us the fact that there must be a war on somewhere. After about 30 minutes Dieppe appeared through the heat haze and we turned down the coast towards Le Havre.

'Our airfield at Havre lay north-east of the town on the edge of 400-ft cliffs. It was new and spacious, with an unfinished hangar on one side. On the other side, surrounded by trees, was a long, low, building that turned out to be a convent that had been commandeered to billet us. The squadron closed in, broke up into flights of six, then sections of three, and, after appropriately saluting the town, came in to land individually. We taxied in to a welcome from out troops: No 1 Sqn had arrived in France, the first British fighter squadron to do so.'

The fighters had been the first units within the Air Component despatched to France in order to cover the disembarkation of the ground troops, and their equipment. Once the BEF was safely on the continent, No 60 (Fighter) Wing's quartet of squadrons commenced their assigned escorting role within the Air Component. However, following a series of losses to the Battle force during armed reconnaissance missions into Germany during late September, senior air force commanders within the BEF realised that the medium bombers of the AASF could not operate independently of dedicated RAF fighter escorts over enemy territory – their promised French fighter escorts had not proven up to the job.

Consequently, on 10 October Nos 1 and 73 Sqns were transferred from the Air Component to the AASF, forming No 67 (Fighter)

No 1 Sqn's L1679 was the regular mount of Flg Off Paul Richey for much of the 'Phoney War', although it was not one of the original 16 Hurricanes flown by the unit from Tangmere to Octeville on the morning of 7 September 1939. This fabric-winged, two-bladed Hurricane was, however, amongst the first batch of 14 Mk Is delivered to No 1 Sqn at Tangmere from the Hawker factory at Kingston in October 1938. The exact date of its transfer to the continent is unknown, but Richey used the fighter to claim a third of a kill against a Do 17Z of 7./KG 3 on the opening day of the *Blitzkrieg*, followed by an unconfirmed victory against a second Dornier bomber (a Do 17P from 3.(F)/10) the following day. However, at the end of the latter combat he was forced to recover at the bombed out French airfield of Meziéres due to a shortage of fuel, and during his landing roll he swerved to miss a crater and dug L1679's port wing in – Richey abandoned the fighter and returned to his unit. Three days later a party of No 1 Sqn riggers was despatched to Meziéres to patch the aircraft up. However, within minutes of their arrival the airfield was attacked, and the Hurricane (along with the 15 French Potez Po 63s based at the site) was summarily strafed for two-and-a-half hours by marauding Do 17s. Paul Richey described how he felt upon hearing the news in *Fighter Pilot* – 'poor old "G" was sieved with bullets. I can only hope she burned before the Huns laid their rude hands on her' (*via Norman Franks*)

Flg Off Richey runs the engine up on L1679 at Vassincourt in October 1939, prior to departing on a gun test over the Maginot Line. Manning the chocks are his fitter and rigger – note the rope attached to each block gripped in their hands. Stuck in the ground beneath the aircraft's left wing is the pilot's then new lucky shooting stick. Richey would get to carve nine notches into it prior to leaving France in June of the following year (*via Norman Franks*)

Fresh-faced Plt Off P W O 'Boy' Mould of No 1 Sqn scored the RAF's first kill in France since 1918 when he downed a Do 17P of 2.(F)/123 on 30 October 1939. Awarded a DFC for this early success, Mould had achieved a tally of 7 and 1 shared destroyed, 1 unconfirmed destroyed and 3 damaged by the end of the *Blitzkrieg* (*via Norman Franks*)

Wing. Pilots within both units were extremely happy to hear this news, as up until this point in the war all they had been doing was performing convoy patrols in between long periods of rain. No 1 Sqn moved to Vassincourt, some 50 miles east of Reims, whilst No 73 Sqn went to Rouvres, which was even closer to the German border.

Things hotted up for both squadrons almost immediately, although their first taste of combat involved avoiding overzealous French fighter pilots who, on several occasions, attempted to shoot down patrolling Hurricanes. Paul Richey remembers;

'I was in a dive at 10,000 ft when I saw what I took to be six Hurricanes about five miles away on my starboard side, flying in the same direction. I went over to have a look and made the mistake of approaching at the same level, thinking they were friendly.'

'I soon saw the fighters were not Hurricanes. I thought it was unlikely they were Messerschmitts this far over France. While I was studying them the number two aircraft saw me, waggled his wings beside his leader and dived below and towards me. He pulled up, and as he did so I saw the tricolour on his tail. He was a French Morane fighter. Then he opened fire, taking a full deflection shot at me as he climbed. A second Morane attacked.

'I had by this time turned steeply left towards the first Frenchman and passed over him. I then dived in a turn to the right, did an Immelmann to the left which took me above a small cloud, stood on my tail, stall-turned and dived in a vertical left-hand spiral at full throttle. One Morane got on my tail, but I reckoned he was out of effective range, and knowing the Hurricane to be less manoeuvrable but faster than the Morane, I straightened out 200 ft above ground and kept a straight course at full throttle. I had shaken off both Frogs but was now lost.'

On 30 October the RAF fighter force at last saw action in France when No 1 Sqn's Plt Off P W O 'Boy' Mould downed a Do 17P of 2.(F)/123 that had been sent to photograph various French airfields near the German border. The bomber had first been sighted over Vassincourt at 20,000 ft by No 1 Sqn pilots, two of whom (Paul Richey and future 10-kill Hurricane ace Sgt F J Soper) scrambled after it but lost the high-flying Dornier in cloud.

Meanwhile, back at Vassincourt, 'Boy' Mould had just returned from a morning patrol when the same Do 17P appeared again over the airfield. As per standard RAF operational procedures, Mould's groundcrew had immediately refuelled his Hurricane (L1842) as soon as the pilot had vacated the cockpit, so without waiting for the order to scramble, Mould jumped back in, hastily fired the aircraft up and pulled the boost override 'plug' in the cockpit so as to increase the boost pressure of the air being fed through the engine's supercharger.

Thanks to the extra 'panic boost', Mould climbed skyward in impressive fashion, but initially lost sight of the elusive Dornier. However, he spotted it again at 18,000 ft and closed in and fired a long burst at the bomber from astern. The Do 17 quickly caught fire and spiral dived into the French countryside some ten miles west of Toul.

Much was made by the British press of this initial success in France, with 'Boy' Mould eventually being awarded a DFC and then going on to become an ace during the *Blitzkrieg* of May 1940. He was rested until the spring of 1941, when he was sent to Malta to fly firstly with No 261 Sqn, then take command of the newly-formed No 185 Sqn. He enjoyed more success over the beleaguered island before being lost in action on 1 October 1941.

Air Component fighter units also opened their accounts at around this time against Luftwaffe recce aircraft, which were venturing more regularly over France. No 87 Sqn was the first to enjoy success on 2 November when Flt Lt R Voase-Jeff (in L1614) downed a He 111H-2 of 2.(F)/122 after a 20-minute chase – Robert Voase-Jeff claimed a further three victories in France before being killed on 11 August 1940.

A second Heinkel from the same unit was engaged less than an hour later by Plt Offs D W David (15 and 2 shared destroyed, 5 unconfirmed destroyed and 4 damaged) and C C D Mackworth, again from No 87 Sqn. However, on this occasion a spirited defence by the He 111's rear gunners caused Mackworth to force-land at Seclin with his fuel and oil lines shot up, and David's aircraft was also superficially damaged. The Heinkel returned to its Münster-Handorf base with minimal damage.

After three days of very poor weather, Tuesday, 6 December 1939, dawned misty but dry in northern France, which enabled His Majesty King George VI (seen here in the light-coloured overcoat), the Duke of Gloucester and the Commander-in-Chief of the BEF, Viscount Lord Gort, to carry out their planned inspection of the Air Component at Lille/Seclin. As this panoramic view shows, six pristine Hurricanes from the locally-based Nos 85 and 87 Sqns were neatly parked within the gaze of the airfield watch tower. Opposite them were Gladiators from No 615 Sqn and Blenheim IVs from Nos 53 and 59 Sqns. Although the Hawker fighters had had their serials, painted out, squadron records indicate that the second Hurricane in the line-up was the mount of future No 85 Sqn ace, Flt Lt 'Dickie' Lee, whilst the No 87 Sqn aircraft parked farthest from the camera was Plt Off Dennis David's regular machine (L1630). After talking to a number of pilots, His Majesty then inspected the Operations Room at Lille/Seclin, where he witnessed a genuine section scramble (*via Phil Jarrett*)

No 85 Sqn got its first score later that month when future ace Flt Lt R H A 'Dickie' Lee downed a He 111 of *Stab./*KG 4 over the Channel off Cap Griz Nez on 21 November – he was credited with at least nine kills before being lost in action on 18 August 1940. Earlier that same day No 79 Sqn, based at Biggin Hill, had also registered its premier kill when two Hurricanes were scrambled to patrol over Hawkinge. They were soon vectored onto a Do 17P of 3.(F)/122, and Flg Off J W E Davies and Flt Sgt F S Brown shared the kill. The former pilot went on to score 6 and 2 shared destroyed, 1 unconfirmed destroyed and 1 damaged prior to falling victim to Bf 109Es over the Channel on 27 June 1940.

These skirmishes were all flown exclusively against bombers or reconnaissance aircraft, and they proved an ideal way to 'blood' RAF fighter pilots for the actions that lay ahead. Just as the French-based Hurricane units were beginning to take a steady toll of Luftwaffe aircraft, so Fighter Command assets again began to engage armed reconnaissance patrols attempting to bomb Allied convoys in the North Sea.

Whilst the quartet of BEF/AASF Hurricane squadrons infrequently sparred with Luftwaffe reconnaissance bombers over France, No 11 Group's fighter units were usually restricted to performing standing patrols, or practising interceptions against compliant Blenheims and Battles in conjunction with coastal radar sites. This photograph of No 79 Sqn Hurricanes in line abreast formation near the unit's Biggin Hill base was taken by the *Kent Messenger* during the RAF's last peacetime air exercises, held in August 1939. Three months later, on 21 November, No 79 Sqn scored the first of more than 1600 kills credited to units based at Biggin Hill during World War 2

Amongst the most successful Hurricane squadrons during this period were Nos 43, 111 and 605 Sqns, with future aces of the calibre of Sqn Ldr Harry Broadhurst, Flt Lt Caesar Hull and Flt Sgt Frank Carey all being exposed to combat between November 1939 and April 1940.

Another of the future aces to smell the distinctive aroma of cordite in his nostrils as a result of an engagement with the enemy was Flt Lt Peter Townsend, who was serving as a flight commander with No 43 Sqn at Tangmere when war broke out. His unit had been posted north in November 1939 to help protect coastal convoys, and on 3 February 1940 he achieved considerable fame by shooting down the first German aircraft to fall on English soil – a He 111H-3 of 4./KG 26. Townsend had shared the victory with future 16-kill Hurricane ace Sgt H J L 'Darkie' Hallowes. The former pilot's second kill was achieved just 19 days later, and he described it in rather bleak terms in his classic work, *Duel of Eagles* (Weidenfeld & Nicolson, 1990 edition);

'On 22 February, one of KG 26's Heinkels ran the gauntlet of No

43 Sqn once again – a black speck etching a white vapour trail across the blue sky. Pat Christie (Canadian Flg Off G P Christie also achieved 'acedom' by the end of 1940, and was subsequently killed in a flying accident back in his native land in July 1942), my No 2, saw it first.

'Four miles above our heads the enemy bomber flew eastwards towards home. In it were four young airmen oblivious that death was creeping up on them and that they had only a few more minutes to live. Fate had picked me as their executioner. The horrible reality never struck me during those last seconds as the Heinkel grew larger in my sights. The Heinkel was my target, not the man inside it.

'The effect of my guns was devastating. The bomber staggered, emitting a cloud of oily vapour which obscured my windscreen. Then, as if the pilot had collapsed over the controls, it tipped into a steep dive at a terrifying speed. Suddenly both wings were wrenched off with fearful violence and the dismembered fuselage plummeted straight into the sea, followed by a trail of fluttering debris. Only at that moment did I realise what I had done to the men inside. I felt utterly nauseated.'

HURRICANE V *EMIL*

The limited endurance enjoyed by single-seat fighters on both sides at the start of World War 2 meant that Fighter Command and the *Jagdwaffe* rarely met during the eight months of the 'Phoney War'. Although pleased to have had the chance to engage German bombers on their own terms in the final months of 1939, most RAF fighter pilots realised that the true test of their mettle would only come when they finally encountered their German counterparts, and their preferred weapon of war – the Bf 109E.

Bomber Command crews had felt the wrath of the *Emil* within 24 hours of Prime Minister Neville Chamberlain's declaration of war with Germany, whilst French fighter pilots had experienced their first combat with the Bf 109 as early as 8 September in the hotly contested airspace over the Saarland region of the Franco-German border. A series of running battles was fought between the agile French Hawk H-75s and Morane MS.406s and the faster, better armed, *Emils* throughout the 'Phoney War', with honours being generally shared – French pilots had also encountered the less impressive Bf 109D on several occasions, inflicting a heavy toll on this obsolescent variant.

From a technical standpoint, the Hurricane Is used by the squadrons based in France during the early months of war were inferior to the Bf 109E-1s and E-3s that sat just across the border from them. Many of the BEF aircraft were still equipped with wooden 'Watts' two-bladed propellers, had fabric-covered wings, lacked cockpit armour for the pilot, or boasted anything more effective than a World War 1-vintage ring-bead gunsight. On the positive side, early clashes with Luftwaffe bombers had shown the Hurricane to be both an exceptionally steady gun platform and capable of withstanding substantial battle damage.

No 73 Sqn's Plt Off P V Ayerst was thankful for this latter trait on 6 November 1939 when he inadvertently became the first RAF fighter pilot to encounter the Bf 109E. His account of this action was printed in Don Minterne's *The History of 73 Squadron - Part One* (Tutor Publications, 1994);

'I was duty pilot and I took off after a Dornier which had flown over Rouvres at about 25,000 ft. I pulled the boost override straight from take-off and climbed flat out in an easterly direction as the Jerry was heading back to Germany. By the time I got close to him we were well across the border and he found some thick cloud before I could get in a shot. I gave up and turned for home when I spotted nine single-engine kites in a loose formation, and thinking they were one of our two squadrons, I went to join them. Just as I was settling down to slot in at the rear I saw the black crosses on their wings – '109s!

'I took a wild squirt at the nearest then stood the Hurricane on its nose and pulled the boost override again. There was some light cloud to the west at about 3000 ft and I headed for that, with tracers whistling past my ears. Out of the corner of my eye I spotted another nine '109s (and I learned later that the total was in fact 27), but I got into the cloud and relaxed a little, until I realised that I had spent practically the whole flight with the "plug" pulled, and was just about out of fuel. I spotted a field (Nancy) with French fighters underneath, and landed – as I finished my run the prop stopped.'

Peter Ayerst (who would survive the war with a score of 3 and 2 shared destroyed, 1 probable, 3 damaged and 2 destroyed on the ground) had escaped with just five bullet holes in his Hurricane, and he would later go one to reap his revenge by downing two Bf 109Es in April 1940. Sadly, No 73 Sqn's next meeting with the *Emil* was to prove fatal.

By 22 December 1939, a number of three-bladed, variable pitch (VP) propeller-equipped Hurricane Is had arrived in France, and the increased performance (both in terms of rate of climb and straight-line speed) that this modification bestowed on the Hawker fighter was greatly appreciated. On this fateful day, a section of three No 73 Sqn Hurricanes (two with VP propellers) had been ordered to fly along the now-familiar patrol line between Metz and Thionville. Once on station, the section leader, Plt Off P B Walker, was instructed to investigate an unidentified aircraft at the northern end of the patrol line.

Ordering his formation into echelon starboard at 17,000 ft, Walker commenced turning towards the contact when the section was bounced from above by a quartet of diving III./JG 53 Bf 109Es led by ranking *Condor Legion* ace, *Gruppenkommandeur* Hauptmann Werner Mölders. Using their greater height and speed to full effect, Mölders and future 34-kill ace Oberleutnant Hans von Hahn made short work of the Hurricanes flown by Sgts R M Perry and J Winn, each sending an aircraft down in flames on their first pass – neither pilot survived. Walker managed to get onto the tail of one of the *Emils*, and despite claiming a probable kill upon his return to Rouvres, none of the Bf 109s suffered as much as a scratch in the brief action.

This inauspicious start for the Hurricane in combat with its German rival seemed to confirm the rather contemptuous opinion held by Werner Mölders (who would down a fair number of Hawker fighters during the course of 1940 whilst achieving his final score of 101 kills) in respect to the threat it posed to the *Jagdwaffe*. After having had the opportunity to fly captured examples of both the Hurricane and Spitfire following the fall of France in June 1940, Mölders made the following comments to his former *Gruppe* colleagues within III./JG 53;

'The Hurricane is a bit of a tugboat (*Jagddampfer*) with a retractable undercarriage. In our terms both are very easy to fly, the Hurricane particularly good-natured, steady as a rock in the turn, but well below the Bf 109 when it comes to performance – it's heavy on the rudder and the ailerons are sluggish. Take-off and landing of both types is child's play.'

Although Mölders may have been right about his beloved *Emil* being able to outperform the Hurricane when *he* was at the controls, throughout the 'Phoney War' period the Hawker fighter more than held its own on the continent. No 73 Sqn was to suffer just two fatalities in combat (the two sergeant pilots on 22 December 1939) and fellow AASF unit No 1 Sqn a solitary loss (Plt Off J S Mitchell on 2 March 1940 after being hit by return fire from a Do 17P of 4.(F)/11) up to 10 May 1940. A further six Hurricanes either force-landed or were abandoned in flight as a result of combat with *Emils*.

In reply, the RAF credited the pilots of Nos 1 and 73 Sqns with the destruction of 18 Bf 109Es – being based near the border, the two AASF units were ideally placed to oppose the *Emils* of III./JG 53 in particular, this *Gruppe* having been entrusted with protecting the vital Saar sector. Although this official figure may be slightly inflated thanks to the tradition of overclaiming in the heat of combat, it nevertheless shows that the Hurricane was far from outclassed by the Bf 109E.

The first *Emil* to fall to a Hurricane pilot was a III./JG 53 machine reportedly shot down in flames by no less an aviator than No 73 Sqn's Flg Off 'Cobber' Kain during a joint patrol with French fighters along the Franco-German border on 2 March 1940 – this was Kain's third kill, although German records indicate that no aircraft were lost on this date. Flying one of three Hurricanes involved in the sortie, Kain was then forced to crash-land his badly shot up L1808, a fate which also befell the remaining two No 73 Sqn aircraft.

As described in the opening chapter of this volume, 'Cobber' Kain became the RAF's first ace by scoring two Bf 109 kills on 26 March – the second pilot to achieve 'acedom' also downed a pair of *Emils* on this date, and like Kain was a No 73 Sqn pilot. Flg Off N 'Fanny' Orton had claimed his first victories against He 111s on 23 November 1939 (Kain had scored his second kill – a Do 17 – on this date too), and 'made ace' on 21 April 1940. He went on to claim 17 destroyed, 8 unconfirmed destroyed or probables and 3 and 1 shared damaged by the time he was killed on 17 September 1941 – he was also the first pilot to win a Bar to his DFC during World War 2, the award being gazetted on 17 July 1940.

Although the caption for this official Air Ministry photograph describes the aerial battles of 26 March 1940, during which 'Cobber' Kain scored his fourth and fifth kills before being wounded and forced to bale out of his blazing Hurricane, it is likely that this shot was taken *before* the historic engagement had taken place. This conclusion can be drawn from the fact that Kain (second from left) appears to have no bandaging on his hands – he burnt his right hand quite badly whilst attempting to shut off the fuel cock in his burning Hurricane. Photographed outside the No 73 Sqn Officers' Mess at Rouvres are, from left to right, Flt Lt R E 'Unlucky' Lovett, Flg Offs E J 'Cobber' Kain and N 'Fanny' Orton, and Sgt T B G 'Titch' Pyne. All four pilots had joined No 73 Sqn prior to the outbreak of war, and all four had been killed by September 1941 (*via Jerry Scutts*)

No 1 Sqn achieved their premier *Emil* kill on the morning of 29 March, when a fighter from III./JG 53's 9.*Staffel* was downed by Paul Richey near Saarbrücken. This evened up the day's score, for No 73 Sqn had lost Plt Off J G 'Tub' Perry earlier that morning when he crashed in a bog after becoming separated from his patrol (running low on fuel, he had attempted to land in what he though was a field, but as soon as the Hurricane touched down, its undercarriage dug in and the fighter flipped onto its back, instantly killing its pilot). Richey describes his first victory in the following extract from *Fighter Pilot*;

'I was on patrol near Metz at nine in the morning with Pussy (US born Plt Off C D Palmer, who was downed by Werner Mölders just four days later, but fortunately baled out over Allied lines – he went on score 2 and 2 shared destroyed before being lost in action on 27 August 1942) leading and Pete Matthews (Flg Off G P H Matthews survived the war with 6 and 3 shared destroyed, 2 unconfirmed destroyed, 2 probables and 4 and 1 shared damaged) No 3 behind me. At 20,000 ft I sighted flak north-east at 15,000 ft, and flew towards it as Pussy couldn't see it. Pussy then spotted the aircraft that was drawing the flak. I never saw it and Pussy lost it shortly afterwards. We were searching vainly, by now at 25,000 ft, when I saw two '109s left above us flying in the opposite direction. I reported them and we climbed to attack, but suddenly Pete called "Look out behind!" Three other '109s were attacking from the rear. Pete behind me was fired at and blacked out pulling out of the way, coming to at 10,000 ft. Pussy ahead of me dived steeply left, spiralled and then spun. Thinking Pussy had mistaken me for a Hun, I called "It's only me!", but I was alone by then and continued to climb in a left-hand turn, watching my tail.

'I saw an aircraft climbing up behind me, but wasn't sure whether he was friend or foe so waited to see whether he opened fire. He did, at longish range, and I twisted down underneath his nose. As I flattened out violently, either he or one of the '109s I had seen above dived on my port side and whipped past just above my cockpit. He was so close that I heard his engine and felt the air-wave, and I realised that he must have lost sight of me in the manoeuvre. He pulled up in front of me, stall-turned left and dived steeply in a long, graceful swoop with me on his tail. He was much faster and I couldn't get within range, so I held my fire. He went down about 10,000 ft, pulled up violently at an angle of 50° or so, then throttled back at the top of a long straight climb, and I started gaining on him.

'Waiting until he was in range and sitting pretty, I let him have it. My gun button was sticking and I wasted ammunition, but he started to stream smoke. The pilot (Leutnant Joseph Volk) must have been hit for he took no evasive action, merely falling slowly in a vertical spiral. I was very excited and dived on top of him using my remaining ammunition. I then pulled out and saw another '109 about 2000 ft above me. He headed for me, but knowing his speed to be superior I didn't dive away but turned on him, partly to stop him getting on my tail, and partly to bluff him. Either he had finished his hardware, which was unlikely, for the Germans carried 1000 rounds for each gun to our 300, or he'd witnessed his chum's fate and wasn't feeling so brave. Anyway, he beat it – and so did I, at ground level until I reached

Nancy. I calculated my '109 must have fallen near Merzig, in Germany, and it therefore could not be confirmed from the ground. Bad luck.'

Richey's victory (in Hurricane I N2382) was somewhat overshadowed later in the day when his flight commander, Flt Lt P R 'Johnny' Walker (3 and 2 shared destroyed, 2 unconfirmed destroyed and 1 damaged), downed the first of the much-vaunted Bf 110C *Zerstörer* to fall to an Allied fighter whilst on a patrol over Metz – he used the very same Hurricane to achieve this notable success that Richey had flown that morning! Some nine Messerschmitts of V.(Z)/LG 1 were engaged by the section of three Hurricanes at an altitude of 25,000 ft, and although the British pilots later reported that their opponents had been both fast and manoeuvrable, they also concluded that the Bf 110 was no match for the Hawker fighter in a turning fight.

Walker shared his victory with New Zealander Flg Off W H Stratton (who survived the war with a score of 2 and 1 shared destroyed and 1 damaged), whilst the third pilot, Sgt A V 'Taffy' Clowes (9 and 1 shared destroyed, 1 shared unconfirmed destroyed, 3 probables and 2 damaged), claimed two probables, which were later upgraded to confirmed – German records show that only Walker and Stratton were successful, however, 'their' machine crashing in Allied territory. Further Bf 110s were successfully encountered by No 67 (Fighter) Wing during April and May, further exposing the vulnerability of the type.

On the morning of 9 May two No 87 Sqn Hurricane had taken off from their new base at Senon, near Metz, and headed west to commence a patrol over the nearby Maginot Line. Leading the flight was Plt Off H J R 'Jimmy' Dunn, with Sgt G L 'Garry' Nowell as his wingman. Soon after arriving over the French fortifications, the British pilots spotted a Bf 110C of II./ZG 1 near the town of Longwy, and it wasn't long before they had inflicted mortal damage on the *Zerstörer* – it duly crashed landed just over the German border.

Pleased to have at last experienced combat after months of tedious patrols, Dunn and Nowell were each credited with a half-share of No 60 (Fighter) Wing's first victory over a Luftwaffe fighter. Unbeknown to them at the time, this lone Bf 110 was also significant for being the last BEF kill of the 'Phoney War' – the quartet of Hurricane units in France were credited with having destroyed some 60 Luftwaffe aircraft up to 10 May 1940 by the RAF.

Less than 24 hours after No 87 Sqn's *Zerstörer* kill, the skies over western Europe were filled with more enemy aircraft than could have possibly been repelled by the combined might of both the RAF fighter wings in France.

Taken in the first days of *Blitzkrieg*, this wonderfully informal shot shows a mixture of air- and groundcrew conducting an impromptu post-flight briefing outside No 73 Sqn's Operations Building – these gatherings had also been the norm at Rouvres during the spring months of the 'Phoney War', although the Ops building at the latter site had consisted of little more than a draughty Nissen hut. Again Kain seems to be the centre of attention, and to his right is 'Fanny' Orton. Standing across from him with his arms folded, map neatly tucked into in his lower leg pocket and right epaulette undone, is 'Titch' Pyne, whilst to Kain's left is Plt Off Des Roe, who was shot down and killed by a Bf 110C of III./ZG 26 near Namur on 14 May 1940 – the same day that 'Titch' Pyne was lost. The pilot with his back to the camera in conversation with Kain is OC No 73 Sqn, Sqn Ldr J W C 'Hank' More (four and two shared destroyed and a least one unconfirmed), and the individual obscured by More (to the right of Orton) is Flg Off H G 'Ginger' Paul (four and one shared destroyed and one destroyed for which there are no confirmed). Note the sheer variety of the flying clothing worn by the half-dozen pilots visible in this photograph (*via Norman Franks*)

21

HOME FLEET DEFENDERS

Prior to examining the Hurricane's role in the Battle of France, mention must be made of the series of actions fought by Nos 43, 111 and 605 Sqns in defence of the Royal Navy's Home Fleet, and its ports in the Scapa Flow and Shetland Islands region, in early April 1940. Anxious to neutralise any threat posed by Royal Navy vessels to their surprise invasion of Scandinavia on 9 April, the German High Command ordered *X Fliegerkorps* to despatch armed raiders to search out and sink any warships off the Orkney or Shetland islands 24 hours prior to launching their assault on Denmark.

Some two-dozen He 111H-3s from II./KG 26 duly departed their base at Lübeck-Blanksee for the long overwater flight to Scapa Flow

The ubiquitous triple-hose Albion bowser is strategically positioned between a recently returned section of No 111 Sqn Hurricanes at Wick in late February 1940. An 'erk has already jumped up on the wing of Mk I L2001 and started to unscrew the fuel filler cap for the starboard tank. Each wing tank could hold 34.5 Imperial gallons (157 litres) of fuel, whilst the precariously placed fuselage reserve tank immediately ahead of the cockpit topped off at 28 Imperial gallons (127 litres). Prior to serving with 'Treble One', L2001 was on strength with No 56 Sqn, having been delivered to the latter unit as a 'two-blader' in early 1938. After being fitted with a vp propeller, the fighter was issued to No 111 Sqn, who flew it in action firstly from northern Scotland in defence of the naval base at Scapa Flow, and then from France in May 1940 – it was the regular mount of ace Flg Off Henry Ferriss during this time. L2001 was finally written off in a fatal crash at Hatfield on 19 June 1940 (*via Phil Jarrett*)

late on the afternoon of the 8th. Detected by coastal RDF Stations at dusk, the raiders immediately provoked a response from Nos 43 and 111 Sqns, who were already at readiness at Wick and Drem respectively. Closing in on the Heinkels in rapidly fading light, 'Treble One's' Green Section attacked one of the bombers, but this failed to deter its progress westward – Flg Off D C Bruce (who had scored 6 and 1 shared destroyed, 2 and 1 shared unconfirmed destroyed and 3 damaged by the time he was killed in action on 4 September 1940) and Flg Off H M Ferriss (who was also to die during the Battle of Britain, being shot down on 16 August 1940 after having been credited with 9 and 2 shared destroyed, 1 shared unconfirmed destroyed, 1 probable, 2 damaged and 1 destroyed on the water) were both subsequently credited with a shared probable kill. However, German records confirm both pilots' suspicions that they had inflicted no damage on the bomber in question.

The formation immediately broke up some 40 miles east of the Orkney Islands as No 43 Sqn entered the fray. The latter unit enjoyed more success than 'Treble One', downing three of the now fleeing Heinkels. One of these fell to Peter Townsend;

'To airmen (friend and foe) the sea was a common grave. On the night of 8 April it claimed more victims. That evening we were at stand-by strapped in our cockpits. Enemy jamming was heavy on our wavelength and that meant a raid. The nerve-racking tension made us

During the months of 'Phoney War', Fighter Command hastily established, or re-equipped, a further eight squadrons with Hurricanes, the bulk of these units being declared available to No 11 Group following just weeks of operational flying training. One of the new units based in the south-east was No 253 Sqn, who painted their Hurricanes with 'SW' codes. Originally reformed at Manston on 30 October 1939, No 253 Sqn finally received its first batch of early-production Hurricane Mk Is on 23 January 1940, having initially flown Battles and Magisters for a number of weeks. On Valetine's Day the unit moved to Northolt, and when this photo was taken at the Middlesex fighter station on 19 April 1940, No 253 Sqn was just four days away from being declared operational by both day and night. This anonymous Hurricane is seen taxying past one of Northolt's hangars, the latter having been draped with camouflage netting. The air station's commander, Grp Capt S F Vincent, was personally involved in the successful camouflaging of 'his' base, and he later played an active part in defending it during the summer of 1940. Indeed, Vincent became the only British pilot to score victories in both World Wars when he added two Bf 109Es destroyed and a Do 17 damaged to his 1916/17 tally of two kills and 'one out of control' – he used his own personal Hurricane throughout the Battle, often flying into combat with Northolt-based Nos 1 (RCAF), 303 'Polish' and 229 Sqns (*via Andy Thomas*)

sick. Then suddenly, "Off you go", called the controller. And I was heading out to sea, Hallowes following. "Twenty plus", the controller called, and then the darkening sky above Scapa was an inferno of anti-aircraft fire.

'In the north-west the "afterglow" of the sun (long since set) provided a luminous background, but I searched that sector of the sky in vain. Then the vague silhouette of a Heinkel appeared high above me heading south-east into darkness. His mission was accomplished, but not mine. All through the long, stealthy climb my eye was riveted immovably on the retreating bomber. The minute of truth was upon us. In the next few moments someone would die. The chances were – and it was certainly my intention – that it should be they, but one never knew. You never even thought of it as killing men. All you could see was the aircraft.

'My fire blasted into it. Down came the undercarriage – a frequent phenomenon with Heinkels – and the usual clouds of Glycol vapour poured from the engines. I pulled aside, followed by a stream of tracer. The rear gunner could see me against the "afterglow" and now it was going to be a desperate gun-battle. The Heinkel came alive. Someone in it was out to kill me. The fight became personal. Him or me.

'On my second attack I flew straight down the cone of fire marked by his (the gunner's) darting red tracer bullets – for every one there were four others, invisible, of ball and armour-piercing. Our fire crossed until it met at point blank range. At that moment I actually heard the MG 15 firing just above my head as I dodged below the Heinkel to avoid a collision.

'The Heinkel was now doomed. Its navigation lights came on and I could just discern it in the dark as it settled on the water. Then the lights disappeared.'

Sgt Hallowes had also enjoyed success of a more tangible nature on this sortie, his Heinkel actually crash-landing neatly inside the flare-path back at Wick! Two of the gunners aboard the bomber had been killed during the action, and the survivors insisted that they had been shot up by a Spitfire.

'It was the first sign of the Luftwaffe's "Spitfire snobbery" – there were no Spitfires for miles', commented Townsend in *Duel of Eagles*.

Elements of the Home Fleet immediately sailed for the Norwegian coast upon receiving news of the Germany invasion on 9 April. The following day a series of sorties was undertaken by *X.Fliegerkorps* bombers off northern Scotland, with the first contact between the RAF and the Luftwaffe taking place off Ronaldshay Island, north-east of the Orkneys. No less than seven No 43 Sqn Hurricanes attacked a lone He 111P of 3.(F)/Ob.d.L, sent out on a armed reconnais-

sance mission in advance of ten Heinkel bombers from KGr 100 and 35 from KG 26. Peter Townsend was again in the thick of things;

'The weather that afternoon was too lovely for dying, for the sea placidly reflected the sky's rich blue. Led by our squadron commander George Lott (a pre-war veteran who had first been posted to No 19 Sqn as a sergeant pilot in 1927, Lott survived the war with a score of 2 and 3 shared destroyed and 1 unconfirmed destroyed), we were a formation of seven, as we flew out to sea toward the island of Ronaldshay. "Tally ho!" I think we all bellowed at once: a lone Heinkel was dodging among the clouds just ahead. With seven of us lining up for a crack at that pitiful target the attack was a shambles. As I came in I could see the tail unit was already wobbling and the engines streaming vapour. I turned aside and as the Heinkel glided down I flew very close alongside it. Caesar Hull stationed himself on the other side. The rear cockpit bore the signs of a charnel house with the gunner slumped inside it mutilated beyond recognition. His fair hair streaming in the slipstream which rushed through his shattered windscreen, the young pilot bent over the controls trying to urge his stricken machine to fly. Through the window panels the two other members of the crew regarded me in silent despair.

'I pushed back my hood and signalled them to turn toward the coast. Those men were no longer enemies but airmen in distress. If only we could have borne up their doomed aircraft with our own wings. But there was nothing we could do to help. I knew I was watching the last moments of three brave men as they went down to perish in the sea. I watched the Heinkel until, unable to fly any more, it alighted awkwardly on the sea. The fuselage broke in half. One wing tipped up crazily in the air then slithered under the surface.'

Meanwhile, the KGr 100 force had located naval vessels of the 2nd and 3rd Cruiser Flotillas returning to their base at Scapa Flow and immediately attacked. The bombers missed their targets, however, and were intercepted by Hurricane Is of No 605 'County of Warwick' Sqn, who had scrambled from Wick. Only Plt Off I J Muirhead (who had scored 5 and 3 shared destroyed and 3 damaged by the time he was killed in action on 15 October that same year) was able to confirm hits on a He 111, and he was duly credited with having damaged one of the bombers – a 1./KGr 100 aircraft returned to base with a dead flight engineer and minor damage. No 605 Sqn's Red Section enjoyed greater success almost an hour later, downing one of two 4./KG 26 He 111H-4s engaged off Fraserburgh.

Having received reports from their armed reconnaissance flights that naval vessels were indeed at sea, *X.Fliegerkorps* hastily despatched the largest raid yet sent against Britain. Some 40 bombers headed for Scapa Flow, and in their way stood 10 Hurricanes from Nos 43, 111 and 605 Sqns. Yellow Section of 'Treble One' was the first to 'draw blood', destroying a He 111 of *Stab* I./KG 26 – Flt Lt R P R Powell (whose final wartime tally was 7 and 2 shared destroyed, 1 unconfirmed destroyed, 3 probables and 4 damaged), Flg Off H M Ferriss and Sgt W L Dymond (who had been credited with 10 and 1 shared destroyed, 1 probable and 6 damaged by the time he was killed on 2 September 1940) were each credited with a third of a kill.

No 605 Sqn's Flg Off G R Edge.and Plt Off C F Currant also attacked the He 111s, but seemingly without any success – two Heinkels later succumbed to battle damage inflicted by RAF Hurricanes over Scapa Flow during the long return flight. Both men would go on to become leading aces within this squadron, 'Gerry' Edge (who was credited with having damaged three He 111s on this date) scoring at least 20 kills, 3 or more probables and at least 7 damaged, whilst 'Bunny Currant (who made no claims after this sortie) finished with 10 and 5 shared destroyed, 2 probables and 12 damaged. Edge and Currant survived the war.

The German raiders had achieved little success on 10 April, losing four bombers to the Hurricanes and a further three to anti-aircraft fire.

The final victories gained by the Wick-based units came late in the morning of Thursday 9 May, less than two hours after No 87 Sqn had got its Bf 110 over the Maginot Line. Two *Wekusta Ob.d.L.* reconnaissance Do 17Zs had been sent to overfly Scapa Flow to check on the disposition of the Home Fleet, but unfortunately for them six No 605 Sqn Hurricanes were already in the air on a routine exercise when the Dorniers were detected by RDF. A thick cloud layer blanketed the region on this day, so two No 43 Sqn Hurricanes were also scrambled to patrol below the cumulus while No 605 Sqn stayed above it. The latter unit had soon located one of the snooping Dornier bombers, and this was swiftly despatched by Flg Offs Edge and Austin after several firing passes.

Leading the No 43 Sqn patrol was Flt Lt John Simpson, who would go on to score 9 and 1 shared destroyed, 1 unconfirmed destroyed, 1 probable and 1 damaged. He had already been credited with a shared kill on 3 February, and was looking to increase his score. His account of the what happened next is taken from *Combat Report*, written by Hector Bolitho (B T Batsford, 1943);

'We were to patrol the aerodrome below the clouds while another flight had to patrol above. The cloud was grey and thick. We were told that they were nearing the aerodrome. We had just got up to 3000 ft when I heard the other flight give a Tally ho! I rather thought we were out of it. One Hun was already being fired on by the six aircraft above us and it was no use my joining in. We flew on under the clouds out to sea and I felt a bit peeved at not being able to fire my guns.

'I was about to turn back to base when I saw another Hun, a long, slim, green aircraft, flying beneath a cloud, hugging it and just staying enough in the open to be able to see the water. We must have been about 40 miles out to sea. It was beautifully calm. I was terribly lucky because I was in a perfect position to open fire with a full deflection shot, almost the moment I saw him. Unfortunately, I was out of range with my first burst and I think that I missed. He tried to climb back into the cover of the cloud, but I got him with my next burst before he disappeared. It was terrific. I blew his nose right off. I must have killed the pilot. It burned furiously and dived into the sea and exploded. A terrible but a wonderful sight.'

The focus of Fighter Command's attention now shifted some 700 miles south-east to the Low Countries.

Whilst serving with No 43 Sqn at Wick during the early months of 1940, future ace Flt Lt John Simpson was credited with a shared kill against a He 111 from II./KG 26 on 3 February, and a Do 17Z of *Wekusta Ob.d.L* on 9 May – the latter victory was the last scored by Fighter Command during the 'Phoney War'. This photograph of Simpson sat in his personally-marked Hurricane (W9145) was taken in December 1940 after he had assumed command of Northern Ireland-based No 245 Sqn (*via Jerry Scutts*)

BLITZKRIEG

The first eight months of World War 2 had seen the RAF produce just two aces, both of whom flew Hurricanes with No 73 Sqn. 'Cobber' Kain had achieved this feat on 26 March, followed by his great friend, and rival, 'Fanny' Orton, on 21 April. No better an indication of the escalation of the conflict can be given by the bare statistic that in the seven days following 10 May 1940, a further 27 Hurricane pilots scored five or more kills. The bulk of these (19 in fact) came from the six units already based in France – ex-Gladiator units Nos 607 'County of Durham' and 615 'County of Surrey' Sqns had started their transition to Hurricanes as part of No 61 (Fighter) Wing in March/April 1940.

Few shots from the *Blitzkrieg* better encapsulate the dogged fighting spirit of Hurricane pilots in France than this photograph of No 501 Sqn at Bétheniville on 11 May 1940. The unit saw near-constant action in support of the AASF's No 67 Wing throughout the battle, remaining in France until 21 June. Of the seven pilots featured here, five 'made ace' in Hurricanes – from left to right, Flg Off E J Holden (7 destroyed, 1 and 1 shared probable and 3 damaged);

The remaining five pilots hailed from Nos 3 and 501 'County of Gloucester' Sqns, which had been rushed across the Channel, along with Nos 79 and 504 Sqns, as reinforcements for the BEF within hours of the Germans instigating Operation *Yellow* – the all-out attack on Holland, Belgium and ultimately France.

The French government had been expressing its disappointment at the lack of Hurricane and Spitfire squadrons committed to the BEF from the time the British had arrived on the continent the previous September. Commander in Chief of Fighter Command, Air Chief-Marshal Sir Hugh Dowding, had fought a long battle with politicians in Whitehall throughout the 'Phoney War' in an effort to stop more of his precious squadrons being despatched to France. Indeed, two additional Fighter Wings had been planned (Nos 62 and 63) for the BEF in the early spring of 1940 to oversee the operations of Nos 3, 79, 46 and 501 Sqns, but the Air Staff took the view that commitments elsewhere (in Norway and northern Britain) took precedence at the time.

Sgt D A S McKay (14 destroyed plus 2 and 1 shared no details, 1 unconfirmed plus 3 no details, and 4 damaged); Sgt J H Lacey (28 destroyed, 5 probables and 9 damaged); Sqn Ldr A V Clube; Flg Off M F C Smith, who was killed on 12 May when shot down by a Bf 110C of I./ZG 2; Plt Off K N T Lee (7 destroyed and 1 damaged); and Sgt P C P Farnes (7 and 2 shared destroyed, 1 possibly destroyed, 2 probables and 11 damaged)

However, now that the *Blitzkrieg* had begun, the British government got their way, and promptly sent these units (with the exception of No 46 Sqn, which was fighting for its survival in Norway) to France. By the time the last battle-weary Hurricanes of No 501 Sqn had departed St Helier, on Jersey, for Croydon on 21 June, some 452 Hawker fighters had been committed to the Battle of France. Of this number, just 66 returned to Britain following the withdrawal of the Air Component.

Although on paper 452 Hurricanes seems a considerable fighting force, these aircraft were ranged against almost 3500 serviceable German machines, 1100 of which were Messerschmitt Bf 109E and Bf 110C fighters. It must also be borne in mind that the former figure represents an accumulated total that covered 42 days of near-constant fighting, rather than an available number of aircraft opposing the Luftwaffe onslaught on any one day during the *Blitzkrieg*. This latter fact is brought into sharp focus when the Air Component loss figure of 203 Hurricanes (about half of these were the result of combat) between 10 and 20 May is worked into the equation. The examination of these bare statistics would have one believe that Air Component and AASF Hurricane units were little more than cannon fodder for the *Jagdwaffe* in May/June 1940, but a closer examination of the campaign reveals a rather different story.

'BLITZED!'

Based almost in sight of the Belgian border at Lille/Seclin, and therefore directly in the path of the German push westward towards the Channel coast, No 85 Sqn was embroiled in the thick of the action from the early hours of 10 May. Pilots were first alerted to the invasion at 0410 when 'innumerable Hun aircraft' were heard flying overhead. Amongst those No 85 Sqn pilots to enjoy initial success in the first minutes of the *Blitzkrieg* were 'Dickie' Lee, who had scored the unit's first kill of the war the previous November, and future aces Plt Off P P Woods-Scawen (10 and 3 shared destroyed, 2 unconfirmed destroyed and 1 probable – killed on 1 September 1940), Flg Off K H Blair (6 and 2 shared destroyed, 5 and 1 shared probable and 3 damaged), Sqn Ldr J O W Oliver (8 destroyed) and Sgt G 'Sammy' Allard (whose score stood at 19 and 5 destroyed and 2 probables by the time he met his death in a flying accident on 13 March 1941).

Ten minutes prior to No 85 Sqn entering the fray, No 73 Sqn pair Flt Lt R E Lovett (having scored 3 destroyed, 1 probable and 1 and 1 shared damaged, he was killed 7 September 1940) and 'Fanny' Orton became the first RAF pilots to encounter the

Two of the most effective fighter pilots on either side during May 1940 were No 85 Sqn's Flt Lt 'Dickie' Lee (left) and Plt Off Albert Lewis. Between them they scored at least fifteen victories during the *Blitzkrieg*, with Lee claiming three and one shared in the first forty-eight hours of the invasion and South African Lewis five destroyed on 19 May. This photograph was taken at Castle Camps in July 1940 (*via Phil Jarrett*)

Although not of the best quality, this photograph is one of the few taken of No 73 Sqn pilots *after* 10 May 1940. It shows 'Phoney War' veterans (from left to right) Sgt L S Pilkington (KIA with No 111 Sqn on 20 September 1941); Plt Off H G G Paul (4 and 1 shared destroyed, plus 1 destroyed no details); Flg Off N Orton (17 destroyed, plus 6 no details, 8 unconfirmed destroyed, plus 5 no details, and 3 and 1 shared damaged); and Flg Off E J Kain (16 destroyed and 1 damaged (*via Norman Franks*)

enemy on 10 May, although on this occasion their target – one of three Do 17Zs of 4./KG 2 spotted over their airfield at Rouvres – escaped with battle damage. Orton was not so lucky, having to effect a force-landing. A similar fate befell 'Reg' Lovett on his second sortie of the day flown just an hour later, his Hurricane being caught in a cross-fire from a formation of Do 17Zs again from 4./KG 2. However, unlike Orton, 'Unlucky' Lovett suffered severe burns to his hands after his Hurricane burst into flames during its descent – he never flew again in France.

In 'a day too crammed with incident to do anything like justice to it', as it was described in No 73 Sqn's operations book, a number of pilots claimed multiple kills as the AASF was credited with 6 aircraft destroyed (in 47 sorties) and the Air Component 36 (in 161 sorties) – significantly, none of these were fighters. Although seven Hurricanes had been lost in reply, no pilots had been killed.

Perhaps the most significant contribution to the first day's action was made by No 3 Sqn, whose pilots had awoken on the morning of the 10th at their No 11 Group base at RAF Kenley, south of London. Along with No 79 Sqn, sighted less than 15 miles away due east at Biggin Hill, the unit had been earmarked for immediate despatch to France to form No 63 (Fighter) Wing in support of the BEF should the war escalate.

Like the bulk of Fighter Command units in Britain, No 3 Sqn had seen no action since the declaration of war, but it had been commanded since December 1939 by a veteran of the early 'Phoney War' skirmishes off Scotland in Sqn Ldr Pat Gifford. He had scored two shared kills (including the first Luftwaffe aircraft to fall to Fighter Command on 16 October 1939) and won the DFC whilst serving as flight commander with the Spitfire-equipped No 603 'City of Edinburgh' Sqn – Gifford survived just six days in action, being shot down and killed by a Bf 110C of 1./ZG 1 on 16 May. The unit had also welcomed the recently-commissioned Plt Off Frank Carey into its ranks just the month before, the South Londoner having already been awarded a DFM as a sergeant pilot with No 43 Sqn for his part in the destruction of three He 111s the previous winter.

That Carey had a penchant for Heinkel's twin-engined bomber was graphically shown soon after the squadron had completed their move to Merville, just west of the Belgian border. Flying one of three Hurricanes (L1932) that comprised 'Blue Section' of 'B' Flight on a patrol over Lille at 1930, Carey engaged a force of about 25 He 111Ps from III./KG 54 – Hurricanes from Nos 85 and 607 Sqns also participated in this action. His combat report later stated;

'R/T being useless, we chased after the enemy aircraft (e/a) independently. I attacked several e/a, taking a different one each time, but eventually settled on to one, which I attacked until both engines were put out of action and wheels were down, when it spun round to the right sharply and dived towards the ground. It eased out of the dive, but I observed what appeared to be a large cloud of dust as e/a apparently hit the ground. I resumed attack on other e/a until all ammunition was expended. During attacks, my fire was obviously damaging e/a as several were emitting black smoke or had wheels lowered. Other squadrons and remainder of section were still attacking and many e/a observed losing height on easterly course and almost certainly did not reach their base.'

Having been credited with two victories following this action, Carey was airborne once again less than 90 minutes later when He 111Hs of I./KG 27 bombed Merville soon after 2100. Along with Flg Off 'Dickie' Ball (who died on 4 June 1940 in a PoW camp as a result of wounds he suffered in action three days later) and Plt Off M M Stephens (18 and 3 shared, 1 probable, 5 damaged and 2 unofficially destroyed), Carey engaged the bombers (again in L1932) in rapidly fading light almost immediately after take-off. He quickly despatched one of the Heinkels and returned to base before it was swallowed up by the darkness. This final kill of 10 May made him only the third RAF ace of the war

The contribution made by the newly-arrived units, combined with those BEF fighter elements experiencing sustained combat for the first time (Nos 607 and 615 Sqns plus, to a lesser degree, Nos 85 and 87 Sqns) was one of the few plus points for the Allies on 10 May. The Battle and Blenheim units had suffered fearful losses in their attempt to stem the German invasion, particularly at the hands of the deadly mobile flak units that accompanied the Wehrmacht's push westward. On the fighter front, although the Hurricane squadrons had not faired anywhere near as badly, the AASF squadrons had nevertheless been forced to vacate their bases at Rouvres and Vassincourt for sites further west after a series of well executed bombing raids had rendered their former homes inoperable.

Although the Dutch Air Force had encountered both Bf 109s and Bf 110s in significant numbers on 10 May, the Hurricane units had 'feasted' almost exclusively on a diet of Luftwaffe bombers on the first day of Operation *Yellow*. However, within 24 hours this had changed, as No 11 Group sent squadron-strength patrols from bases in southeast England across the Channel to assist the hard-pressed Dutch.

Operating over foreign territory, with few maps for guidance and at the extremity of their range, the inexperienced Hurricane units enjoyed mixed success on this day. No 17 Sqn was despatched on a patrol from Martlesham Heath during the afternoon of the 11th, fellow No 11 Group units Nos 32 and 56 Sqns also simultaneously conducting operations off the Dutch and Belgian coasts. However, only the former unit saw any real action, with both its flights (12 aircraft in total) engaging large formations of Bf 109Es of I./JG 51 in a series of bitter dogfights.

Like most other UK-based fighter units, No 17 Sqn was still employing regulation pre-war tactics based around the tight three-air-

The Hurricane soon proved itself capable of withstanding considerable battle damage once combat was joined over France. According to details kept in the RAF Museum's photographic archive, this shot shows a No 17 Sqn aircraft that returned to the unit's Norrent-Fontés forward base following a patrol between Cambrai and Valenciennes on the afternoon of 19 May 1940. The unit had engaged a Do 17P (of 3.(F)/11) and its Bf 109E escorts whilst aloft, downing the Dornier and claiming a further three *Emils* (from I.(J)/LG 2) destroyed. No 17 Sqn had in turn lost two Hurricanes to the Messerschmitt fighters, with one pilot being killed and the second captured. This particular aircraft, coded 'YB-S', was also apparently damaged in the melee, with machine gun fire exposing the the starboard wing trailing edge ribs and a cannon shell blowing apart a section of flap. Fortunately for the anonymous pilot, the starboard wing main fuel tank (immediately in front of the battle damage) appears to have escaped unscathed. The panel covering the aircraft's radios and oxygen bottles is also missing, but judging by the lack of damage in its immediate vicinity, this may have been removed by the groundcrew upon the Hurricane's return to its dispersal. Damage of this magnitude usually meant that the aircraft had to be taken out of the frontline and sent to a dedicated repair facility (*via RAF Museum*)

craft vic, or section. With individual aircraft spaced just 12 yards apart, four vics made up a squadron, the leading section of which was headed by the commanding officer. The vics were usually colour-coded, the leader's being red, the second section yellow (which combined to form 'A' Flight), the third blue and the final one green (the latter two comprised 'B' Flight). The vic had been adopted by the RAF simply because air force tacticians believed that the days of fighter-v-fighter combat had passed due to the high speeds attainable by modern fighters. The 1938 edition of the RAF Manual of Air Tactics curtly explained the air force's reason for the adoption of new fighter techniques in the following passage;

'Manoeuvre at high speeds in air fighting is not now practicable, because the effect of gravity on the human body during rapid changes in direction at high speed causes a temporary loss of consciousness, deflection shooting becomes difficult and accuracy is hard to obtain.'

Bombers were now considered to be the primary targets for RAF fighter pilots, and as they tended to fly in close three-aircraft vics stepped back in echelon, then a similar formation would be ideal to combat them. Unfortunately for Fighter Command's pilots, their German equivalents had soon learned during the Spanish Civil War that fighter-v-fighter engagements were far from being a thing of the past, and leading ace of the conflict, then Leutnant Werner Mölders, created a whole series of combat techniques based around the loose, widely-spaced, two aircraft *Rotte* formation.

By the time No 17 Sqn had run into the four *Schwarm* (a *Schwarm* was made up of two *Rotten*) of I./JG 51, patrolling The Hague-Rotterdam sector, the German pilots were far more confident of the merits of their tactics than their inexperienced British counterparts. This quickly showed as the Bf 109Es exacted a heavy toll on their first pass through the unwieldy Hurricane formation – whilst frantically trying to either avoid colliding with each other, or stay with their section leaders as they reacted to the shout of 'enemy aircraft behind you', three Hawker fighters (all from the leading 'A' Flight) were mortally hit. 'B' Flight was also badly shot up in the opening seconds of the engagement, losing two Hurricanes in quick succession.

Of the five pilots shot down, two had been killed, two were captured and one (the unit's OC, Sqn Ldr G C Tomlinson) eventually returned to Martlesham Heath some 48 hours later. In reply, No 17 Sqn claimed three *Emils* destroyed and a fourth as a probable, plus two Hs 126 observation aircraft destroyed soon after the fighter combat had broken up.

The AASF units had long since abandoned the vic when dealing with the Germans, instead adopting tactics very similar to those employed by both their Luftwaffe opponents and French allies. These stood No 1 Sqn, in particular, in good stead in the early evening of 11 May, as the unit enjoyed its most successful single action of the entire Battle of France. 'A' Flight, comprising five Hurricanes, was scrambled from its base at Berry-au-Bac to intercept a raid approaching nearby Reims. Led by flight commander, Flt Lt 'Johnny' Walker, the modest Hurricane force soon spotted the raiders – 30 Do 17Zs from III./KG 76, escorted by 15 Bf 110Cs of I./ZG 26. Realising that surprise was still on their side, Walker deftly manoeuvred his force into a position above and behind the fighter escorts before giving the 'tally ho'. Paul Richey was one of the attackers;

'We went in fast in a tight bunch, each picking a '110 and manoeuvring to get on his tail. I selected the rear one of the two in line-astern who were turning tightly to the left. He broke away from his No 1 when he had done a half-circle and steepened his turn, but I easily turned inside him, holding my fire until I was within 50 yards and then firing a shortish burst at three-quarters deflection. To my surprise a mass of bits flew off him – pieces of engine-cowling and lumps of his glasshouse (canopy) – as I passed just over the top of him, still in a left-hand turn, I watched with a kind of fascinated horror as he went into a spin, smoke pouring out of him. I remember saying "My God, how ghastly!" as his tail suddenly swivelled sideways and tore off, while flames streamed over the fuselage. Then I saw a little white parachute open beside it. Good!

'Scarcely half a minute had passed, yet as I looked quickly around me I saw four more '110s go down – one with its tail off, a second in a spin, a third vertically in flames and a fourth going up at 45° in a left-hand stall-turn with a little Hurricane on its tail firing into its side, from which burst a series of flashes and long shooting red flames. I shall never forget it.

'All the '110s at my level were hotly engaged, so I searched above. "Yes – those buggers up there will a nuisance soon!" Three cunning chaps were out of the fight, climbing like mad in line-astern to get above us to pounce. I had plenty of ammunition left, so I climbed after them with the boost-override pulled. They were in a slight right-hand turn, and as I climbed I looked around. There were three others over on the right coming towards me, but they were below. I reached the rear '110 of the three above me. He caught fire after a couple of bursts and dived in flames. Then I dived at the trinity coming up from the right and fired a quick burst at the leader head-on.

'I turned, but they were still there; so were the other two from above. In a moment I was in the centre of what seemed a stack of '110s, although there were in fact only five. I knew I had scarcely the speed or height in my wooden-blader (L1685) to dive away and beat it, so I decided to stay and make the best of it. Although I was more manoeuvrable at this height than the Huns, I found it impossible to get in an astern shot because every time I almost got one lined up tracers came whipping past from another on my tail. All I could do was to keep twisting and turning, and when a '110 got behind me make as tight a turn as possible, almost spinning with full engine, and fly straight at him, fire a quick burst, then push the stick forward and dive under his nose. I would then pull up in a steep climbing turn to meet the next gentleman.

'Obviously they couldn't all attack at once without colliding, but several times I was at the apex of a cone formed by the cannon and machine gun fire of three of them. Their tactics consisted mostly of diving, climbing and taking full deflection shots at me. Their shooting seemed wild. This manoeuvre was easily dealt with by turning towards them and popping over their heads, forcing them to steepen their climb until they stalled and had to fall away. But I was not enjoying this marathon. Far from it. My mouth was getting drier and drier, and I was feeling more and more desperate and exhausted. Would they run out of ammunition? Would they push off? Would help come? I knew I couldn't hold out much longer.

'After what seemed an age (actually it turned out to be at least 15 minutes, which is an exceptionally long time for a dogfight) I was flying down head-on at a '110 which was climbing up to me. We both fired – and I thought I had left it too late and we would collide. I pushed the stick forward violently. There was a stunning explosion right in front of me. For an instant my mind went blank. My aircraft seemed to be falling, limp on the controls. Then, as black smoke poured out of the nose and enveloped the hood, and a hot blast and a flicker of reflected flame crept into the dark cockpit, I said "Come on – out you go!", pulled the pin out of my harness, wrenched open the hood and hauled myself head-first out to the right.'

Richey survived this experience with minor injuries, and was returned to No 1 Sqn the following day, where he was credited with two kills. The remaining quartet of pilots (Flt Lt P R Walker, Flg Offs M H Brown and J I Kilmartin and Sgt F J Soper) had all made it safely back to base following the engagement, where they too were each credited with having destroyed a pair of Bf 110s apiece – all five pilots involved in this memorable action had achieved ace status by 20 May. As a footnote to this action, recent studies of Luftwaffe records have since revealed that I./ZG 26 only reported the loss of *two* Bf 110s during the clash.

No 73 Sqn also enjoyed much success on the 11th, with 'Fanny' Orton and 'Kobber' Kain both adding further victories to their respective tallies. Another 'antipodean' enjoying a rich vein of success in these early days of *Blitzkrieg* was South Australian Flg Off Leslie Clisby of No 1 Sqn, who became an ace on this date following the destruction of two I./ZG 2 Bf 110s – he had destroyed a pair of Do 17s 24 hours earlier, plus a *Zerstörer* and a Bf 109E on consecutive days on 1/2 April.

Although undoubtedly oblivious to the fact at the time, No 60 (Fighter) Wing's Nos 85 and 87 Sqn's also got their first aces on 11 May. The latter unit's Sgt 'Garry' Nowell was credited with the destruction of a Do 17 – he claimed to have shot down a further four Dornier bombers (all from *Stabsstaffel* StG 2), but these could not be confirmed. As noted in the previous chapter, Nowell had been involved in the last 'Phoney War' kill by the BEF on 9 May, which had brought to an end seven months of combat inactivity for both himself and his unit. In the intervening 72 hours since his first kill, Nowell had downed 2 Hs 126s and $2^1/2$ (possibly $7^1/2$) Do 17s, plus had had to force-land battle-damaged Hurricanes on consecutive days!

No 85 Sqn's Flt Lt 'Dickie' Lee added four kills in 48 hours to his solitary victory on 21 November 1939, although he too was shot down (by flak this time) soon after securing his fifth victory and briefly captured by the Wehrmacht, before escaping back to Allied territory.

BOMBER ESCORT

At the heart of *Blitzkrieg* was mobility, and to facilitate this the Germans had to ensure that vital road bridges over the various rivers and canals in Belgium and Holland remained intact. Two key structures (the Vroenhoven and Veldwezelt bridges) spanning the Maas at Maastricht were the primary arteries through which the Wehrmacht's Panzer divisions flowed into the Low Countries, and the RAF quickly realised that the only way to impede the Germans' progress long enough to perhaps regroup the rapidly recoiling Allied armies, and then launch a counter-offensive, was to destroy those bridges.

On the morning of 12 May five volunteer crews from the Battle-equipped No 12 Sqn duly set out from their base at Amifontaine with the express purpose of 'dropping' the Vroenhoven and Veldwezelt, which had been surrounded by literally hundreds of mobile flak batteries soon after their capture. Providing fighter escort for this operation were eight No 1 Sqn Hurricanes, led by their charismatic OC, Sqn Ldr P J H 'Bull' Halahan.

As the formation approached Maastricht, the Hurricanes were engaged by 16 Bf 109Es of 2./JG 27, and the two forces merged in battle. The following report on the action was entered in the official No 1 Sqn Operational Record Book;

'The Hurricanes (except Kilmartin) engaged five of the Messerschmitt 109s. Flg Off Brown's aircraft was hit twice and dived into cloud and he made his way back to base. Flg Off Clisby saw a 109 crash after it had been attacked by Soper, then attacked another and saw it crash. Flg Off Lorimer and Soper attacked a 109 which dived to ground level and was last seen with smoke coming out. Plt Off Boot attacked two 109s and fired a long burst at one, but was then attacked by others and had his starboard wing damaged. Meanwhile, Kilmartin attacked two He 112s (actually Bf 109s) as they dived on the Hurricanes – he fired at one and saw it roll and dive vertically through the clouds. Then attacked by two 109s and remaining He 112, he did a few steep turns and fired a burst at the He 112, but no damage noticed. Plt Off Lewis was shot down in flames and was seen to bale out by Clisby and Soper.'

Whilst all this was occuring, the Battles pushed on towards the bridges at low level, but two of their number were quickly shot down by the attacking *Emils*. The remaining bombers got within sight of their targets before two more succumbed to groundfire – the third Battle, riddled with flak holes, crash-landed on the return flight home. Neither bridge received as much as a scratch during the suicidal mission, but six aircrew from No 12 Sqn had been killed and seven captured. The leader of the raid, Flt Lt Donald Garland, and his observer,

Sgt Tom Gray, were both posthumously awarded the Victoria Cross for their part in the operation.

No 1 Sqn had also sustained losses over the Maas bridges, with both Lewis and Halahan being shot down, although both pilots were returned to the unit within 24 hours. The aircraft of Soper, Brown and Boot had all suffered varying degrees of damage during the combat with the Bf 109s, but they had all recovered safely at Berry-au-Bac. At least four *Emils* and two Hs 126s were credited to No 1 Sqn pilots in the aftermath of this operation, with 'Killy' Kilmartin's 'He 112' (one of the quartet of 2./JG 27 Bf 109Es claimed destroyed – Luftwaffe records claim that only one *Emil* was lost) bringing him ace status.

A second raid on the Dutch bridges had also been planned by No 2 Group in England, some 24 Blenheim IVs of Nos 15 and 107 Sqns being despatched from their base at RAF Wattisham, in Suffolk, just minutes prior to the 'massacre' of the Battles over the Maas. The bombers were to be escorted to their target by Hurricane Is from Nos 85 and 87 Sqns, and like No 1 Sqn, these units were soon embroiled in a desperate battle with a mixed force of Luftwaffe aircraft that included He 111Ps, Do 17s, Ju 87s, Ju 88s and Bf 109Es of JG 27.

Despite their best efforts, the Hurricane pilots could not prevent a repetition of the earlier Battle and Blenheim missions of that morning, where no less than 12 bombers had been shot down. No 15 Sqn lost exactly half of its force to flak, some six Blenheim crashing around the target, whilst No 107 Sqn also saw two of its bombers downed by groundfire and a further pair claimed by 2./JG 27.

No 87 Sqn also suffered losses when two Hurricanes were bounced out of the sun north-west of Liége – both kills were credited to the Adjutant of *Geschwaderstab* JG 27, Hauptmann Adolf Galland. His victims were Sgt Frank 'Dinky' Howell and Flg Off Jack Campbell, the latter pilot being killed in the attack. Galland later described his first victories of World War 2 in his best-selling autobiography, *The First and the Last* (Methuen & Co, 1955);

'It is true to say that the first kill can influence the whole future career of a fighter pilot. Many to whom the first victory over the opponent has been long denied either by unfortunate circumstances or by bad luck can suffer from frustration or develop complexes they may never rid themselves of again. I was lucky. My first kill was child's play.

'We did not see much of the English in those days. Occasionally we met a few Blenheims. The Belgians for the most flew antiquated Hurricanes (seeing their two-bladed propellers, Galland assumed that these Hurricane Is were Belgian aircraft, when in fact they were BEF machines), in which even more experienced pilots could have done little against our new ME-109E. We outstripped them in speed, in rate of climb, in armament, and above all in flying experience and training.

'Therefore, it was not particularly heroic when, some five miles west of Liége my flight companion and I dived from an altitude of about 12,000 ft on a flight of eight Hurricanes flying 3000 ft below us. The route had been practised innumerable times. The Hurricanes had not yet spotted us. I was neither excited nor did I feel any hunting fever. "Come on, defend yourself!" I thought as soon as I had one of the eight in my gun sight. I closed in more and more without being noticed. "Someone ought to warn him!" But that would have been even more stupid than the strange thoughts which ran through my head at that moment. I gave him my first burst from a distance which, considering the situation, was still too great. I was dead on the target. The poor devil at last noticed what it was all about. He took rather clumsy avoiding action which brought him into the line of fire of my companion.

'The other seven Hurricanes made no effort to come to the aid of their comrade in distress, but made off in all directions. After a second attack my opponent spun down in spirals minus his rudder. Parts of the wings came off. Another burst would have been a waste of ammunition. I immediately went after another of the scattered Hurricanes. This one tried to escape by diving, but I was soon on his tail at a distance of 100 yards. The Belgian did a half-roll and disappeared through a hole in the clouds. I did not lose track of him and attacked again from very close quarters. The plane zoomed for a second, stalled, and dived vertically to the ground from a height of only 1500 ft.'

Slightly tempering No 87 Sqn's first flying fatality of the Battle of France was Plt Off W Dennis David's claim for a He 111 destroyed, which took his tally to 5 1/2 kills in just 72 hours. He was the unit's second ace. Fellow No 60 (Fighter) Wing members No 85 Sqn also crowned their second ace of the war when Sgt 'Sammy' Allard claimed two He 111Ps from KG 54, bringing his tally of Heinkel bombers to five in 72 hours.

A third unit had accompanied Nos 3 and 79 Sqns across the Channel to France on the opening day of the *Blitzkrieg*, although

This No 501 Sqn Hurricane I is in the process of being speedily turned around between sorties at Bétheniville during the first days of the *Blitzkrieg*. Note that all the groundcrew have donned steel helmets in anticipation of a surprise visit by marauding Bf 109Es. The cloth patches pasted over the gun ports of this Hurricane have been shot through, indicating that the pilot saw action on his previous flight. Indeed, he is probably relaying a verbal report of his actions to the unit's Intelligence Officer (IO) whilst the aircraft is being serviced – both the pilot (in his dirty white overalls) and the IO can be seen deep in conversation at the extreme right of the photograph (*via Frank Mason*)

unlike them, it had been allocated to the AASF rather than the Air Component. No 501 'County of Gloucester' Sqn moved to Béthenville, east of Reims, from its base at Tangmere on the afternoon of the 10th, and scored its first kill before the day was out. The unit had been in constant action from that point onwards, and on the 12th its pilots had single-handedly provided the available fighter strength for No 67 (Fighter) Wing due to No 1 Sqn being predisposed on the Maastricht bridges operation and No 73 Sqn preoccupied with patrols further west.

Eleven victories were credited to No 501 Sqn pilots on this day, one of which fell to future seven-kill ace Plt Off K N T 'Hawkeye' Lee, as he recounted in *Twelve Days in May* by Cull, Lander and Weiss (Grub Street, 1995);

'I was ordered to fly rear cover (arse-end Charlie) and I observed bomb bursts below and then spotted four Dornier 17s flying 4000 ft below. I flew up in front of the section and waggled my wings, pointing down (full radio silence was being maintained so as not to advertise our presence in France). I peeled off towards the enemy and followed the classic procedure: tighten straps, switch on gun button, lower seat, set sight with wingspan of target and range 300 yards. Whilst this was going on, the Dorniers assumed vic, with one in the box. I turned in towards them, looking confidently over my shoulders for my supporting friends, assuming a similar formation on me as practiced *ad infinitum* for No 2 Fighter Attack – but no one was there! I was committed and went on alone, with one Dornier down (as confirmed by French artillery) and one damaged – and 37 strikes on my own aircraft.'

Lee's section-mates had been bounced by the Do 17Zs' (from II./KG 3) Bf 110C escorts, I./ZG 2 downing both his section leader, Flg Off Cam Malfroy (who some sources claim later achieved ace status), and Flg Off Michael Smith – the latter pilot was killed in the attack. Although No 501 Sqn had achieved numerous successes on this day, they had come at the cost of two pilots killed and four Hurricanes shot down.

Although fewer Hurricanes (13) had been lost on 12 May than on the previous two days of Operation *Yellow* (15 per day), some five pilots had been killed. Significantly, 6 of the 13 fighters shot down had fallen to the guns of the Bf 109E, which had been encountered by BEF units for the first time in significant numbers. In an attempt to make good the losses, No 504 'County of Nottingham' Sqn was sent from Debden to two Air Component airfields at Bapaume ('A' Flight) and Vitry ('B' Flight).

On 13 May the Wehrmacht commenced its attack on the heart of France by breaking through the defences at Sedan with no less than five Panzer Divisions. Further north, British and French commanders realised that the situation in Holland was hopeless, and duly pulled their forces back into north-western France. Things were no better in neighbouring Belgium, where the Allies were steadily retreating towards the Channel coast.

Three AASF stalwarts all achieved 'acedom' during interceptions of the now traditional early-morning German bombing raids on 13 May. No 73 Sqn's 'B' Flight commander, Flt Lt John Scoular, led a section

Roughly a third of all Hurricane pilots involved in the Battle of France were NCOs, these five hailing from No 501 Sqn. Seen studying maps of the Bétheniville area for the benefit of the attendant photographer, all of these pilots went on to become Hurricane aces with this unit. They are, from left to right, Sgt J H Lacey (28 destroyed, 5 probables and 9 damaged); Flt Sgt A D Payne (5 destroyed); Sgt P C P Farnes (7 and 2 shared destroyed, 1 possibly destroyed, 2 probables and 11 damaged); Sgt P F Morfill (6 and 1 shared destroyed and 4 damaged); and Sgt D A S McKay (14 destroyed plus 2 and 1 shared no details, 1 unconfirmed plus 3 no details, and 4 damaged). During the early stages of the *Blitzkrieg* it is likely that this informal scene was regularly repeated prior to each flight involving NCO pilots, as these men would rarely have been involved in flight briefings. A veteran of both the 'Phoney War' and the *Blitzkrieg*, No 73 Sqn's Sgt Ken 'Tubby' Campbell (who later rose to the rank of squadron leader) had the following to say about the role of a good NCO;

'Hard though it might be to believe, in those days the NCO pilots did not attend flight briefings, nor did we have any maps! Our job was to follow our (officer) leader and always stick with him even in combat.'

However, as more and more officers were lost in action, so combat-seasoned NCOs were called upon to lead surviving pilots into the fray in both section and flight strength (*via Norman Franks*)

of three Hurricanes against a 36-aircraft formation heading for Reims, claiming one He 111P of KG 55 destroyed. The trio of RAF fighters was then pounced on by escorting Bf 110Cs, who shot down an already crippled Hurricane that had been hit by return fire from another *Zerstörer*.

Less than an hour later No 1 Sqn's 'B' Flight also encountered a substantial force of He 111Ps and escorting Bf 110Cs south-east of Vouziers. The five Hurricane waded into the 40+ aircraft, and by the time the engagement had ended some 30 minutes later, four Heinkels of KG 55 had been destroyed, plus a further two *Zerstörer*. Australian ace Les Clisby had claimed two He 111s and a Bf 110 (to add to his reported six kills – three Hs 126s and three Bf 109Es – scored on the previous day), whilst Flg Off P W O 'Boy' Mould downed single examples of each type to take his tally to 5¹/₃. Leading the attack had been Flt Lt P P Hanks, flight commander of 'B' Flight, who shared the remaining He 111 with two other pilots, and thus take his score to five (see *Aircraft of the Aces 16 - Spitfire Mark V Aces 1941-45* for more details). Four Hurricanes had been written off during these interceptions, three from No 1 Sqn and a solitary aircraft from No 73 Sqn.

Two further engagements of significance on this day saw a small, red-headed, sergeant pilot from No 501 Sqn encounter the enemy for the first time. Sgt J H 'Ginger' Lacey overcame his feelings of excitement to swiftly despatch a He 111H of KG 53 and an unidentified Bf 109E (the first by his unit), followed by a Bf 110C on a second sortie later in the afternoon. Lacey's first two kills had been achieved whilst he was patrolling over Sedan alone, having been separated from his section following a delayed departure from Bétheniville after his engine had refused to start. An astute comment regarding the relationship between officers and NCO pilots at this early stage in the war was made by author Richard Townshend Bickers when describing the events on 13 May in his volume, *Ginger Lacey - Fighter Pilot* (Pan Books, 1969 edition);

'He was horrified to find himself suddenly staring down at a Heinkel 111 bomber. "A big, fat Heinkel all on its own", as he recalls with relish. But it was truly a moment of horror for him; not because he was immediately confronted with the prospect of being shot at, but because he was unexpectedly called on to exercise initiative and decision for which he had not been trained. He was a sergeant pilot and therefore not supposed to think for himself. He wanted his flight commander badly. At least, he wanted the leadership of some experienced section leader whatever the latter's rank. At 23 years of age, despite 600 hours of flying in his log book and a year of professional instructing to his credit, a sergeant pilot who was inexperienced of combat and comparatively a novice in the Service could legitimately yearn for his flight commander.'

A further six Hurricanes had been lost to German fighters on 13 May, and although RAF pilots claimed to have downed ten fighters in reply, only five were in fact destroyed. An additional 32 pilots (and their Hurricanes) were allocated for use in France as attrition replacements on this date, although their value was somewhat reduced by the fact that most of them were fresh out of operational training units.

Aside from the new aircrew and aircraft, the BEF was further strengthened by the arrival of three- or six-aircraft sections from units still based in England with No 11 Group. No 615 Sqn welcomed pilots from Nos 229, 151 and 601 Sqns; No 607 Sqn, men from Nos 242, 245, 151 and 601 Sqns; No 3 Sqn aircrew from Nos 32, 56 and 253 Sqns; and No 85 Sqn pilots from Nos 145 and 213 Sqns. Despite receiving this mixed bag of 'men and machines', the French-based squadrons had to make do with no extra groundcrews, which appreciably increased their workload in respect to servicing and effecting battle damage repairs.

DAY OF DISASTER

The fourth day of Operation *Yellow* saw the BEF's fighter component suffer heavy losses in combat, with some 27 Hurricanes being shot down – 22 of these fell to Messerschmitt fighters. No less than 15 pilots had also been killed (with a 16th succumbing to wounds inflicted on this day on 19 May), including No 1 Sqn's leading ace, Les Clisby – historians dispute whether he was killed on 14 or 15 May. He had scrambled along with five other Hurricanes of 'B' Flight to engage a large formation of Bf 110s that had overflown No 1 Sqn's airfield at 15,000 ft, and like his squadron-mates, had initially struggled to intercept the high flying Messerschmitts of I./ZG 26.

The formation eventually changed course, which allowed the Hurricane pilots to at last dive into their midst. In the ensuing melee, a number of Bf 110s were claimed, but No 1 Sqn also lost Flg Offs Clisby and L R Lorimer – Prosser Hanks was also shot down, as he detailed in *Twelve Days in May*,

'We got above them and I dived vertically on the leader and fired a burst, allowing deflection, and he just blew up. Nothing left of him but a few small pieces. Then I pulled up in a climbing turn to the left and saw a bugger coming up at right angles towards me from the left firing at me. He wasn't allowing enough deflection and all his shots were going behind me.

'I was just turning over him when my aeroplane was hit by some other bugger behind me and I was suddenly drenched in hot glycol. I didn't have my goggles down and the bloody stuff com-

This early-build Hurricane I is believed to be one of two Hawker fighters lost by No 615 Sqn's 'A' Flight at Le Touquet airfield during a dawn raid by He 111s of II./KG 27 on 10 May 1940 – a fighter in this condition would have been classified Aircraft Category E (write-off on the ground following enemy bombing) according to the RAF. The unit was in the process of re-equipping with Hurricanes at the time, having been previously equipped with Gladiator IIs. Indeed, the bulk of the squadron was still situated at their 'Phoney War' base of Abbeville when the Heinkels struck at Le Touquet – a raid which signalled the start of the *Blitzkrieg* for No 615 Sqn, as OC, Sqn Ldr J R Kayll (7 and 1 shared destroyed, 2 unconfirmed destroyed, plus possibly 5 more confirmed/unconfirmed destroyed, 2 probables and 6 damaged), described in *Twelve Days in May*;

'We were bombed very early in the morning. The pilots were billeted at an unoccupied château a few miles from the aerodrome and we were woken up by the bombs. As we had received no warning of any kind we assumed that it was the French practising. It wasn't until we received a call from the aerodrome that we realised the war had started' (*via Norman Franks*)

pletely blinded me. I didn't know where I was and somehow got into a spin. I could see damn all and the cockpit was getting bloody hot, so I undid the straps and opened the hood to get out, but I couldn't. Every time I tried I was pressed back. I started to scream then, but stopped screaming and then somehow or other I got out.'

Clisby was not so lucky, being hit by a cannon shell which set his Hurricane (P2546) alight just forward of the cockpit and caused him to dive to his death. As with the date of his demise, Clisby's score is also contentious, official sources crediting him with 16 and 1 shared destroyed and 1 unconfirmed destroyed, whilst recent historians have scaled his tally down to 9 and 3 shared destroyed. Whatever the final figure, the RAF had lost its first ace.

It had almost lost another three hours earlier when Plt Off Frank Carey was hit in L1932 whilst despatching a Do 17P of 3.(F)/11 south of Louvain;

'I was attacking a Dornier 17 and it did a snap half-roll, which was an extraordinary thing for a kite of that size to do. I did the same and followed it closely down. It was nearly vertical; in fact, the pilot was dead, I think (he was only wounded, Ed.), because it just went straight on in. But before I'd realised that, the rear gunner fired and hit me well and truly.'

Wounded in the leg, Carey had to stay with his aircraft because of the immense speed he had built up whilst diving after the Do 17. He eventually succeeded in crash-landing his fighter, but he would not fly again during the Battle of France – the Do 17 brought his score to 13 and 2 shared destroyed and four unconfirmed destroyed. Carey would be back in action with No 3 Sqn come the Battle of Britain. As the unit lost (albeit temporarily) their most successful ace, a new pilot was thrust to the fore to fill the void – Plt Off M M Stephens achieved 'acedom' in style on the afternoon of 14 May by downing a trio of aircraft (a Bf 109E, a Ju 87 and a Hs 126) over Sedan to take his score to six. His score had risen to 11 destroyed by the time his unit evacuated France on 20 May.

Other No 3 Sqn pilots also enjoyed success on this sortie, with a further 14 aircraft being claimed as destroyed to add to Stephens' trio of kills. Amongst those credited with victories were future aces Flt Lt W M Churchill (4 and 3 shared destroyed and 2 inconclusive – 3 Ju 87s and a fourth inconclusive on 14/5), Sgt R C Wilkinson (7 and 2 shared destroyed and 1 damaged – 2 Bf 109Es on 14/5), Flg Off C A C Stone (5 and 2 shared destroyed – 1 Bf109E and 1 Ju 87, plus a second Stuka as a probable, on 14/5), Sgt A H B Friendship (6 and 2 shared destroyed and 1 and 1 shared damaged – 1 Bf 109E and 1 Ju 87 on 14/5) and Plt Off C G St D Jeffries (3 or 4 and 2 shared, 2 or 3 probables, 2 damaged, 6 shared destroyed on the water, 4 shared damaged on the water – 1 Bf 110 on 14/5). Amazingly, all of these pilots survived the war.

The aerial clashes stretched along the whole of the frontline, many of the BEF fighter squadrons performing multiple patrols that saw them in action on each occasion. One of the biggest engagements took place between Nos 85, 87 and 607 Sqns (the latter unit also including a handful of No 242 Sqn pilots who had arrived less than an hour earlier from England) and a large formation of Hs 123s of II.(S)/LG 2 at low level, He 111Ps of I. and III. /KG 27 at medium altitude and a powerful force of escorting Bf 109Es of II./JG 2. The battle broke out near Louvain, with No 607 Sqn tackling 15 Hs 123s and 45 *Emils*, whilst the remaining Hurricane pilots waded into the Heinkels.

One of the newly-arrived attrition replacements soon made his mark, Australian Flg Off I B N 'Hack' Russell – formerly of No

245 Sqn – claiming five successes, although exactly what type of aircraft these were has never been ascertained (the following day he shared in the destruction of two Do 17s, but was in turn shot down and wounded – Russell was posted to No 609 Sqn upon recovering from his wounds at the end of May, where he downed a further two kills before being lost on 1 June over Dunkirk when bounced in his Spitfire by a Bf 110). No 607 Sqn pilots were credited with the destruction of nine aircraft, future ten-kill ace Flg Off J M Bazin claiming one of these. Nos 85 and 87 Sqns downed six He 111s, with aces Angus, David and Lee scoring two apiece.

These successes came at a price, however, with No 607 Sqn losing three pilots killed (plus one from No 242 Sqn) and No 87 Sqn two – the latter unit lost a third pilot during an early-evening patrol some hours later. Other units badly hit on this day included No 73 Sqn, who lost three pilots killed during a series of pitched battles with Ju 87s, and their Bf 109E escorts, over the Sedan battlefield, and No 504 Sqn, who also had three fatalities, including their OC, Sqn Ldr J B Parnall (the first fighter squadron commander to be lost).

Over the next three days (15-17 May) the bitter fighting for control of the skies over the rapidly encroaching German army tapered off as both sides attempted to make good their respective losses suffered since the 10th. Despite a noticeable lessening in aerial combat, no fewer than 51 Hurricanes were lost through a combination of enemy action and operational accidents – the latter figure had risen appreciably since 10 May due to ever-increasing levels of fatigue taking a toll on pilots who had been in action since the start of the *Blitzkrieg*. This weariness manifested itself in different ways, with No 85 Sqn ace 'Sammy' Allard being found asleep by his groundcrew in the cockpit of his Hurricane after he had landed his fighter at the completion of yet another patrol. They decided to leave him there until the dawn patrol of the following day, but as he was still asleep when the time came to send him aloft again, Allard was packed off to hospital suffering from exhaustion.

For No 73 Sqn ace 'Cobber' Kain, combat fatigue took another, more sinister, shape. He misidentified photo-reconnaissance Blenheims IVs as Do 17s on two days running, damaging both aircraft on each occasion. Despite his fratricidal tendencies, the Kiwi ace had continued

By 20 May 1940 this sight had become commonplace in northern France, the BEF's Hurricane squadrons being overwhelmed both in the air and on the ground by Luftwaffe fighters, bombers and attack aircraft. Hurricane I L1898 of No 85 Sqn was shot down north-west of Lille whilst being flown by Sgt H H Allgood from Lille/Seclin to Merville for servicing – it had been declared u/s the previous day. Replacement pilot Allgood, who had arrived at No 85 Sqn fresh from an OTU just 48 hours earlier, miraculously escaped from his blazing, and upturned, Hurricane with minor injuries – he was, however, later killed in action (in Hurricane L1928) on 10 October 1940 whilst flying from Kenley with No 253 Sqn. Allgood's victors on 16 May were *Emil* pilots Oberleutnant Helmut Bolz and Unteroffizier Hans-Joachim Hartwig of 5./JG 2. Aside from Sgt Allgood and his aircraft, No 85 Sqn had a further two pilots killed, two injured and six Hurricanes destroyed on this day (*via RAF Museum*)

to exact a heavy toll on the Luftwaffe from 10 May onwards, downing eight kills in the first nine days of Operation *Yellow*, including a triple score on 19 May. By this stage, his close friend 'Fanny' Orton had been repatriated to England after being wounded in the shoulder during an engagement with Bf 110Cs from I./ZG 2 on the afternoon of 15 May. He did, however, claim two Messerschmitts destroyed before being shot down himself.

Despite Air Chief-Marshal Dowding's continued protestations, the equivalent of four fighter units were despatched to France on 16 May, the Air Ministry deciding to send eight separate flights from a commensurate number of Hurricane squadrons so that if a unit was lost in action, the surviving half back in England could be used as a core around which it would be rapidly rebuilt. These flights combined into the following composite units once in France – 56/213, 111/253 and 145/601. Further flights from Nos 229, 242 and 245 Sqns combined with BEF units already established. Their arrival on the continent now meant that every frontline Hurricane unit within the RAF, aside from No 46 Sqn, was involved in aiding the French cause.

So horrified was Dowding at this fact, that he sent a frank letter to his 'bosses' in Whitehall stating his position on the 'Hurricane crisis'. The air chief-marshal made it clear that if more fighters were sent to France, then the security of Britain could not be guaranteed. The following two paragraphs from this historic note clearly detail his position in respect to the outcome of the Battle of France, and the impending Battle of Britain;

'I must point out that within the last few days the equivalent of ten squadrons have been sent to France, that Hurricane squadrons remaining in this country are seriously depleted, and that the more squadrons are sent to France the higher will be the wastage and the more insistent the demand for reinforcements. I must therefore request that as a matter of paramount urgency the Air Ministry will consider and decide what level of strength is to be left to Fighter Command for the defence of this country, and will assure me that when this level has been reached, not one fighter will be sent across the Channel however urgent and insistent the appeals for help may be.

'I believe that, if an adequate fighter force is kept in this country, if the fleet remains in being, and if Home forces are suitably organised to resist invasion, we should be able to carry on the war single-handed for some time, if not indefinitely. But, if the Home Defence Force is drained away in desperate attempts to remedy the situation in France, defeat in France will involve the final, complete and irremediable defeat of this country.'

Aside from the extra Hurricanes sent to the BEF, 20 experienced pilots were also sent across the Channel to replace an equal number of war-weary aviators. One of those despatched was Flt Lt Ian 'Widge' Gleed, who had actually been posted to No 87 Sqn on 12 May as a replacement flight commander, but who had not arrived until the 17th due to the fact that he had not been allocated a Hurricane, and had therefore had to come by troopship! He quickly made up for lost time, however, as he explains in his autobiography *Arise to Conquer* (Victor Gollancz, 1942 edition);

Flt Lt Ian 'Widge' Gleed and 'Figaro' (P2798), from Walt Disney's *Pinocchio*, pose for the camera soon after the former's arrival as replacement flight commander for No 87 Sqn's 'A' Flight at Lille/Seclin on 17 May 1940. Future ace Plt Off R P 'Bee' Beamont had the following to say about Gleed's impact on the battle-weary unit; 'Gleed was one of our replacement pilots and he came out from the UK to tell us exactly how to run the war – all 5 ft 6 ins of him! He was immediately as good as his word and tore into the enemy on every conceivable occasion with apparent delight and entire lack of concern. His spirit was exactly what was needed to bolster up the somewhat stunned survivors of the week following 10 May' (*via Jerry Scutts*)

'It was my first day of readiness (18 May) with 87. We were to do a dawn patrol across the lines towards Brussels. 85 Squadron was to have two sections to meet us over Lille; they were operating from the 'drome south of us. We wandered to our planes. They had already been warmed up. We checked that our parachutes and helmets were handy, then there was nothing to do but wait. We sat by the 'phone; it might ring at any time, giving us patrol orders.

'Gradually, steadily the time passed. Six o'clock was zero hour. At ten to the engines were started; we clambered in. The 'plane (P2798/LK-A) I had got only arrived from England the day before – a brand-new one, with the latest variable-pitch Rotol airscrew. Already a black cat – my mascot – was painted on its side. We taxied out. On the other side of the aerodrome (Lille/Seclin) we saw "B" Flight turning into wind for the take-off. Soon we roared across the ground. Airborne, we swung southwards for the centre of town . . .

'. . . In the distance I can see a haze of smoke, steeples and towers. Brussels . . . Christ! There they are – five specks coming towards us well below. I waggle my wings, "Line astern, line astern. Go." Messerschmitt 110s (of I./ZG 26); nine of us against five of them. This looks easy. What the hell are the leading sections (from No 85 Sqn) doing? Still in vic formation, they sail on. "Well, here goes, boys." I bank over for a right-hand diving turn. Out of the corner of my eye I see "B" Flight's section in line astern, wheeling towards us. The enemy are flying in rather a wide vic formation. I decide on the right-hand 'plane, "Echelon port, echelon port. Go." "Watty" (Flg Off R F Watson) and Chris (Plt Off C W W Darwin) swing up on my left. They still haven't seen us. We are diving steeply now, doing about 300 on the clock.

'"Throttle back a bit; otherwise you'll overshoot them. Hell! they've broken. What the hell! They have turned to meet us. Steady, now; get your sights on before you fire. Rat tat tat, rat tat tat. Hell! you can hear their cannon firing. Blast it! I am going too fast: they are past me, on either side – so close I thought we would hit."

'As they pass, their rear-gunners fire at me; their tracer goes over my head.

'"A quick left-hand turn. Steady or you'll black out."

'As I turn, the sky seems full of black crosses; another one overshoots me.

'"Hell! they must have dived out of the sky!"

'To my right a Hurricane goes down in flames; by it there's a white puff as a parachute opens.

'"Keep turning – tighter, tighter. God! They turn badly. I wonder if

I'll get out of this alive? Another couple of turns; it's only a question of time before one of those rear-gunners hits me."

'At last I can get my sights on – a full deflection on the inside of the turn. I thumb the firing-button: a tearing noise as my guns fire.

'"Got him."

'My bullets hit his petrol tanks, a stream of white vapour pours from his wing tanks, a whouf! Almost in my face – his wings on fire. He turns on his back, trailing fire and smoke behind, plunges into a wood below.

'"Keep turning."

'My lips crack, my cockpit smells of the oily compressed air that fires my guns.

'Only 3000 ft up now. Three of the bastards are at me – seem to be the centre of their circle; their rear gunners banging away at me. Silly bastards! One of them overshoots me – in front of me; only 25 yards' range. Brrrrrrr, brrrrrrr. God! I can't miss. Brrrrrr – a blur of white and black.

'My windscreen is covered with muck. I've hit his oil and glycol tank. I still turn tight as I can. A flash from below – that last one just hit the deck; no parachutes.

'"God! I wonder if I am going to get out of this. Not a sight of another Hurricane in the sky. Far above there seem to be a lot of 'planes; those damn Huns are bloody bad at turning."

'A few more turns and one of them is in my sights again. I thumb the gun-button. Nothing happens. I press again.

'"Oh, Hell! I am out of ammo."

'A shiver runs down my spine. Still turning as steeply as I possibly can, I dive for the deck.

'"Down, down. Thank God they've broken away from me."'

The following day Flt Lt Gleed downed two Do 17s, a Bf 109E (plus a second as a probable) and shared in the destruction of a He 111. He was also credited with half a kill against a Ju 88 on the 20th, then ordered back to England with the rest of No 87 Sqn. In just 72 hours of combat Gleed had achieved 'acedom'

THE BEGINNING OF THE END

'Widge' Gleed's first action on 18 May was just one of many in a day packed with aerial combat that started at dawn with a Do 17 kill for No 56 Sqn/'B' Flight's Flt Lt I S Soden (who added 3 1/3 victories to his two kills scored 24 hours earlier – he was lost later that same day defending Vitry, shot down by a Bf 110C of II./ZG 76 whilst on his fifth sortie since the initial dawn patrol) and ended with Plt Off B Van Mentz of No 504 Sqn damaging a Bf 109E at dusk. In between, some 57 German aircraft were claimed destroyed by Hurricane pilots, with a further 20 as probables – Luftwaffe losses were actually 39.

After two comparatively quiet days, the Luftwaffe had reappeared in significant numbers, supporting the Panzers' rapid push westward into France through Cambrai. There was little the Hurricane units could do to stem the Wehrmacht tide on the ground, despite the impact made by the additional flights from No 11 Group – No 56 Sqn/'B' Flight, which included elements of No 229 Sqn, had downed five He

Lacking its outer wing panels and the entire tailplane and fin assembly, L2045 of No 501 Sqn has been loaded onto a French goods train for carriage to a coastal harbour. No details are available as to where this photo was taken – or when, for that matter. Similarly, why the Hurricane ended up in a dismantled state is also a mystery, as there appear to be no signs of crash or battle damage on its fuselage. Delivered to No 501 Sqn at Filton in July 1939, the fighter accompanied the unit to France on 10 May 1940. It saw its first action 24 hours later during a lone reconn-aissance sortie to Sedan, with future ace Flg Off 'Gus' Holden at the controls; 'I glanced back to find a whole squadron of Messerschmitt 109s forming a line astern behind me, at which point I felt the need for some immediate action. I turned on my back and went down vertically under maximum power'. He escaped at tree-top height, having been shot through the wing! Patched up, the fighter was used by Sgt Paul Farnes to claim 1 and 1 shared kills (He 111Ps of II./KG 55) the following day. L2045's subsequent history in France is unknown, but upon its return to England the Hurricane was issued to No 6 OTU and then No 9 FTS, before ending up with the Fleet Air Arm (*via Bruce Robertson*)

111s in their first combat 24 hours earlier. In an attempt to further bolster the BEF's flagging fighter strength, British-based units were instructed to temporarily operate from French airfields during daylight hours, before returning to their bases in the south-east of England at dusk. Again, these fresh units also met with some success on their first day in action, Nos 151 and 17 Sqns claiming the destruction of no less than 11 'fighterless' Ju 87s in two separate actions whilst patrolling from Abbeville and Merville respectively.

Of the dozen No 11 Group units that flew from the continent on a daily basis during the final days of the Battle of France, Nos 17 and 151 Sqns were amongst the most effective, pilots from the former unit being credited with 16 kills to finish in joint top place with No 56 Sqn.

Amongst those to score in the Ju 87 massacre of III.StG 51 and IV.(St)/LG 1 were future No 151 Sqn aces Sqn Ldr E M Donaldson (5 and 1 shared destroyed, 3 unconfirmed destroyed and 1 damaged – 2 and 1 probable on 17/5), Flg Off R M Milne (14 and 1 shared destroyed, 1 unconfirmed destroyed, 1 probable and 11 damaged – 1 on 17/5) and Plt Off J R Hamar (4 destroyed, 2 unconfirmed destroyed and 1 damaged – 1 probable on 17/5), and future No 17 Sqn aces Plt Offs K Manger (5 and 3 shared destroyed and 3 and 3 shared damaged – 1 destroyed and 1 damaged on 17/5) and R C Whittaker (6 and 2 shared destroyed, 1 unconfirmed destroyed and 2 damaged – 1 on 17/5).

These few highlights were far outweighed by the overall losses suf-fered by the Hurricane force on 18/19 May, however, for no less than 68 fighters were either shot down or forced to crash-land as a result of sustaining battle damage. Fifteen pilots had been killed, eight taken prisoner and a further eleven wounded. Of the Hurricanes lost, two-thirds had fallen victim to the ever increasing number of Bf 109Es and

Bf 110Cs being encountered over the frontline. The situation was becoming even more desperate on the ground, as airfields were subjected to repeated aerial attacks. Many units were caught by marauding Messerschmitts just as they were either taking off or landing, one such raid on Vitry on 18 May resulting in the death of No 56 Sqn/'B' Flight's Flg Off F C Rose, who had been shot down in error during the 'Battle of Barking Creek' the previous September.

In an effort to stave off these surprise attacks, squadrons began moving ever closer to the Channel coast on a near-daily basis, often having to leave unserviceable Hurricanes behind. This tactic adversely affected the units' operability, and stretched supply routes and communication lines to breaking point.

Despite the seemingly hopeless situation now facing the BEF, Hurricane squadrons continued to take the fight to the Luftwaffe at every possible opportunity. The trio of AASF units were given the thankless task of escorting the remnants of the bomber wings as they forlornly attempted to attack German positions along the rapidly approaching frontline, and on 19 May Nos 1 and 73 Sqns again exacted a heavy toll. The former unit claimed seven aircraft destroyed – 'Cobber' Kain got three and Flg Off H G Paul (4 and 1 shared destroyed) two, whilst Flt Lt J E Scoular (15 and 1 shared destroyed, 1 unconfirmed destroyed and 4 damaged) destroyed one and shared a second with Sgt A E Marshall (16 and 2 shared destroyed, 2 probables, 1 damaged, 1 V1 destroyed, 8 shared destroyed on the ground and 2 damaged on the ground).

No 1 Sqn's pilots got five – Paul Richey (10 and 1 shared destroyed, 1 unconfirmed destroyed, 1 and 1 shared probable and 6 damaged) three, Flg Off M H Brown (15 and 4 shared destroyed, 1 probable and 2 damaged) one and one probable, and Flg Off P W O Mould (8 and 1 shared destroyed, 1 unconfirmed destroyed, 5 damaged, 6 shared destroyed on water and 4 shared damaged on water) one shared with Flg Off C D Palmer (2 and 2 shared destroyed). Fellow No 1 Sqn aces Walker, Kilmartin and Soper also claimed probable kills or were credited with having damaged their target – all He 111s of III./KG 27.

This engagement was the last flown by the original 'Phoney War' members of No 1 Sqn, as the request by their OC, 'Bull' Halahan, to have the survivors of his outfit repatriated to England was duly granted on 20 May. During the previous ten days the unit had claimed the destruction of 63 enemy aircraft for the loss of two pilots killed, one a PoW and two in hospital – both returned to active duty in due course. Its record in France was unequalled by the many other units that participated in the *Blitzkrieg*, and its pilots were subsequently honoured with the unique mass-awarding of ten DFCs and three DFMs.

Sitting strapped into their fighters at the edge of the vast Lille/Seclin airfield, two No 85 Sqn pilots 'sweat it out' in the warm spring sunshine whilst at immediate readiness towards the end of the *Blitzkrieg*. During the preceding week a number of Hurricane squadrons had been caught on the ground by roaming Bf 109 and Bf 110 *Staffeln*, so in order to try and negate the potentially devastating effect of these surprise raids, RAF fighter units had started keeping a section of aircraft at readiness, manned and plugged into starter trolley accumulators. Should enemy aircraft be reported in the vicinity, either a flare would fired or word rung through to the alert section ordering them to scramble. Following a thumbs up from the pilots, the groundcrew would press the power switches on the trolleys, thus sending electricity flowing from the latters' batteries into the idle Merlins. With the Hurricanes coaxed into life, the accumulators were swiftly unplugged and the fighters cleared for take-off. Aircraft on readiness were usually dispersed into wind, so all the pilot had to do was open the throttle and commence his take-off run from where he was parked (*via Norman Franks*)

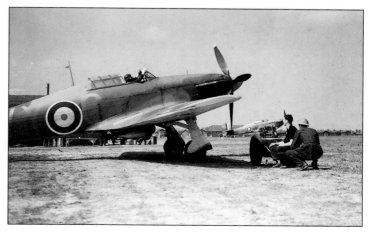

Despite the return of most of its original pilots, No 1 Sqn stayed on in France with a new crop of aircrew.

On 21 May German Panzers reached the Channel near Abbeville, thus cutting the northern Allied armies off from their compatriots in the central and southern regions of France. Twenty-four hours earlier Air Component commanders had realised the gravity of the situation and ordered the surviving Blenheim and Lysander squadrons to return to England. Later in the afternoon of the 20th the Hurricane units in northern France also received the signal to abandon their airfields and return to Britain as best they could. One pilot tasked with flying an operationally unserviceable Hurricane (of No 87 Sqn) to England from Merville was Kiwi Flg Off Derek Ward of No 151 Sqn, who had ferried a Hawker fighter to France just four days before. Lacking a gunsight, and with only the compass, oil and petrol gauges working, the Hurricane was in desperate need of an overhaul, and in no fit state for battle;

'The engine was badly overheating. Seven guns were loaded but there was no incendiary tracer. I intended to land at Abbeville to collect some kit which I had left there on the way out. On approaching Abbeville I saw the town was in flames and two Do 215s were dive-bombing the town. I climbed and attacked one of the machines and got in two bursts at 300 yards, pointing my guns in the general direction of the e/a. The e/a dived into cloud and I followed and gave the e/a some more bursts in the cloud. I came out and circled for ten minutes and saw another Dornier between clouds and attacked again. My engine began to overheat badly and some '109s attacked me from behind. I dived into cloud and eventually landed at Abbeville.

'I found that my machine had a puncture in the starboard tank and the petrol was spraying out. The aerodrome was being evacuated – u/s machines were being burned, chiefly Lysanders. The aerodrome crews were about to be evacuated and wished to burn my machine rather than take the risk of starting it again owing to the petrol spraying out of the starboard tank. I stuck a bayonet several times into the starboard tank to empty it and managed to persuade two airmen to fill my port tank. I had to leave without being rearmed. I took off and two miles east of the aerodrome I encountered six Do 17s and six '109s. I attacked the leader of the '109s, which were coming head-on towards me, and gave the leader a burst. He swerved left and I dived past him towards the ground. Fortunately the '109s continued to escort the bombers and did not give chase. I then flew the aircraft to North Weald and landed.'

Ward's score stood at 6 and 1 shared destroyed, 1 probable and 4 damaged when he was shot down and killed by German ace Oberleutnant Hans-Joachim Marseille (see *Aircraft of the Aces 2 - Bf 109 Aces of the Mediterranean and North Africa* for more details) whilst commanding No 73 Sqn in North Africa on 17 June 1942.

Many of the Hurricanes that returned to airfields in south-east England were in a similar condition (or worse) to the fighter nursed across the Channel by Derek Ward. Some, like the trio flown into Croydon by escaping No 607 Sqn pilots, were scrapped in situ – one of the Hurricanes had 87 bullet holes in it. By the evening of 21 May

Left

As mentioned earlier in this chapter, South African-born Plt Off Albert Lewis enjoyed great success with No 85 Sqn during the *Blitzkrieg*, being credited with the destruction of six Bf 109Es (five of these on 19 May) and a He 111 – although a further two claims have been awarded to him, no specific details pertaining to these kills are available. Lewis's penchant for Messerschmitt fighters continued on into the summer of 1940, as he was credited with a further five Bf 109Es and two Bf 110s destroyed, plus an additional two *Zerstörers* as probables. His greatest day in combat came on 27 September whilst flying with No 249 Sqn when he completed four sorties and claimed six kills, a probable and a damaged – this herculean effort took his score to 18 destroyed, 2 and 1 shared probable and 1 damaged. Lewis's victories on this day were to be his last, however, for he was badly burned whilst baling out of his shot up Hurricane (V6617) high over the Thames Estuary barely 24 hours later. It is likely that he had become the 20th victim of Knight's Cross holder Hauptmann Rolf Pingel, *Staffelkapitän* of 2./JG 26 – Pingel had only received the coveted *Ritterkreuz* two weeks earlier. Lewis returned to flying in May of the following year, and after a stint as an instructor with No 52 OTU, he was given command of No 261 Sqn in Ceylon. He lasted just a month in back in the frontline, however, as on 9 April 1942 his Hurricane II (Z4961) as shot down by Zeros soon after he had taken off in response to a surprise raid on China Bay. Wounded yet again, Lewis was repatriated back to the UK in June and saw no further operational flying (*via* Phil Jarrett)

the only operable Hurricanes remaining in France belonged to the three AASF units, which had moved further south to temporary strips around Troyes. Many others could, however, be found abandoned at Merville, Abbeville, Lille/Seclin and other recently vacated Air Component airfields – 178 in fact, as only 66 Hurricanes had physically made it back to England.

PERFORMANCE ANALYSIS

Despite the Battle of France ending in a swift route for the forces of the BEF, RAF Hurricane squadrons (AASF, Air Component and No 11 Group reinforcements) had inflicted significant losses on the Luftwaffe which proved to be a portent of things to come later that summer. Pilots claimed at least 499 kills and 123 probables between 10 and 21 May, whilst contemporary German records, examined post-war, attributed 299 aircraft destroyed and at least 65 seriously damaged to RAF fighters. As mentioned earlier, the most successful AASF unit was No 1 Sqn with 63 kills, whilst No 3 Sqn topped the Air Component list with 67 victories. Nos 17 and 56 Sqns shared top spot in No 11 Group with 16 kills apiece.

As has historically been the case in virtually all aerial conflicts, a fair percentage of the kills scored by Hurricane squadrons during this period were credited to a small clutch of pilots – the aces. Some 41 aircrew scored five or more kills during the *Blitzkrieg*, with the leading ace being No 1 Sqn's Flg Off Leslie Clisby with 16 and 1 shared destroyed (notwithstanding recent studies into his combat successes, as detailed earlier in this chapter). Whatever his final score, Clisby was one of just three aces killed between 10 and 21 May 1940, Canadian Flg Off A B Angus of No 85 Sqn and Flt Lt I S Soden of No 56 Sqn being the other two.

More than a quarter (12 in total) of the 41 aces to emerge hailed from No 1 Sqn, followed by No 87 Sqn with seven, Nos 3 and 85 Sqns with five, No 607 Sqn with four, No 73 Sqn with three and solitary aces for Nos 56, 79, 111, 501 and 601 Sqns.

As these raw statistics show, Hurricane pilots had acquitted themselves well in conditions that would have proven daunting for any aviator, either Allied or Axis. Always outnumbered, severely hampered by the employment of obsolete tactics that saw squadrons committed to combat in rigid sections of three or flights of six, and often led by men that had little or no combat experience, British and Commonwealth pilots nevertheless held their own in the vicious skies over Belgium, Holland and France. A strict adherence to the RAF Manual of Air Tactics, which favoured tight formation flying over the more critical aspects of aerial combat like deflection shooting and effective offensive/defensive tactics based on the fighting pair, cost squadrons dearly, as future ace Roland 'Bea' Beamont (6 and 1 shared destroyed, 1 probable, 2 damaged and 32 V1s destroyed), then a pilot officer with No 87 Sqn, recounted after the war;

'We were operating from a grass field at Lille/Marque and had been ordered off at three-squadron strength to patrol the ground battle area at Valencienne at 10,000 ft.

'We made a fine sight as 36 Hurricanes formed up in the late after-

At just 19 years of age, Plt Off R P 'Bea' Beamont was one of No 87 Sqn's youngest pilots during the Battle of France. The start of the *Blitzkrieg* found him in the unit's sick quarters battling with dysentery, but by 15 May Beamont had recovered enough to score his first kill, as he describes in the following quote;

'I got so excited, I opened fire well out of range. My flight commander (Flt Lt R Voase Jeff) tore me off a strip afterwards. He said he was in front of me and still out of range and there I was firing behind him and nearly hitting him. We closed in on the Dorniers (Do 17Zs of I./KG 76). I hit one pretty hard. While I was wondering what was happening to everybody else, I suddenly noticed some stuff coming down past me, like bright rain. It was tracer bullets. There was a Messerschmitt 110 (Bf 110Cs of II./ZG 76) very close, doing a very tight turn on me from above.'

Having survived his 'baptism of fire', Beamont finally departed France with the survivors of his unit on 20 May, being forced to return to England by RAF transport due to a shortage of serviceable Hurricanes (*via Norman Franks*)

noon sun in three squadrons line astern, with four sections of vic threes to a squadron.

'I was flying No 2 to the right of the commander of No 87 Sqn who was leading the wing, and it made one feel quite brave looking back at so many friendly fighters. Then, without fuss or drama, about ten Messerschmitt 109s appeared above the left rear flank of our foramation out of some high cloud.

'The Wing Leader turned in towards them as fast as the big formation could be wheeled, but the 109s abandoned close drill and pulled their turn tight, diving one after the other on to the tail section of the wing. Their guns streamed smoke and one by one four Hurricanes fell away. None of us fired a shot, some never saw it happen, and the enemy disengaged while we continued to give a massive impression of combat strength over the battle area with four less Hurricanes that we had started.

'We had more than three times the strength of the enemy on this occasion and had been soundly beaten tactically by a much smaller unit led with flexibility and resolution.'

Aside from generally poor tactics, Hurricane pilots also had to

Left
'Bea' Beamont used Hurricane I L1963 to score his first victory on the evening of 15 May 1940, this fighter having been passed to No 87 Sqn by No 1 Sqn sometime prior to the commencement of the *Blitzkrieg*. The fighter was one of the few squadron aircraft to return to England following the pull out directive of 20 May. Once back in the UK, L1963 remained with No 87 Sqn for a short while before being sent to a maintenance unit for an overhaul. It was whilst landing from a post-rectification check flight that this minor accident occurred, the port undercarriage collapsing and tipping the fighter up on its nose. Once repaired, L1963 was issued to No 43 Sqn at Tangmere on 27 August 1940 as an attrition replacement for the quartet of Hurricanes lost in action 24 hours earlier. After having sustained heavy casualties in late August and early September, No 43 Sqn was finally pulled out of No 11 Group and ordered north to Usworth, south of Newcastle. L1963 accompanied the unit to No 13 Group, but was written off in a training accident on 27 October when recent arrival Sgt L V Toogood inexplicably power-dived the fighter into the ground from a height of 20,000 ft. It is believed that the 20-year-old pilot may have suffered an attack of anoxia, caused by the failure of the aircraft's oxygen system, whilst he was undertaking high altitude aerobatics (*via Bruce Robertson*)

endure a performance gap between their fighter and their opponents' most effective mount, the Bf 109E. The latter type could climb higher than the Hawker fighter and dive faster, thanks to a combination of its fuel-injected Daimler-Benz engine and thinner wing section. Both attributes were used to full effect by the *jagdflieger* in a series of 'hit-and-run' engagements, German pilots usually bouncing their quarry from above, using the sun to mask their presence. One swift pass was all that was required for an *Experten*, and often the victim would only become aware of the presence of a Bf 109E when the machine gun and cannon rounds hit him. By the time the Hurricane pilot reacted, his German counterpart would have used his superior diving speed to race away. The *Jagdwaffe* knew that the Hurricane could out turn an *Emil* in a dogfight, so avoided tackling them in the horizontal plane.

Despite their abundance in numbers, the Bf 109E had not been the Hurricane's major opponent during the *Blitzkrieg* – postwar analysis of the combats that did take place between the two types clearly indicate that losses to the Hurricane force would have been far greater had the *Emils* ventured into the British sectors in greater numbers. Instead, the RAF encountered the Bf 110 on a near-daily basis, and although the the *Zerstörer* inflicted heavy losses on the Hurricane squadrons on occasion, this was usually achieved through sheer weight of numbers. In a one-to-one fight, the Hurricane could easily out-turn the cumbersome Bf 110, and as the latter rarely used the 'hit-and-run' tactics so favoured by their single-seat counterparts within the *Jagdwaffe*, the *Zerstörer Gruppen* suffered particularly heavy losses.

As a 'bomber destroyer', the Hurricane really came into its own, as it was a superb gun platform and had a wide spread of fire. Its eight .303-in machine guns were perhaps a little lightweight for downing heavily-armoured bombers fitted with self-sealing fuel tanks, but the adoption of different attacking methods (head-on attacks were considered to be amongst the most effective at the time, striking at the unprotected cockpit area of the bomber) resulted in both the *Kampfgeschwader* and *Stukageschwader* coming off second best against the numerically inferior Hurricane force. Pilots also quickly realised that the harmonisation of their guns was way out at 400 yards convergence (as stipulated in the RAF Manual of Air Tactics), as they were having to get much closer to their targets to ensure critical hits were achieved – squadron armourers were therefore instructed to 'toe in' the Colt Brownings to a harmonisation distance of just 120 yards.

In light of their closer proximity to their targets, pilots were thankful that Hawkers had built the Hurricane in such a way that it could withstand significant battle damage, and the fitment of head and back armour, plus toughened windscreen glass, saved many lives. The fighter's wide-track landing gear was also most welcome when operating from austere French airfields – particularly those encountered towards the end of the campaign, which were little more than farmers' fields. Ease of maintenance also meant that hard-pressed groundcrews could achieve remarkable serviceability rates with just a modicum of spares.

OPERATION DYNAMO

Whilst the BEF retreated towards the Channel port of Dunkirk, the

RAF continued to send patrols to France comprising No 11 Group Hurricanes and, ever increasingly, Spitfires. For many pilots who had flown almost exclusively from bases on the continent, the prospect of firstly a water crossing, and then a limited sweep over what was now almost certainly enemy territory, filled them with trepidation. However, many of the war-weary crews were spared this torture thanks to their ravaged units being posted north to rest and reform.

Although a considerable number of the Hurricane pilots now tasked with protecting the BEF during Operation *Dynamo* (the evacuation from Dunkirk) were seeing action for the first time, they soon proved up to the demanding task. Between 26 May and 3 June, when the evacuation was deemed to have been completed, the 14 Hurricane units committed to *Dynamo* were credited with the destruction of 108 aircraft for the loss of 22 pilots killed and 3 captured.

This was the first real operation where the RAF's two principal fighters flew side-by-side, and it is therefore prudent to include the Spitfire's statistics for the same period. Some 13 units saw action, and they were credited with 109 victories for the loss of 24 pilots killed and 4 captured. As these figure show, the success rates for both types were remarkably similar.

The RAF's performance over Dunkirk during *Dynamo* was heralded as a victory by senior commanders and politicians alike, as the Luftwaffe had essentially suffered its first reversal of the war through the fact that it had not been able to prevent significant numbers of BEF personnel escaping back to England. *Reichsmarschall* Hermann Göring's boast that not a single British soldier would leave French soil alive was proven to be totally false, and although many of the returning men complained bitterly once back in England that the RAF had done precious little to secure their safe passage, nothing could be farther from the truth.

Weather conditions often meant that fighter patrols had to stay above the blanket cloud that often covered the area in an effort to avoid being bounced by the high-flying Messerschmitt escorts, while Luftwaffe bombers struck from below the cumulous – smoke also aided the cause of the attacking German aircraft. This effectively meant that the soldiers and sailors at ground level often only saw their attackers, who seemed to be able to consistently carry out their bombing and strafing runs totally unmolested. Fighter patrols also ventured inland away from the beaches in an effort to break up and repel attacking formations prior to them reaching their targets. Again this resulted in their actions going unobserved by their sister-services.

The tatics employed by Fighter Command over Dunkirk changed as *Dynamo* progressed. Initially, units were ordered to maintain fighter patrols in single flight or squadron strength only from dawn to dusk, but this often resulted in them suffering serious casualties. Eventually, after much protesting by Air Vice-Marshal Keith Park, OC No 11 Group, this order was rescinded and units were permitted to fly in formations numbering two, three or four squadrons strong. However, these 'wings' were less impressive than they seemed as units had had little training in flying in such numbers, and the ever-present cloud cover made station keeping even more haphazard. Once over Dunkirk,

Lower right
Flg Off The Hon J W M 'Max' Aitken was one of six 'B' Flight/No 601 Sqn pilots despatched to Merville from Tangmere on the afternoon of 18 May to help swell the ranks of No 63 Wing – the flight was paired with 'A' Flight/No 145 Sqn to form a composite unit upon its arrival in France. One of the prominent pre-war members of the 'The Millionaires' Squadron', as No 601 'County of London' Sqn was unofficially known by both the RAF and the British media, Aitken enjoyed immediate success during his very first patrol from Merville, as he his combat report for 18 May 1940 recounts;

'I attacked one (He 111P of I. and II./KG 4) from astern, which broke away. I followed it down into a cloud firing one burst before entering. On emerging I fired another burst and hit his port motor. He tried to climb back to the clouds, but could not make it, so he dived. I followed and hit the starboard motor, which caught fire. His rear gunner continued firing. He (the pilot) retained control of the plane though losing height rapidly. We were now over German lines and I was out of ammunition, so I broke away. I did not see him crash, but one side of the plane was blazing and the other belching smoke. I landed back at Merville. My machine (N2568) was hit in the spinner and tailplane.'

After being credited with two He 111 kills on this day (the second is likely to have been a probable), Aitken went on to achieve 'ace status' just 24 hours later when he claimed another He 111, a Bf 110 and two Ju 87s. He enjoyed further successes over the Channel in the wake of the French evacuation, and had risen to the position of OC No 601 Sqn (plus been awarded a DFC) by the time he left the unit for non-operational duties on 20 July. Aitken went on to gain further victories with Nos 68 and 46 Sqns (Beaufighters) and the Westhampnett Wing (Spitfire IIs), finishing the war with a tally of 14 and 1 shared, 1 probable and 3 damaged (*via RAF Museum*)

the unit commanders couldn't converse with each other either, as they were out of radio (and radar) range for the controllers back in England.

Many pilots also felt that being locked into a wing formation hindered there ability to fight the enemy, as three or more squadrons would be too unwieldy to react if attacked by the Germans. This often meant that once the enemy was sighted, squadrons would effectively split up and 'do their own thing'.

The majority of kills claimed by Fighter Command during *Dynamo* were against Bf 109Es and Bf 110Cs, units flying the former type in particular being present in greater numbers in the skies over Dunkirk than had been the case during the *Blitzkrieg*. Nevertheless, some 27 Hurricane pilots achieved ace status whilst covering the evacuation, or whilst patrolling the Channel in its immediate aftermath, and a further 50 future aces also claimed kills in the late May/early June period. The two top scorers of the period were Canadians Plt Offs W L 'Willie' McKnight (10 kills) and P S 'Stan' Turner (7 kills), who flew with the predominantly Canadian-manned No 242 Sqn. Both men had seen action as reinforcements with Nos 605 and 615 Sqns during the last days of the *Blitzkrieg* (McKnight had scored his first kill – a Bf 109E – in an aircraft from the latter squadron on 19 May), and then returned to French skies with No 242 Sqn proper from the unit's Biggin Hill base.

McKnight and Turner, along with squadron-mates Flt Lt G H F Plinston (7 and 1 shared destroyed) and Plt Off R D Grassick (7 and 1 shared destroyed, 3 probables and 2 damaged), attained 'acedom' during a frantic 48-hour period between 31 May and 1 June when No 242 Sqn pilots claimed the destruction of 13 aircraft. McKnight got the bulk of these, being credited with two Bf 110s and a Bf 109 on the 31st, and two Ju 87s (plus a further two unconfirmed) the following day. He and Turner added further kills to their score following the unit's temporary return to France on 7 June to help cover the evacuation of BEF troops withdrawing through the Biscay ports.

Other high-scorers during *Dynamo* included Flg Off G R Edge of No 605 Sqn with 7 kills (approximately 20 and two shared destroyed, 3 or more probables and at least 7 damaged), Flt Lt M N 'Red Knight' Crossley of No 32 Sqn with 6 (20 and 2 shared destroyed, 1 unconfirmed destroyed and 1 damaged) and Flt Lt A H 'Ginger' Boyd of No 145 Sqn also with 6 (15 and 3 shared destroyed, 3 and 1 shared destroyed unconfirmed, 2 probables and 4 damaged). The following five pilots all scored five kills apiece; Sgt S L Butterfield of No 213 Sqn (5 and 2-4 shared destroyed and 1 unconfirmed destroyed), including four on 28 May alone, after which he was forced to bale out of his stricken Hurricane at low-level over the Channel; Plt Off V G Daw of No 32 Sqn (6 destroyed); Flt Lt R G Dutton of No 145 Sqn (13 and 6 shared destroyed, 2 probables and 8 and 1 shared damaged); Plt Off I J Muirhead of No 605 Sqn (5 and 2 shared destroyed and 3 damaged); Flt Lt R D G Wight of No 213 Sqn (5 and 2 shared destroyed and 6 and 1 unconfirmed destroyed); and Flt Lt J W C Simpson of No 43 Sqn, who recounted the sortie in which he had 'made ace' on 7 June 1940 in *Combat Report*;

'Coming towards us, in layers of twenty, were what seemed like a

No 242 Sqn's Plt Off 'Stan' Turner was one of a handful of Hurricane pilots to 'make ace' during the final stages of the BEF's involvement in France. The Devon-born Canadian only scored his first kills (two Bf 109Es) on 25 May, despite the fact that he had been flying over France since the 12th of the month. Making up for lost time, he had destroyed a further five *Emils* (plus three unconfirmed and one damaged) by 8 June. Turner added two Do 17s to his tally during the Battle of Britain, and went on to enjoy further success with Nos 145, 249 and 417 Sqns. His final score was 10 and 1 shared destroyed, 3 unconfirmed destroyed, 1 probable and 8 damaged

hundred of the enemy, looking like bees in the sky. Some were level with us. Some above. Some below. My CO (Sqn Ldr C G Lott – 2 and 3 shared destroyed and 1 unconfirmed destroyed) climbed up with us to 16,000 ft and there, while we were being circled by all of those hungry fighters, he gave the order to break up and engage. Forty were bombers. They flew south: perhaps to bomb Rouen. I singled out a Messerschmitt 109 and had a very exciting combat with him. He was a good pilot and he hit me several times. We began to do aerobatics and while he was on his back, I got in a burst which set him on fire. He jumped out, but I did not see his parachute open. His machine was almost burned out before it hit the ground. There were scores of fighters about me, but I still had plenty of ammunition. I got on the tail of another '109 and while I was firing at him two Messerschmitt 110s fired at me from either side. I continued to fire at the '109 which was badly winged. He suddenly stall turned sharply to the right, went into a spin and crashed straight into one of the other Messerschmitts which was firing at me.

'I couldn't resist following them down. It was wonderful sight. They stuck together in a sort of embrace of flames, until they were a few hundred feet above the ground. Then they parted and crashed, less than 20 yards apart.'

Fighter Command patrols along the French coast did not stop once *Dynamo* had officially ended on 3 June, however, as Hurricane and Spitfire units continued to escort both Blenheim bombers on raids against the Channel ports and coastal convoys running the gauntlet of Luftwaffe bombers (and E-boats) in the confined waters between southern England and France. Operating at the limit of their range, Hurricane squadrons were often bounced by overwhelming numbers of enemy fighters operating from newly-established bases closer to the coast. Losses were sometimes heavy – No 43 Sqn lost seven Hurricanes in two sorties on 7 June, including those flown by aces Sgts H J L Hallowes and P G Ottewill (4 and 2 shared destroyed and 1 unconfirmed destroyed or damaged), and Flg Off C A Woods-Scawan (7 destroyed, 1 unconfirmed destroyed, 4 probables and 1 damaged), whilst No 32 Sqn had three Hurricanes shot down the following day, including the aircraft flown by Plt Off D H 'Grubby' Grice (5 destroyed, 1 unconfirmed destroyed, 2 damaged and +3 destroyed according to his DFC citation).

Involved in the latter patrol as a flight commander with No 32 Sqn was future ace Flt Lt P M 'Pete' Brothers who, like many seasoned Fighter Command pilots at that time, could not understand why good men and aircraft were being sacrificed in these pointless patrols;

'After Dunkirk we were flying these utterly stupid patrols in wing strength to demonstrate air superiority. We would be detailed to fly down the French coast, cross in at Calais and then fly down to Amiens, before turning around and coming back. All of the Bf 109 chaps at Merville and Abbeville would simply rub there hands and say, "Oh, there they go", and then they would take-off just as we returned towards Calais. By this stage, invariably the sun was behind us and we would have to get home sharpish because we were by then short of fuel. They would then simply climb up and jump us. This happened

If No 87 Sqn's Plt Off 'Bea' Beamont was one of the youngest pilots involved in the Battle of France, then No 43 Sqn OC Sqn Ldr C G Lott must have been amongst the oldest. Born in 1906, his first flying posting was as a sergeant pilot with No 19 Sqn flying Grebe IIs from Duxford in 1927. He assumed command of No 43 Sqn in October 1939, and had scored 2 and 3 shared destroyed and 1 unconfirmed destroyed by the time he was wounded in action on 9 July 1940 – Lott lost the sight in his right eye, and was therefore removed from the frontline (*via N Franks*)

A highly experienced pre-war Hurricane pilot, Flt Lt J G Sanders had become No 615 Sqn's top scorer (16 destroyed and 5 damaged) by the time he left the unit in late September 1940 (*via N Franks*)

time and time again, and we were getting hammered for no reason at all. In mid-July we were sitting on the ground at Hawkinge waiting to perform one of these sorties, and we were getting short of pilots – just seven of us by this stage – when "Stuffy" Dowding arrived suddenly and came over to ask us what was going on. By then I was getting rather tired and I duly told him what I thought of these bloody silly patrols. We did one the next day and then they were stopped.'

AASF

Whilst No 11 Group was doing its best to defend the BEF evacuation to the north, the trio of AASF squadrons that had stayed in France after the Air Component units had pulled out between 21 and 23 May tried their best to protect the remnants of the British Army still on the continent. They continued their struggle until finally admitting defeat on 21 June, when the last surviving Hurricane of No 501 Sqn left the Channel Islands for England. In the intervening month, Nos 1, 73 and 501 Sqns (plus Nos 17 and 242 Sqns from 7 June onwards) had moved bases on innumerable occasion and inflicted significant losses on the ever-present enemy, but at a high price – eight pilots killed and two PoWs.

Two of those to lose their lives were aces, and both were killed within hours of one another on 7 June 1940. No 17 Sqn's Plt Off R C Whittaker (6 and 2 shared destroyed, 1 unconfirmed destroyed and 2 damaged) was downed during an engagement with Bf 109Es just inland from the coast between Le Treport and Aumale, and No 73

No 32 Sqn's 'B' Flight commander, Flt Lt 'Pete' Brothers, scored his first victories in the final days of the *Blitzkrieg*, before going on to achieve 'acedom' in the Battle of Britain (*via Tony Holmes*)

With its tail propped up on a trestle, a battle weary No 501 Sqn Hurricane I (note the wing edge chipping and oil streaked lower engine cowling) is serviced at Anglure in late May 1940 (*via N Franks*)

Combat veteran of both the 'Phoney War' and the *Blitzkrieg*, Flg Off Paul Richey is seen at Châteaudun on 14 June 1940 following his return to No 1 Sqn after a three-week spell in the American Hospital in Paris. Prior to being wounded in the neck by return fire from a He 111P of III./KG 27, Richey had downed three bombers during the 19 May action (*via Norman Franks*)

Sgt J E Proctor was No 501 Sqn's sole ace of the *Blitzkrieg*, achieving exactly five kills – he claimed two more victories in June. Commissioned and posted to No 32 Sqn upon his return to England, Proctor scored two and one shared and a probable during the Battle of Britain (*via M Sheppard*)

Sqn's Flg Off E J Kain (16 destroyed and 1 damaged) was killed in a flying accident soon after taking off from Echemines airfield, west of Troyes.

The latter's loss was felt particularly keenly within Fighter Command primarily because of the circumstances in which it had occurred, and of course because 'Cobber' Kain had been the RAF's first fighter ace of World War 2. By the time of his death, the New Zealander had become the last of the original batch of pilots sent to France with No 73 Sqn in September 1939 to still be flying in the frontline – indeed, he had been involved in the fighting almost continuously since the first day of the *Blitzkrieg*. Kain had scored 11 kills in that time, but by the end of the first week of June it was obvious he needed a rest. He received orders on 6 June to return to England to take up an instructor's post, so prior to his departure a hastily-arranged sending off party was held at *Maxim's* in Paris – a favourite AASF fighter pilots' haunt. Paul Richey, who had himself only recently left hospital after being shot in the neck on 19 May, was amongst the guests;

'I noticed, but without surprise in the circumstances, that he seemed nervous and pre-occupied, and kept breaking matches savagely in one hand while he glowered into the middle distance. Like the rest of us, he'd had enough for a bit.'

Kain was given an old two-bladed Hurricane (probably L1826) to fly back to England, this aircraft being the last of its type within No 73 Sqn, and probably as war-weary as its pilot. Some weeks earlier, the Kiwi ace, and several other pilots, had visited the French fighter squadron *Escadrille Lafayette*, where they had seen a Czech pilot performing flick rolls in a Curtiss Hawk. Renowned for his stunning aerobatics in peacetime, Kain could not resist adding this new manoeuvre to his repertoire, and soon after departing Echemines he proceeded to perform one last airfield 'beat-up'. The following report, submitted by No 73 Sqn's OC, Sqn Ldr J W C More (4 and 2 shared and 1 unconfirmed at least), to his superiors at HQ AASF RAF on 12 June 1940, starkly reveals what happenned next;

'Flg Off E J Kain took off from Echemines in a fixed-pitch Hurricane at approximately 11.15 hours on 7th June 1940, en route for Le Mans. He passed over the aerodrome at about 800 ft and went into a series of "Flick" Rolls to the left. At the third roll the aircraft lost speed very rapidly and went into a spin to the right. The spin was very fast and the aircraft straightened with a burst of engine, but was completely stalled and hit the ground.

'The aircraft burst into flames on impact and the pilot was thrown out some distance ahead of it.

'Death was instantaneous from Head injuries.'

Kain was buried at Troyes at midday on the following day, and the many newspapers which had generated so much publicity about the RAF's 'Ace Air Fighter' in the spring months, mournfully reported his death. The burnt-out wreckage of the Hurricane was left where it had fallen at the edge of the airfield, where it served as a stark reminder to the folly of such stunts – particularly to the incoming Canadian pilots of No 242 Sqn who arrived at Echemines the following day.

On a more positive note, eight pilots achieved ace status during the AASF retreat through France; No 17 Sqn's Flg Off Count M B Czernin who claimed 1 kill (13 and 5 shared destroyed, 2 unconfirmed destroyed, 3 and 1 shared probables and 3 and 2 shared damaged) and Plt Off K Manger with 4 victories (5 and 2 shared destroyed and 3 and 3 shared damaged; No 1 Sqn's Plt Off P V Boot with 2 kills (6 destroyed and 1 damaged) and Flt Sgt F G Berry with a single victory (5 destroyed and 1 unconfirmed destroyed); and No 501 Sqn's Sgt J H 'Ginger' Lacey with 2 kills (28 destroyed, 5 probables and 9 damaged) and Plt Off K N T Lee also with 2 victories (7 destroyed and 1 damaged).

NORWAY

The Hurricane was also involved in attempting to stem yet another *Blitzkrieg* attack in the spring of 1940, although in far fewer numbers than was seen in French skies. The Germans relied heavily on Swedish iron ore to feed their war effort, and in order to ensure a continued supply of this vital raw material, it was decided that the occupation of both Denmark and Norway was desirable. The occupation of both Scandinavian countries would also increase the security of Germany's northern flank when the invasion of the Soviet Union eventually commenced in May 1941.

Neither country possessed a particularly strong air arm, and the Wehrmacht marched into Denmark virtually unopposed on 9 April 1940. The Allies had realised the importance of Norway long before the Germans showed their hand, and were in the process of sending an expeditionary force to the strategically vital port of Narvik when the first Wehrmacht troops invaded neutral Denmark. The latter country was effectively captured in a day, and Norway would have gone the same way had it not been for the timely intervention of the Royal Navy.

The first RAF fighter presence in the area comprised 18 obsolescent Gladiator IIs of No 263 Sqn flown onto the frozen Lake Lesjaskog from HMS *Glorious*. Although putting up a valiant defence, the few surviving Gloster fighters still airworthy by 25 April were lost following the bombing of the lake by overwhelming Luftwaffe forces.

With the south of the country in German hands, the Allies now decided to counter-attack at Narvik, and to help provide vital fighter cover for the assault, a restocked No 263 Sqn was joined by the Hurricane-equipped No 46 Sqn again aboard *Glorious*. After an uneventful sea crossing, 17

Watched by an anxious pilot, visible in the lower right-hand corner of the photograph, an anonymous No 46 Sqn Hurricane I is carefully hoisted from Blackburn's wharf at Abbotsinch onto a lighter moored alongside in the Clyde. This process was repeated some 17 times on 10/11 May 1940 as the squadron was embarked aboard HMS *Glorious*, anchored some 20 miles down the Clyde. No 46 Sqn had been expecting to go to France (indeed, its OC, Sqn Ldr K B B 'Bing' Cross and flight commander Flt Lt P G 'Pat' Jameson had already visited the continent in search of suitable landing sites), but instead received orders for immediate embarkation to Norway. They duly flew their aircraft from their Digby base, south of Lincoln, to Abbotsinch, west of Glasgow, on 9 May, the pilots completing their journey by taxying their mounts through fields to the wharf for loading. Kiwi Jameson made the following observations in respect to the latter operation;

'The sight of our beloved Hurricanes being hauled up on the end of a rope, swinging around, wings and tails nearly hitting the side of the ship, was sickening.'

Sqn Ldr Cross had insisted that each pilot accompany his aircraft from the wharf to the carrier in order to make a note of any damage incurred during the loading operation (*via RAF Museum*)

'PO-C' has safely made the crossing from terra firma to its awaiting lighter. Although none of the Hurricanes suffered serious damage during the loading, the squadron discovered *after* the carrier had sailed that wing mainplane locking bolts for four or five aircraft had been taken back ashore by the slinging party! Rendered unflyable, the aircraft were soon returned to airworthiness, however, by the ship's engineers, who made new bolts for the forlorn fighters (*via Jerry Scutts*)

Flt Lt 'Pat' Jameson and his OC, Sqn Ldr 'Bing' Cross, were the only RAF pilots to survive the sinking of HMS *Glorious* on 8 June 1940. During his brief time in Norway he had downed a Ju 88 and shared in the destruction of two Do 26 flying boats alighted on the water (*via Phil Jarrett*)

Hurricane pilots were led off the carrier by their OC, Sqn Ldr K B B Cross, and recovered at Bardufoss on 26 May.

Despite the German presence in Narvik being quickly eliminated by the Allied force, the collapse of resistance in central Norway released more aircraft and naval vessels to aid the struggling Wehrmacht in the north.

No 46 Sqn soon found itself down to 15 serviceable aircraft even before the Germans had fired a shot, as poorly prepared runways wreaked havoc with the Hurricanes' normally sturdy undercarriage. First blood was drawn by the unit 48 hours after their arrival when a Ju 88A of 6./KG 30 was shot down. Over the next 13 days, the Hurricane pilots would destroy 11 German aircraft during 249 sorties for the loss of two fighters (and their pilots) in combat. Despite this success, combined with the significant contribution made by No 263 Sqn, Allied commanders realised that the Germans could no longer be denied their victory in Scandinavia.

On 7 June word was passed to No 46 Sqn to prepare for evacuation, and in a final stroke of brilliant airmanship (performed only after Sqn Ldr Cross had convinced his RAF and Royal Navy commanders of the feasibility of his plan) all ten surviving Hurricanes were flown back aboard *Glorious* with the minimum of fuss in the early hours of the following day. However, later that afternoon the carrier was intercepted by the German battlecruisers *Scharnhorst* and *Gneisenau* and swiftly sunk. Only two air force pilots survived the sinking of the *Glorious* out of the 59 RAF personnel aboard – Sqn Ldr Cross and Flt Lt P G Jameson, both of No 46 Sqn.

A further three pilots also survived the virtual annihilation of No 46 Sqn by escaping Norway aboard the troopship MV *Arandora Star* due to a shortage of aircraft. Amongst this lucky trio was the campaign's leading scorer on Hurricanes, Plt Off J F Drummond, who was credited with four kills, plus a further two damaged. He went on to become an ace flying Spitfires with No 92 Sqn during the Battle of Britain, and was finally killed on 10 October 1940 when in collision with fellow squadron ace Plt Off D G Williams during an attempted interception of a Do 17 over Tangmere – the latter pilot also lost his life.

A second member of the troopship party, Plt Off P W Lefevre, who gained a shared kill over Norway, would also become an ace later in the war (5 and 5 shared destroyed, 1 shared probable and 1 damaged), as did *Glorious* survivor Flt Lt P G Jameson (9 destroyed, 1 and 1 shared probable, 1 shared probable, 2 damaged and 2 shared destroyed on water) – his Norwegian claims comprised a Ju 88 destroyed and the shared destruction of two prototype Do 26V flying boats spotted unloading field artillery in a fjord.

COLOUR PLATES

This 13-page colour section profiles many of the aircraft flown by the leading Hurricane Mk I aces of the 1939-40 period, as well as the mounts of some of the lesser known pilots who scored five or more kills. All the artwork has been specially commissioned for this volume, and profile artist Keith Fretwell and figure artist Mike Chappell have gone to great pains to illustrate the aircraft, and their pilots, as accurately as possible following exhaustive research by the author. The majority of the 42 Hurricanes depicted in profile over the following pages have never been illustrated in colour before, and the schemes shown have been fully authenticated either by surviving aces like 'Pete' Brothers and Dennis David, or through comparison with contemporary images taken by serving personnel, or press photographers, in 1939-40.

1
Hurricane Mk I L1679 of No 1 Sqn, flown by Flg Off Paul Richey, Vassincourt, late 1939

2
Hurricane Mk I P3395 of No 1 Sqn, flown by Flt Lt A V Clowes, Collyweston, early November 1940

3
Hurricane Mk I P3878 of No 17 Sqn, flown by Plt Off H A C Bird-Wilson, Debden, 24 September 1940

4
Hurricane Mk I P3144 of No 32 Sqn, flown by Sqn Ldr J Worrall and Flt Lt M N Crossley, Biggin Hill/Hawkinge, mid-July 1940

5
Hurricane Mk I P2921 of No 32 Sqn, flown by Flt Lt P M Brothers, Biggin Hill/Hawkinge, July 1940

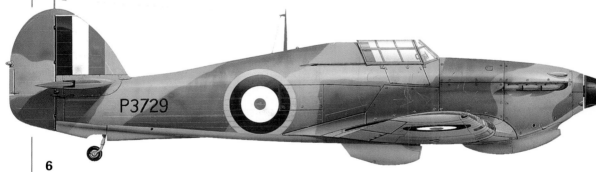

6
Hurricane Mk I (Trop) P3729 of No 33 Sqn, flown by Flg Off V C Woodward, Fuka, Egypt, October 1940

7
Hurricane Mk I P2970 of No 56 Sqn, flown by Plt Off A G Page, Rochford, 12 August 1940

8
Hurricane Mk I R2689 of No 56 Sqn, flown by Flt Lt E J Gracie, North Weald, 30 August 1940

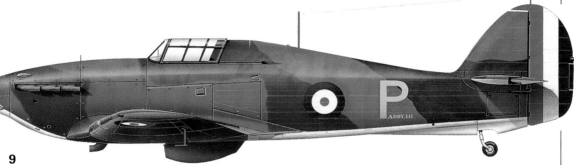

9
Hurricane Mk I (serial unknown) of No 73 Sqn, flown by Flg Off E J Kain, Rouvres, France, early spring 1940

10
Hurricane Mk I P2569 of No 73 Sqn, flown by Flt Lt R E Lovett, Rouvres, France, 19 April 1940

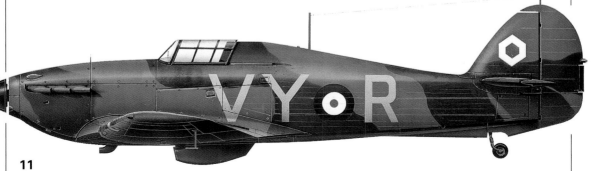

11
Hurricane Mk I (serial unknown) of No 85 Sqn, flown by Flt Lt R H A Lee, Lille/Seclin, France, 6 December 1939

12
Hurricane Mk I P3854 of No 85 Sqn, flown by Sqn Ldr P W Townsend, Church Fenton, September 1940

13
Hurricane Mk I P2923 of No 85 Sqn, flown by Flg Off A G Lewis, Castle Camps, June 1940

14
Hurricane Mk I L1630 of No 87 Sqn, flown by Plt Off W D David, Lille/Seclin, May 1940

15
Hurricane Mk I P2798 of No 87 Sqn, flown by Flt Lt I R Gleed, Exeter, August 1940

16
Hurricane Mk I P3394 of No 87 Sqn, flown by Plt Off J R Cock, Hullavington, 26 July 1940

17
Hurricane Mk I L2001 of No 111 Sqn, flown by Flg Off H M Ferriss, Wick, February 1940

18
Hurricane Mk I P3221 of No 145 Sqn, flown by Flt Lt A H Boyd, Westhampnett, August 1940

19
Hurricane Mk I P3039 of No 229 Sqn, flown by Plt Off V M M Ortmans, Northolt, September/October 1940

20
Hurricane Mk I P3462 of No 238 Sqn, flown by Plt Off C T Davis, Middle Wallop, September 1940

21
Hurricane Mk I V7467 of No 242 Sqn, flown by Sqn Ldr D R S Bader, Coltishall, September 1940

22
Hurricane Mk I P2961 of No 242 Sqn, flown by Flg Off W L McKnight, Coltishall, December 1940

23
Hurricane Mk I W9145 of No 245 Sqn, flown by Sqn Ldr J W C Simpson, Aldergrove, December 1940

24
Hurricane Mk I P3870 of No 249 Sqn, flown by Plt Off R G A Barclay, Church Fenton, July 1940

25
Hurricane Mk I V6555 of No 257 Sqn, flown by Sqn Ldr R R S Tuck, North Weald, October 1940

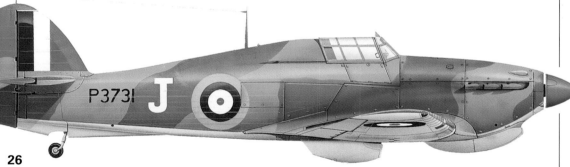

26
Hurricane Mk I (Trop) P3731 of No 261 Sqn, flown by Sgt F N Robertson, Luqa, Malta, December 1940

27
Hurricane Mk I (Trop) V7474, No 261 Sqn, flown by Flt Lt J A F MacLachlan and Sgt F N Robertson, Malta, November 1940

28
Hurricane Mk I (Trop) P2544 of No 274 Sqn, possibly flown by Flg Off E M Mason, Amiriya, Egypt, November 1940

29
Hurricane Mk I P3931 of No 302 'Polish' Sqn, flown by Flg Off W S Król, Northolt, 15 October 1940

30
Hurricane Mk I P3975 of No 303 'Polish' Sqn, flown by Sgt J Frantisek, Northolt, September 1940

31
Hurricane Mk I R4175 of No 303 'Polish' Sqn, flown by Sgt J Frantisek, Northolt, September 1940

32
Hurricane Mk I P3901 of No 303 'Polish' Sqn, flown by Flg Off W Urbanowicz, Northolt, September 1940

33
Hurricane Mk I P3120 of No 303 'Polish' Sqn, flown by Flg Off Z K Henneberg, Northolt, September 1940

34
Hurricane Mk I V6665 of No 303 'Polish' Sqn, flown by Flt Lt J A Kent, Northolt, September 1940

35
Hurricane Mk I P3700 of No 303 'Polish' Sqn, flown by Plt Off M Feric, Northolt, September 1940

36
Hurricane Mk I V7503 of No 303 'Polish' Sqn, flown by Flg Off M Pisarek, Leconfield, November 1940

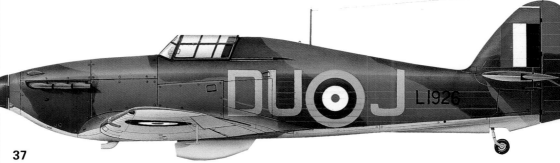

37
Hurricane Mk I L1926 of No 312 'Czech' Sqn, flown by Plt Off A Vasatko, Speke, October 1940

38
Hurricane Mk I P3059 of No 501 Sqn, flown by Plt Off K N T Lee, Gravesend, 18 August 1940

39
Hurricane Mk I V6799 of No 501 Sqn, flown by Plt Off K W Mackenzie, Gravesend, 18 August 1940

40
Hurricane Mk I (serial unknown) of No 601 Sqn, flown by Flg Off W H Rhodes-Moorhouse, Tangmere, July 1940

41
Hurricane Mk I P3308 of No 605 Sqn, flown by Acting Sqn Ldr A A McKellar, Croydon, October 1940

42
Hurricane Mk I R4194 of No 615 Sqn, flown by Flg Off A Eyre, Kenley, August 1940

1
Flg Off E M 'Imshi' Mason of No 274
Sqn, Amiriya, Egypt, November 1940

2
Sqn Ldr Douglas Bader, OC No 242
Sqn, Coltishall, September 1940

3
Flg Off V C 'Woody' Woodward of No
33 Sqn, Fuka, Egypt, October 1940

4
Flg Off E J 'Cobber' Kain of No 73
Sqn, Rouvres, France, mid-May 1940

5
Sgt J H 'Ginger' Lacey of No 501 Sqn,
Bétheniville, France, mid-May 1940

6
Flg Off Zdzislaw Henneberg, joint 'A'
Flight commander of No 303 'Polish'
Sqn, Northolt, September 1940

THE BATTLE OF BRITAIN

Although the RAF's Hurricane units had inflicted heavy losses on the Luftwaffe during both the *Blitzkrieg* and the Dunkirk evacuation, as well as the Channel convoy patrols which followed, these successes paled when set against the sheer volume of victories credited to pilots of the Hawker fighter during the 123 days that historians generally recognise as having constituted the Battle of Britain – 1 July to 31 October 1940. During this period, Fighter Command squadrons (those equipped with Hurricanes, Spitfires and Defiants only) claimed 2475 kills, of which 1392 emanated from Hurricane units. Of the latter total, 658.49 were actually awarded to pilots by the RAF – the gulf between claims and actual credits graphically underlines the high level of over-claiming which seemed to plague fighter combat during World War 2, and Fighter Command in particular during the summer of 1940.

RAF pilots knew at the time that overclaiming was rife, due principally to the nature of the engagements in which they were involved. Dennis David, who initially became an ace within the first week of combat in France with No 87 Sqn, and then went on to claim a further seven kills with this unit and No 213 Sqn during the Battle of Britain, had the following explanation for exaggerated kill figures;

'More often than not, I didn't find it possible to confirm aircraft shot down. We shot at a lot. We destroyed a lot. We damaged a lot. But there was too much going on in the sky to see the results. You'd tell the squadron intelligence officer when you landed. You'd fill out a report listing date, time, weather factor, your aircraft number. Then

One in a sequence of photos taken by legendary aviation photographer Charles E Brown during a visit to Tangmere in early July 1940, this view shows a section of No 601 Sqn Mk Is being fuelled (the aircraft to the left also appears to be having its magazines reloaded) prior to undertaking a convoy protection patrol off the south coast. The unit seems to be relying on a towable bowser rather than the ubiquitous Albion three-point truck in this instance. Note also the belts of .303-in ammunition draped over the flat-loader trolley marked '601', the solitary fire extinguisher just forward of the bowser and the fitter holding the radio access panel for the Hurricane parked to the right of the photo. Three pilots are visible in this view, although only two have been identified – the individual in the pre-war white overall standing behind said radio fitter is Flg Off 'Willie' Rhodes-Moorhouse, whilst the pilot in the 'Mae West' behind the ammunition trolley is newly-promoted squadron OC, Sqn Ldr The Hon J W M 'Max' Aitken (*via Phil Jarrett*)

he'd ask, "What did you see? What did you do?" Gradually from the report would emerge a confirmed score, or perhaps not. The system wasn't always accurate. It couldn't be. A list was published throughout Fighter Command once a month. It would list high scores. I was given 17 on that list once. It was really only to boost morale.'

It is not the purpose of this volume (or this series as a whole, for that matter) to deride or re-write the official record books when it comes to discussing the victories credited to aces that flew the Hurricane in 1939/40. Therefore, all the scores that appear herewith are based on those that have been officially accepted by the RAF's Historical Branch over the years, or collated from primary sources produced by such respected aviation historians as Christopher Shores, Clive Williams, Brian Cull and Norman Franks.

With these factors duly taken into consideration, and following lengthy cross-checking with recognised reference works on the RAF's 'finest hour', I have calculated that some 132 Hurricane pilots achieved 'ace status' between 1 July and 31 December 1940 – although the Battle of Britain officially started on 10 July and ended on 31 October, for the sake of completeness, the comparatively small number of kills scored on either side of these dates are also included.

A further 16 pilots who had achieved 'acedom' prior to 1 July 1940 scored five or more victories during the same period. These outstanding successes are tempered by the fact that no fewer than 46 Hurricane aces were killed either in combat or in operational accidents during the same period.

JULY SKIRMISHES

As previously, the Battle of Britian officially commenced on 10 July (aircrew flying in operations with Fighter Command from this date forth through to 31 October are entitled to wear the much coveted 'Battle of Britain Clasp' on their 1939-45 Star) when a large force of Do 17s from KG 2, escorted by Bf 110s of ZG 26 and Bf 109s from JG 3, attacked a coastal convoy in the Straits of Dover. This raid was despatched as a result of the Luftwaffe operation order issued on 2 July which specified the dual objectives of sweeping both the Channel of British shipping and the skies of British fighters.

In the days prior to this first big attack, larger and larger formations of German aircraft had been testing the effectiveness of the RAF's RDF chain along the southern coastline. The sites within No 11 Group had been of particular interest to the Germans, as the 21 single-seat fighter squadrons based within the boundaries of this strategically important group relied heavily on accurate plots from these radar stations due to their close proximity to incoming raids.

In responding to the convoy attacks, Fighter Command's sector controllers attempted to employ their favoured pre-war tactic which saw Hurricane units engaging the bombers whilst Spitifre squadrons attempted to deal with the Messerschmitt escorts. This delineation of roles was occasionally adhered to, but as the raids grew both in size and frequency, Hurricane units 'mixed it' with the Messerschmitt fighters just as often as their Spitfire-equipped brethren. As many of the squadrons involved in this initial phase of the battle were still attempting to return to full strength following the debacle of France, the responsibilty of taking the fight to the enemy over home waters invariably fell to the weary survivors of the *Blitzkrieg* and Operation *Dynamo* – often with fatal results.

One unit which seemed to suffer more casualties than most during the lead up to 10 July was veteran Biggin Hill-based Hurricane outfit No 79 Sqn, whose pilots had seen continuous action from the moment they had been rushed to France to help bolster the Air Component on 10 May. Having lost two aircrew killed, one captured and one injured, plus nine aircraft destroyed, the remnants of No 79 Sqn returned to Biggin Hill on 21 May, where replacement pilots and aircraft were received. However, during clashes over the Channel with marauding Bf 109s in June the unit lost a further two pilots (including 6-kill ace Flt Lt J W E Davies, who died just hours before he was due to receive his DFC from His Majesty King George VI in a ceremony held at Biggin Hill on 27 June – fellow No 79 Sqn aces Plt Off D W A Stones and Sgts H Cartwright and A W Whitby, plus No 32 Sqn aces Flt Lt M N Crossley and Plt Offs V G Daw and D H Grice, did, however, receive their DFCs and DFMs on this date).

Early July proved no better for No 79 Sqn, as firstly one of their NCO aces of the Battle of France (Sgt H Cartwright) was lost over the Channel to Bf 109s on 4 July, followed three days later by their CO of less than two months, Sqn Ldr J D C Joslin (who had seen action whilst serving as a flight commander with No 56 Sqn in France) – the latter was accidently shot down and killed by Spitfires also over the Channel.

Two more pilots were lost in action 24 hours later, these final casualties convincing AVM Keith Park that No 79 Sqn was a spent force. He

Veterans of the *Blitzkrieg*, the survivors of No 79 Sqn returned to their Biggin Hill home on 21 May and immediately started to regroup for the impending defence of Britain. The unit had enjoyed some success over the continent, and two of the pilots in this view (taken outside the squadron dispersal hut in the first days of July) received decorations from the King on 27 June for their exploits in France. Standing at the extreme left is pre-war pilot Sgt Henry Cartwright, who was awarded a DFM for destroying five aircraft, whilst Plt Off D W A 'Dimsie' Stones (fourth from left) was presented with a DFC for scoring 5 and 2 shared, 2 unconfirmed and 1 damaged. No 79 Sqn suffered serious losses during the Channel clashes in June /July, with Sgt Cartwright (on 4 July) and Sqn Ldr J D C Joslin (third from left – on 7 July) being amongst those killed. The pilot with the tin helmet on his head (reportedly disguised as a poached egg!) is Plt Off T C Parker, who scored 2 and 3 shared destroyed, 1 unconfirmed destroyed and 3 damaged with No 79 Sqn in 1940. The remaining two individuals are Plt Off Murray (no details) and squadron intelligence officer, Flg Off Bill Edwards (*via Norman Franks*)

Although this view of No 111 Sqn pilots at Northolt was taken some two years prior to the Battle of Britain, it nevertheless shows six men who used their vast experience on Hurricanes to achieve ace status with the aircraft in 1940. Looking resplendent in their spotless white overalls are, from left to right; Plt Off B A Mortimer; Sgt Smith; Sgt W L Dymond (10 and 1 shared destroyed, 1 probable and 6 damaged – killed on 2 September 1940); Flg Off M L Robinson (16 destroyed, 4 and 1 shared probables and 8 and 1 shared damaged – killed 10 on April 1942); Plt Off J G Sanders (16 destroyed and 5 damaged); Plt Off R G Dutton (13 and 6 shared destroyed, 2 probables and 8 and 1 damaged); Sqn Ldr J Gillan; Flg Off R P R Powell (7 and 2 shared destroyed, 1 unconfirmed destroyed, 3 probables and 4 damaged); Flg Off C S Darwood (killed on 18 May 1940); and Plt Off S D P Connors (12 destroyed, 2 and 1 unconfirmed destroyed and 4 damaged – killed on 18 August 1940) (*via Norman Franks*)

ordered the unit north to the No 13 Group base at Acklington for a period of rest, where it remained until posted south to rejoin the fray from Biggin Hill in late August.

Not all units faired as badly as No 79 Sqn in these early clashes, however, with the pilots of Croydon-based No 111 Sqn in particular quickly earning a fierce reputation for their head-on attacks on bomber formations. This potentially hazardous tactic had been widely employed by Hurricane units in France, as it enabled a small number of fighters to break up a larger bomber force, which then allowed other friendly units to pick off targets individually. Although the attacking pilot ran the risk of colliding with his quarry, and had less time to both take aim and fire as he closed on his target at a combined speed of over 500 mph, the chance of obtaining telling hits was infinitely greater from the front, as German aircraft were less well armed (and armoured) in this area.

A great proponent of this method of attack was Flt Lt 'Pete' Brothers who, whilst serving as a flight commander firstly with No 32 Sqn and then No 257 Sqn, scored ten kills during the Battle of Britain;

'The urgent thing was to get at the bombers before they dropped their bombs, and if you were short of the height you wanted to carry out a stern or beam attack, the best thing to do was take them head-on and go straight through the formation. I always dived underneath the bombers short of impact because I always thought that the instinctive thing for pilots to do was pull up rather than push down when faced with collision, and the last thing I wanted was to meet a Dornier or Heinkel at close quarters. This manoeuvre also produced additional speed, thus enabling me to pull the Hurricane around once clear of the bombers and turn back into them again for a more conventional stern attack.

'Head on shots were the easiest of the lot to perform because there was no deflection needed whatsoever. I would press home the attack

until I thought a collision was almost inevitable. In many respects this was the best form of attack, as most bombers had less protection from both guns and armour at the front. It was often very difficult to confirm whether you had inflicted mortal damage to an aircraft after a single pass, however, as once you had turned back into the bombers the formation had often scattered in response to your initial assault. With a stern attack you would usually look to set an engine on fire, thus denoting some success for your endeavours.'

Another great proponent of the head-on attack was No 253 Sqn's OC, Sqn Ldr G R 'Gerry' Edge, who had earlier perfected his technique with No 605 Sqn over the Dunkirk beaches whilst achieving ace status. Indeed, he got so proficient at tackling bombers as the summer months wore on that of the 11 kills (added to his $7^{1}/2$ over France) he claimed between 7 and 15 September, no less than five of these were Ju 88s (four claimed on 9 September alone), four He 111s and one a solitary Do 17. In the following passage, he describes the intricacies of his favoured method of attack;

'If you left it till your last hundred yards to break away from a head-on attack, you were in trouble. With practice, you got to judge when to break. But once you knew how, a head-on attack was a piece of cake. When you opened fire, you'd kill or badly wound the pilot and the second pilot. Then you'd rake the line of them as you broke away. On one attack, the first Heinkel I hit crashed into the next Heinkel. There was a lot of crashing among the bombers we attacked head-on.'

During these early aerial battles above the Channel convoys, RAF squadrons typically lost one fighter for every three or four German aircraft claimed destroyed, with the bulk of losses and victories being proportionately higher within the Hurricane units primarily because of their greater number within No 11 Group – some 200 Hawker fight-

On 29 July 1940 a Fox Film Unit photographer shot a number of stills at Hawkinge whilst his colleagues were busy making a series of instructional films for the RAF. Some of the images he captured that day are easily amongst the best photos taken during the Battle of Britain, showing pilots at readiness between sorties. His subjects were No 32 Sqn's 'B' Flight, forward based at Hawkinge from Biggin Hill. This unit enjoyed great success during 1940, having claimed some 102 kills by the time it left No 11 Group at the end of August. Indeed, of the seven pilots seen here lounging about at 'B' Flight's dispersal, only Plt Off Keith Gillman (second from left) failed to 'make ace' – he was killed over the Channel on 25 August. The remaining pilots are (l to r); Plt Off R F Smythe (6 destroyed, 2 unconfirmed destroyed, 1 probable and 1 damaged); Plt Off J E Proctor (9 and 1 shared destroyed and 1 probable); Flt Lt P M Brothers (16 destroyed, 1 probable and 3 damaged); Plt Off D H Grice (5 destroyed, 1 unconfirmed destroyed, 2 damaged); Plt Off P M Gardner (8 and 2 shared destroyed and 1 damaged); and Plt Off A F Eckford (8-9 and 3 shared destroyed, 2-3 probables and 5 damaged) (*via John Weal*)

ers were usually available at any one time to controllers responding to raids entering this sector. Although this may seem quite a large number of Hurricanes, it must be remembered that even at this early stage in the battle, fighter pilots were typically being called upon to fly at least three sorties a day, and that this figure would only rise as Luftwaffe raids grew both in size and intensity as the month wore on.

An indication of just how hectic the daily schedule was for 'The Few' can be gauged by the following quote from No 501 Sqn ace,

Flt Lt Eustace 'Gus' Holden (7 destroyed, 1 and 1 shared probable and 3 damaged);

'At dawn one day, the squadron went to 30,000 ft and, on landing, I started to walk to the mess for some breakfast when I was recalled for standby. Relieved ten minutes later, I again made for the mess but just as I got to the door, I was called back and I had to go to 30,000 ft again. Back at the aerodrome in due course, I tried again to get a meal. I was half-way through it when I was wanted for another standby. When that came to nothing, I made for my quarters to have a shave. I'd just lathered myself when the loudspeaker called, "501 Sqn – readiness". So up to 30,000 ft again. Later, I finished shaving and actually had lunch before being called for another standby. Then, about five o'clock, at 30,000 ft again for the fourth time that day.'

This ceaseless cycle of combat patrols and scrambled interceptions quickly took a toll on the pilots, many of whom were experiencing action for the very first time. One of the units heavily embroiled in the early Channel clashes was North Weald-based No 151 Sqn, who daily sent its flights to operate from the day-time coastal airfields at either Rochford or Manston. Like a number of other units that had been mauled during *Dynamo*, and the Channel clashes that followed, No 151 Sqn relied heavily throughout this period on its veteran OC, Sqn Ldr 'Teddy' Donaldson (5 and 1 shared destroyed, 3 unconfirmed destroyed and 1 damaged), who had the uncanny knack of getting the best out even the most fatigued flyer;

'If I thought it was a rest a man needed, I'd give him a fortnight's holiday. If I felt the war had really

Pilots were plagued with poor radio communication throughout 1940, as the pre-war TR.9 equipment proved to be anything but reliable. Here, a radio fitters (note the 'electrical' flash sewn onto the right sleeve of their tunics) from No 601 Sqn tinker with the set fitted in Mk I P3886/ 'UF-K' at Tangmere. This aircraft suffered serious engine problems whilst on a morning patrol on 26 July 1940, forcing its pilot, Flg Off H J Riddle to effect an emergency landing at Tangmere (*via J Scutts*)

Pilots of 'A' Flight, No 17 Sqn, pose for a photo between patrols at Debden in July 1940. Of these six pilots, only Sgt Glyn Griffiths (sitting far right) achieved ace status, scoring 5 and 5 shared destroyed, 3 probables and 1 and 1 shared damaged – all in 1940 (*via N Franks*)

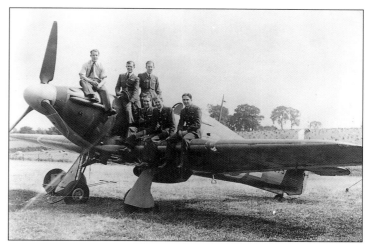

got to him, I'd get rid of him. There weren't many of them. There was one chap who said one day, "I think I'd better stay down today because I've got double vision". He was obviously fatigued; we all were, though we didn't use that word for it then. I looked at him and his eyes really were pointing in different directions. I said, "Look, the Germans don't know you've got double vision so you'd better come with us. The Germans will see 12 Hurricanes, not 11 with one extra chap who can't see

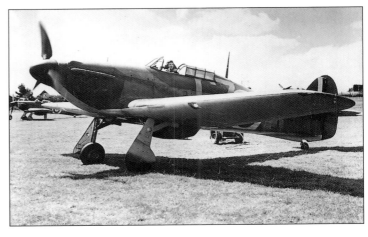

straight". Someone said, "You're a shit, sir". But he survived.'

On 20 July Fighter Command claimed its biggest 'bag' of Luftwaffe aircraft yet (15, of which 13 are confirmed by German records) whilst defending a coastal convoy code-named 'Bosom'. The focal point for the attacking Hurricanes from Nos 32 and 615 Sqns were the Ju 87Bs of II./StG 1, which suffered badly in the near-hour long fight some ten miles off Dover. Two were downed over the convoy itself, a further pair crash-landed in France with battle damage and two more returned to their base at Lannion bearing the evidence of a fight. A quartet of defending Bf 109Es from I./JG 27 (one aircraft, flown by *Gruppenkommandeur* Hauptmann Helmut Riegel) and I./JG 51 (three fighters) were also lost to the Hurricane pilots, who in turn suffered a single fatality.

The success enjoyed by the Hurricane in action over 'Bosom' against a superior number of Bf 109Es was primarily due to the fact that the RAF pilots had bounced the *Jagdflieger* from a superior altitude, using 'hit and run' tactics identical to those employed against them in France.

Five Fighter Command pilots credited with kills during this action went on to achieve ace status later in the battle – No 615 Sqn's Flg Offs A Eyre (8 and 2 shared destroyed, 2 unconfirmed destroyed, 2

Another in the sequence of Fox photos from 29 July 1940, this shot shows Plt Off Rupert Smythe about to taxy away in P3522 after receiving the order to scramble. The Irishman used this fighter to destroy two Bf 109Es (plus a third uncon-firmed) off Deal on 4 July and a Do 17 (claimed as a 'Do 215' by the pilot) again off Deal/ Dover on 12 August. The aircraft had its engine wrecked by return fire from a Do 17 off Selsey Bill three days later, its pilot, Sgt B Henson, having to perform a dead-stick landing at Tangmere. Once repaired, it was issued to No 213 Sqn on 19 September, but was written off in a fatal accident on 10 January 1941 (*via Phil Jarrett*)

A trio of No 32 Sqn Hurricanes 'jockey' for position prior to taking off on 29 July. The middle aircraft (N2459) was the favoured mount of Plt Off 'Grubby' Grice, who used it to down three Bf 109Es – two on 19 May and one on 15 August (*via J Weal*)

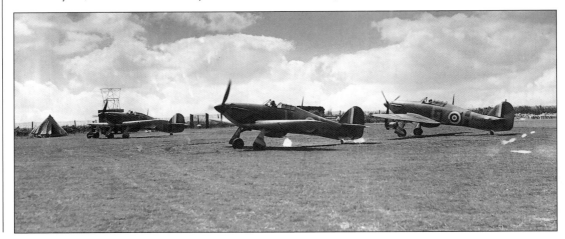

Hurricane I P3878 was regularly flown during the Battle of Britain by Flg Off H A C Bird-Wilson, who used it to down two Bf 109Es (plus a third as a probable) and share in the destruction of a Do 17 and a He 111. He was finally shot down in the fighter over Chatham on 24 September by Major Adolf Galland – that same day Bird-Wilson was awarded the DFC! The Hurricane is seen here parked at Debden in July 1940, with future ace Plt Off J K Ross (2 and 3 shared destroyed and 2 probables) stood in front of it (via Don Healey)

Gloster-built Mk I P2923 is seen moments away from landing at No 85 Sqn's satellite landing ground at Castle Camps on 25 July 1940, Battle of Farnce ace Plt Off A G Lewis at the controls. Note the sky stripes on the aircraft's Rotol propeller spinner and the exhaust anti-glare shield just forward of the cockpit. This aircraft was lost in action on 18 August 1940 (via A Thomas)

probables and 6 damaged) and L M Gaunce (5 and 1 shared destroyed, 2 and 1 shared probable and 6 damaged) were credited with a Bf 109E apiece, as was No 32 Sqn's Flt Lt 'Pete' Brothers. His squadron-mates, Flg Off J B W Humpherson (5 destroyed, 2 probables and 3 damaged) and Sgt W B Higgins (4 and 1 shared destroyed and 1 damaged – killed on 14 September 1940 whilst flying with No 253 Sqn) claimed a Ju 87 and a Bf 110 respectively.

The convoy raids continued into August, with Fighter Command destroying appreciable numbers of enemy aircraft (about 220 German aircraft were lost in action during the month of July), but at a price – some 24 Hurricane pilots had been killed between 1 July and 7 August (phase one of the Battle of Britain). Of this tally, just two were aces – Sgt H Cartwright (No 79 Sqn) and Plt Off J R Hamar (4 destroyed, 2 unconfirmed destroyed and 1 damaged) of No 151 Sqn, the latter being killed when he attempted an upward roll at 120 knots at an altitude of barely 100 ft over North Weald upon his return from an aborted section patrol with Sqn Ldr 'Teddy' Donaldson – the two had flown together on no fewer than 303 occasions in 1940. Hamar, a veteran of France, was decapitated when his Hurricane (P3316) struck the ground inverted. Six days later he was posthumously awarded a DFC.

Although these actions over the Channel were nowhere near as large as the bombing raids flown against London and the airfields in the south-east between mid-August and the end of September, they nevertheless posed their own hazards, as future ace 'Johnny' Kent (12 destroyed, 3 probables, 2 damaged and 1 destroyed on the ground) explained in his autobiography, One of the few (Corgi, 1975 edition);

'These early combats were, in my opinion, the most deadly of all, and many a good fighter pilot was lost who would have been

invaluable in the days that followed. Fighting over England, one always had the comfort of knowing that if one was forced to jump, one would come down on land where medical attention, if required, could rapidly be obtained. Over the sea it was a different matter, as we were only equipped with archaic Mae Wests, the buoyancy of which depended upon wads of kapok and a rubber bladder that had to be inflated by mouth. The chances of being picked up during a convoy attack if one had to bale out were very remote.'

'PEEWIT'

Convoy C.W.9, codenamed 'Peewit' by the RAF, consisted of 20 merchant ships and 9 naval escorts. It had left the Medway on the evening of 7 August and had attempted to pass through the now treacherous Straits of Dover under the cover of darkness. However, it was duly detected by a newly-built German *Freya* radar site on the Calais coast and attacked by E-boats, which sunk three merchantmen. Come the dawn, the Luftwaffe's *Luftflotte 3* was given the task of finishing off the convoy as it sailed past Brighton.

Two days earlier, Reichsmarschall Göring had told *Luftflotten* commanders assembled at his Karinhall home to prepare for the next phase of the battle, which would commence on 10 August – *Adlertag* ('Eagle Day'). According to Luftwaffe strategists, this series of raids would herald the beginning of the end for the RAF, as German bombers struck at key airfields and military installations in both the south and the north. Göring boasted that in just four days all fighter bases in southern England would be rendered unusable, and within four weeks remaining British defences would be obliterated – perfectly timed for the planned invasion, code-named *Seelöwe* ('Sealion'), which was scheduled for mid-September.

With a key part to play in the annihilation of Fighter Command, *Luftflotte 3*'s commander, Generalfeldmarschall Hugo Sperrle, saw the 'Peewit' convoy as an ideal target for his bombers to practice pin-point attacks against, whilst at the same time allowing their escorting fighter *Gruppen* to inflict telling casualties on their RAF opponents as the latter attempted to defend the hapless merchantmen. The key weapon for the Germans would be the 60+ Ju 87Bs of StGs 2, 3 and 77, small formations of dive-bombers being despatched to test Fighter Command's defences throughout the morning of the 8th.

Much to Sperrle's consternation, No 11 Group appeared capable of dealing with the roving Stukas, and their Bf 109E escorts, in a day that saw some 27 German aircraft destroyed or damaged beyond repair for the loss of 12 RAF pilots – 9 of the latter were flying Hurricanes. Indeed, it was only when a large force of 57 Ju 87s swamped the defending fight-

No 17 Sqn's Flg Off 'Birdy' Bird-Wilson is seen relaxing in the civilised surroundings of the Debden Officers' Mess in the early summer of 1940. The bottom photo shows the personal insignia Bird-Wilson had painted on the cockpit door of P3878 sometime in late July. Unlike their contemporaries, No 17 Sqn's COs (the unit had three in as many months) seemed to have adopted a rather laissez faire attitude towards personal markings during the summer of 1940
(*via Norman Franks and Don Healey*)

ers just after midday that the convoy suffered casualties – four merchantmen were sunk and numerous others forced to limp into coastal ports. Only a quartet of vessels actually made it to their destination of Swanage, in Dorset.

Westhampnett-based No 145 Sqn was at the heart of the action throughout the defence of 'Peewit', breaking up dive-bombing attacks on three separate occasions, and claiming the destruction of 21 aircraft (their actual score appears to be 11). Undoubtedly *the* performance of the day by any pilot within Fighter Command came from No 145 Sqn's seasoned *Dynamo* ace, and 'B' Flight commander, Flt Lt A H 'Ginger' Boyd (15 and 3 shared destroyed, 3 and 1 shared unconfirmed destroyed, 2 probables and 4 damaged), who was credited with the destruction of five aircraft (two Bf 109Es, two Bf 110s and a Ju 87), plus a sixth (Ju 87) damaged.

No 601 Sqn's Plt Off J K U B McGrath became the second of six pilots to achieve 'ace in a day' status during the Battle of Britain when he equalled Boyd's haul of five kills on tha afternoon of 13 August (*Adlertag*), again in the Isle of Wight area. He downed two Ju 88s from KG 54, a Bf 110 from LG 1 and a pair of 'anonymous' Bf 109Es – these successes came in the middle of a scoring streak which had seen McGrath increase his tally from 4 destroyed and 2 possibles to 18 confirmed, 2 possibles and 3 damaged.

On 15 August his luck ran out when No 601 Sqn was one of eight units sent to engage 300 raiders approaching the south coast. Having

Four of the six No 601 Sqn pilots seen in this view (taken at a damp Exeter airfield in late September 1940) had 'made ace' by the end of the Battle of Britain. Flt Lt W P 'Billy Clyde (second from left) scored 9 and 1 shared destroyed, 2 probables and 1 and 1 shared damaged; Flg Off Tom Grier (sitting on the tailplane) claimed 8 and 4 shared destroyed, 1 and 1 shared probable and 1 damaged – he was killed in action leading No 32 Sqn on a *Ramrod* over France on 5 December 1941; Flt Lt Sir Archibald Hope (wearing the Irvin jacket) was credited with 1 and 1 shared destroyed, 2 unconfirmed destroyed, 3 and 1 shared probable, 4 damaged, plus 1 or 2 more of which there are no details; and to Hope's left, Flt Lt H C Mayers, who had scored 11 and 1 shared destroyed, 3 and 1 shared probables and 6 damaged by the time he was lost in action leading No 239 Wing in North Africa on 20 July 1942. Note No 601 Sqn's winged sword emblem on the fin flash of this Hurricane, coded 'UF-S' (*via Frank Mason*)

despatched one Ju 88, and damaged a second, McGrath's Hurricane was struck by defensive fire and he was severely wounded in the head – he spent the next six months in hospital recovering.

Returning to No 145 Sqn, other aces to taste success on 8 August were squadron OC, Sqn Ldr J R A Peel (2 and 3 shared destroyed, 1 unconfirmed destroyed, 2 damaged and 2 destroyed on the ground), who got a Bf 109E destroyed and a Ju 87 unconfirmed destroyed, plus damaged a second Stuka; 'A' Flight commander Flt Lt R G Dutton (13 and 6

shared destroyed, 2 probables and 8 and 1 shared damaged), who destroyed three Ju 87s and damaged a Bf 109E; Plt Off P L Parrott (5 and 4 shared destroyed, 1 unconfirmed destroyed, 1 shared possible and 5 and 2 shared damaged), credited with a Bf 109E and a Ju 87 destroyed; Plt Off J E Storrar (12 and 2 shared destroyed, 1 unconfirmed destroyed, 2 and 1 shared probables, 3 damaged and 1 and 8 shared destroyed on the ground), who destroyed two Ju 87s and damaged a third; and Plt Off A N C Weir (4 and 2 shared destroyed and 1 unconfirmed destroyed – he was later killed on 7 November 1940), who got two Bf 109Es and a Ju 87.

The flipside to all this success was the loss of five No 145 Sqn pilots, including 19-year-old ace Plt Off E J C Wakeham DFC (4 and 3 shared destroyed and 2 damaged), who had been with the unit since October 1939, and had scored kills in France, off Dunkirk and over the Channel.

The unit suffered more fatalities during the big raids on Portland and Dover on the 11th (two pilots killed and their OC injured) and whilst defending RDF sites on the 12th (three pilots lost). It was then removed from action and posted north to Drem airfield (east of Edinburgh), within No 13 Group, classified as a spent force.

Seven of the pilots killed flying with No 145 Sqn had only been with the unit for a matter of weeks, and three of them were amongst the first crop of Polish aircrew posted into the frontline. This rising attrition rate was a cause of great concern for both senior RAF commanders and frontline pilots alike, and veterans like Dennis

Two of No 145 Sqn's senior pilots enjoy the summer sun at Westhampnett in early August 1940. Holding the tankard is 'A' Flight Commander, Flt Lt R G Dutton (13 and 6 shared destroyed, 2 probables and 8 and 1 shared damaged), whilst to his left is squadron OC, Sqn Ldr J R A Peel (2 and 3 shared destroyed, 2 damaged and 2 destroyed (or damaged) on the ground). The third member of the trio is Flg Off Antoni Ostowicz, who was amongst the first crop of Polish pilots sent to frontline units within Fighter Command on 16 July 1940. He was also one of the first Poles killed, being shot down over the Isle of Wight on the morning of 11 August in V7294 (via RAF Museum)

David (who was all of 22 years of age!) were shocked at the 'rawness' of their new squadron-mates;

'In those desperate days, if you were 21, you were an old man. It was horrifying to see the youngsters coming along. Some were only 18 years old, but it wasn't their age which scared you. They were so inexperienced. They'd had only eight or nine hours on a Hurricane. We needed chaps with 30 or 40 hours of operational training. We needed chaps who could match the German pilots, who were jolly good.'

Robert Stanford Tuck (27 and 2 shared destroyed, 1 and 1 shared unconfirmed destroyed, 6 probables and 6 and 1 shared damaged) also realised the inadequacies of the replacement pilots reaching the frontline whilst initially flying Spitfires as a flight commander with No 92 Sqn, before assuming command of the Hurricane-equipped No 257 Sqn in early September;

'You told the new men all you could. If you had time, you'd take them up and show them what you meant. You'd show them how to turn correctly, and evasive manoeuvres. Then you'd let them fly alone for a bit and you'd get up sun and make a dummy run at them. If they just floated alone, wondering, "Where is he?" and you knew they hadn't seen you, at the last instant, when in combat you'd open fire, you'd say over the radio, "OK. You've had it". They learnt very quickly from that not to fly down sun if possible. If they got through the first two or three combats, I thought they'd be all right. But it was always the new boys who copped it first. Suddenly something would come up their backside and wham!'

Triple ace 'Pete' Brothers served as a flight commander both with the highly-successful No 32 Sqn and then No 257 Sqn (with 'Bob' Stanford-Tuck) following the former unit's posting north to No 13 Group in late August;

'As a flight commander you tried to give pilots within your flight as many tips as possible, particularly when it came to air combat. I used to try and persuade them that when they were in formation on a patrol looking for the enemy, to always fly with a bit of rudder trim on so that the aircraft was crabbing slightly. Therefore, if you were attacked from above and the chap drew a bead for and aft down your aircraft, when he laid on his aim and fired you weren't exactly flying where he thought you were – i.e. straight ahead. You had to remember to immediately remove the trim after the initial attack so as to allow you to shoot straight.

'The other thing I imparted to pilots was that if you were jumped and you saw tracer rounds flying past you, always turn into them rather than away because if, for example, the rounds are passing on the right, the attacking pilot will see this and correct his aim to the left accordingly. Therefore, if you turn away from the fire, you will only be banking into his now-corrected line of fire. However, if you pull away to the right, you may be hit by a single shell as you pass through the first burst of fire, but after that he will be aiming well to your left, thus throwing his aim off completely.'

CASUALTIES

No 145 Sqn was not the only unit to suffer heavy losses as the

Left
Two more No 601 Sqn aces (the unit produced ten in total during the Battle of Britain) enjoy a quick meal between sorties in early August 1940. On the left is Flg Off G N S 'Mouse' Cleaver, who had scored perhaps as many as 7 destroyed and 2 probables before suffering terrible facial injuries when the perspex hood of his Hurricane (P3232) was shattered by an explosive shell during combat over Winchester on the late afternoon of 15 August. Having suffered serious injuries to both eyes, Cleaver never regained operational status, and was eventually released from the RAF in late 1943. The second pilot in this photograph is Flt Lt M L Robinson, whose details appear in the caption on page 73 (*via RAF Museum*)

As the RAF's first Spitfire ace (a feat he had achieved in just 48 hours over France on 23/24 May), Sqn Ldr 'Bob' Tuck arrived at No 257 Sqn in September 1940 with considerable combat experience under his belt – although he had never even sat in a Hurricane prior to his arrival at his new command! However, Tuck quickly got to grips with the Hawker fighter, and within four days of flying it for the first time, he had scored his premier kill on type. By the end of 1940 Tuck had claimed 7 destroyed, 4 probables and 2 damaged with the Hawker fighter (*via Tony Holmes*)

Luftwaffe shifted the focus of its bombing campaign away from coastal convoys and onto RAF airfields, radar sites and naval bases along the coast of southern England. Between 8 and 19 August some 55 Hurricane pilots were killed in action (a figure which does not include the 10 lost by No 145 Sqn), whilst half as many again were removed from frontline units through hospitalisation for treatment to wounds.

Although the great proportion of these men were 'new' pilots, some ten aces – Plt Off K Manger of No 17 Sqn, Flt Lt R Voase-Jeff of No 87 Sqn and Flt Lt R D G Wight and Sgt S L Butterfield of No 213 Sqn on the 11th, Flg Off R L Glyde of No 87 Sqn on the 13th, Flg Off P Collard of No 615 Sqn on the 14th, Plt Off P W Comely of No 87 Sqn on the 15th, Flg Off H M Ferriss of No 111 Sqn on the 16th, and Flt Lts R H A Lee of No 85 Sqn and S D P Connors of No 111 Sqn on the 18th – were killed during this period of intense action, and a further fifteen wounded.

The dramatic escalation in fatalities was due principally to the fact that more and more Bf 109Es were being committed to escorting the raiding forces, and at this stage in the battle *Jagdwaffe* units were still permitted to fly their much-favoured *Freie Jagd* missions ahead of the incoming bomber formations. With the freedom to operate virtually anywhere within the range constraints of their 'short-legged' *Emils*, German pilots used their mounts' superior performance at heights in excess of 26,000 ft as a perch from which to launch deadly 'hit-and-run' diving

Ale all round! No 85 Sqn's 'B' Flight relax after being stood down from readiness at Castle Camps in early July 1940. Within days of this photograph being taken two of the subjects had been killed, Sgt Leonard Jowitt (third from right with the shaved head – the result of losing a bet during a squadron party!) being lost in action engaging a He 111 over convoy *Booty*, off Felixstowe, on 12 July, and Kiwi Plt Off J L Bickerdike (extreme left) crashing fatally whilst performing aerobatics near the base on 22 July. Later in the battle, aces Flg Off P P Woods-Scawen (second from left) and Flt Lt R H A Lee (centre) would also die in combat (*via RAF Museum*)

attacks on formations of Hurricanes intercepting incoming bombers at around 20,000 ft.

More than two-thirds of the Hurricanes lost in mid-August fell to the guns of Bf 109Es or Bf 110C/Ds, the Messerschmitt fighters also accounting for all bar two of the aces killed during this period – Flg Off H M Ferriss lost his life on 16 August when his Hurricane (R4193) collided with a Do 17Z (from either 3./KG 2 or 7./KG 76) during a head-on pass over Marden, in Kent, whilst Flt Lt S D P Connors (12 destroyed, 2 and 1 shared unconfirmed destroyed and 4 damaged) of No 111 Sqn was shot down in flames (in R4187) over Kenley airfield on 18 August either by a 'friendly' AA battery or by return fire from the Do 17Zs of 9./KG 76 that he was attacking.

Despite the RAF having suffered heavy casualties, they had inflicted a series of telling blows on the Luftwaffe, who had lost over 50 aircraft a day on 15, 16 and 18 August. The hardest hit had been the *Stuka* and *Zerstörergeschwader*, the former having seen 29 Ju 87B/Rs shot down or written off through battle damage, and the latter no less than 49 Bf 110s destroyed. Indeed, the Ju 87 units had been so badly mauled that they never again appeared over Britain in serious numbers (see *Osprey Combat Aircraft 1 - Junkers Ju 87 Stukageschwader 1937-41* for further details pertaining to the role of the aircraft during the Battle of Britain), whilst the surviving *Zerstörer* crews suffered the ultimate ignominy of having to be escorted across the Channel by Bf 109Es.

Although none of the leading aces had been killed in the hectic battles of mid-August, both the high-scoring Hurricane pilots had been wounded so severely that neither of them played any further part in the battle after 18 August. As mentioned earlier, No 601 Sqn's Plt Off J K U B McGrath had become an 'ace in a day' on *Adlertag*, and then gone on to raise his tally to 18 kills (thus becoming the first pilot to pass Clisby and Kain's joint leading score of 16 apiece) before being seriously wounded on 15 August.

Equalling McGrath's score three days later was No 43 Sqn's seasoned campaigner Flt Lt F R Carey, who had downed five aircraft (including three Ju 87s) in five days between 13 and 18 August. He was wounded off the Sussex coast soon after scoring his 18th kill whilst flying Hurricane R4109;

'I took the nine Hurricanes (of No 43 Sqn) head on into a large formation of Ju 87s (from I./StG 77) midway between Chichester and Selsey Bill. After turning round to get behind some of them I found myself in the middle of several Ju 87 formations. I fired at one ahead of me – it stood straight up on its nose with flames coming out of it – when I was hit on the right knee by cross fire, or a stray burst from a Hurricane. It must have been an almost-spent round, for if the bullet had been anything else, I shouldn't have had a knee left! Handing over the Squadron to someone else, I had to drop out of the fight as my

When No 85 Sqn returned from France, it brought with it just three serviceable Hurricanes. Therefore, in order to return the unit to operational strength some 15 new, and used, Hurricanes were issued to the unit at Debden between 24 May and 11 June, one of which was factory-fresh P3408 (it arrived on 30 May, along with two other Mk Is). Having fought throughout the Battle of Britain, the fighter was seriously damaged in a flying accident on 8 October, and sent to a Civilian Repair Unit for rectification work. Once airworthy again, the Hurricane went on to see further frontline service with Nos 306 and 257 Sqns (*via P Jarrett*)

Left
Although not an ace (indeed, his solitary kill was the Bf 110 he attacked on 16 August), Flt Lt J B Nicolson of No 249 Sqn nevertheless became the only member of Fighter Command to be awarded Britain's highest military honour, the Victoria Cross (VC). Seeing combat for the first time on this date, 'A' Flight commander Nicolson was one of three pilots from his unit to engage German raiders striking at Gosport on the afternoon of the 16th. Bounced out of the sun by a *Staffel* of Bf 109Es just prior to engaging the enemy, Nicolson's Hurricane was set alight, but he stayed with the stricken fighter long enough to down a Bf 110. Suffering serious burns to his hands prior to baling out, he was duly awarded the VC for his bravery in November 1940. Nicolson is seen here playing a Jew's harp whilst convalescing – to the extreme left is 'Phoney War' ace Flg Off 'Fanny' Orton, who was shot down in France on 15 May 1940

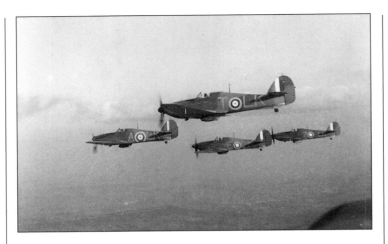

Towards the end of the Battle of Britain Fighter Command's basic combat formations began to change in shape as a result of the lessons learnt earlier in the year. A clear example of this was the adoption of three four-aircraft sections, rather than four three-aircraft vics. In the top photograph, taken in September 1940, No 87 Sqn's 'A' Flight illustrate the new tactical formation, Flt Lt 'Widge' Gleed leading his charges on a patrol between Exeter and Bibury. This 'finger-four' type formation was favoured by the *Jagdwaffe*, as it allowed each of the fighters to manoeuvre as required, whilst still maintaining formation integrity. It also increased the pilots' field of view, thus improving each man's ability to scan the blind areas behind his section mates. Finally, this greater awareness of the evolving combat situation meant that a pilot under attack could expect rapid support from his squadron mates. This formation structure contrasts markedly with the RAF's pre-war 'Battle Formation', illustrated here by No 85 Sqn over Kent. That both shots were taken at about the same time just goes to show how confused many units were in respect to the best tactics to employ in the late summer of 1940 (*via N Franks*)

Despite being one of the most successful pilots of 1940, and the RAF's second-highest scoring Hurricane ace (beaten only by Sqn Ldr M T StJ 'Pat' Pattle) with 25 and 3 shared destroyed, 4 unconfirmed destroyed, 3 probables, 1 'possible' and 8 damaged, Frank Carey's wartime exploits have remained little reported over the subsequent decades (*via Norman Franks*)

knee seemed to be locked and I wasn't feeling too well. My wound made it awkward to control my aircraft, and although one did not use the rudder all that much in the Hurricane, there were times when one needed to waggle it a bit. I called Tangmere but they advised me to stay away with the reply, "There are a lot of bombers heading this way and it looks as if they are going to give us another thumping!" I headed north and flew around for a time, but eventually had to crash-land at Pulborough.'

Carey was helped out of his inverted Hurricane and initially tended by local farmers until an ambulance arrived to take him to Sussex Hospital. His aircraft had a hole blown in its port wing 'big enough for a man to crawl through', whilst its rudder and an elevator had been completely shot off. By the time he returned to No 43 Sqn in mid-September, the unit had been posted north for a rest.

The third Hurricane pilot to pass the previous benchmark of 16 kills was newly-promoted No 32 Sqn OC, Michael 'Red Knight' (a nickname derived from a spell spent as flight commander of 'A', or Red, Flight) Crossley, who had assumed command of the unit after Sqn Ldr 'Johnny' Worrall had been posted as senior controller to Biggin Hill's Control Room. He scored $10^1/_2$ kills between 12 and 18 August, then went on to claim a further two victories on the 25th to raise his tally to

20 and 2 shared, 1 unconfirmed destroyed and 1 damaged. Like Carey and McGrath, he too had been shot down (on 18 and 24 August), but had survived without a scratch on both occasions.

Crossley was duly posted north with his unit to Acklington on 27 August for a well-deserved rest, leaving the action as the top scoring pilot within Fighter Command at that time. The unit he led away from Biggin Hill was also then officially the RAF's most successful fighter squadron, having destroyed 102 aircraft – a feat for which its pilots had been awarded one DSO (for Crossley) and five DFCs. (Brothers, Crossley, Grice, Gardner and Worrall). The cost of this success had been five pilots killed (two of these in its very last combat sortie with No 11 Group) and one a PoW.

The large-scale raids of mid-August tappered off between the 19th and 23rd as the Luftwaffe waited for unfavourable weather conditions to clear. Fighter Command took the opportunity to stand down as many units as possible, but when Saturday, 24 August, dawned clear and fine, the second phase of the Battle of Britain began. For the next 13 days the Luftwaffe was tasked with destroying the seven key sector stations within No 11 Group – Biggin Hill, Kenley, Hornchurch, North Weald, Northolt, Debden and Tangmere. The job of defending these airfields against increasingly larger formations of bombers would

Like Frank Carey, No 32 Sqn's Michael 'Red Knight' Crossley achieved many successes in the spring and summer of 1940, scoring 20 and 2 shared destroyed, 1 unconfirmed destroyed and 1 damaged between 19 May and 25 August (*via Norman Franks*)

fall predominantly to the 500+ frontline Hurricane pilots then available to Fighter Command within Nos 10, 11 and 12 Groups, who, in theory at least, would rely on their Spitfire-equipped brethren to in turn keep the fighters off their backs.

All seven stations were repeatedly bombed during this period, greatly reducing their effectiveness, and thus seriously affecting the ability of Fighter Command to intercept incoming raids. Biggin Hill was particularly badly hit in a series of accurate strikes which saw control of the units based there passed temporarily to Hornchurch, some 20 miles north of the Kent airfield. Commensurate with the increased intensity of the attacks was the alarming rise in the casualty rate within Hurricane units in No 11 Group – some 45 pilots were killed and a further 83 injured. These losses graphically underline just how bitter the fighting was in defence of the sector airfields. Simply put, the RAF was fighting for its survival.

On the afternoon of 18 August Fighter Command suffered one of its most stunning reversals when four No 501 Sqn Hurricane Is were downed in just two minutes over Canterbury by III./JG 26's Oberleutnant Gerhard Schöpfel (who finished the war with 40 kills). Two of the Hurricanes lost in this action are seen scrambling from Hawkinge sometime between 12 and 18 August, the aircraft in the foreground (P3059) being flown by 7-kill ace, Plt Off K N T Lee (he survived the action, baling out at 17,000 ft). Sadly, the pilot of the second machine (P3208), Plt Off J W Bland, was killed – two other No 501 Sqn Hurricanes were also lost on this day (*via Phil Jarrett*)

Above
Rivalling No 501 Sqn on 18 August in respect to the number of Hurricanes lost in action was Kenley-based No 615 Sqn, who suffered casualties not only in the air but on the ground too, as this photograph graphically shows. The unit's Surrey home was badly bombed on the afternoon of the 18th by low-flying Do 17Zs from 9./KG 76, the German raiders knocking out three of Kenley's four hangars, plus numerous other ancilliary buildings. A number of aircraft were also destroyed or damaged, including six No 615 Sqn Hurricanes which were parked in, and around, the unit's hangar when it received a direct hit. Although this particular fighter received serious blast damage to the fabric covering of its rear fuselage and tailplane, its tubular structure seems to have survived the bombing relatively unscathed (*via Dr Alfred Price*)

Above right
One of the No 615 Sqn pilots scrambled on 18 August to defend Kenley was Plt Off K T Lofts (far right), who had been with the auxiliary unit since 1938. He was credited with having damaged one of the marauding Do 17s on this date. Lofts transferred to No 249 Sqn soon after No 615 Sqn was sent north to Scotland for a period of rest, continuing his run of scoring success with his new unit. By war's end Lofts' score stood at 4 and 3 shared destroyed (plus 2 or 3 no details), 1 probable and 5 and 1 shared damaged (*via Norman Franks*)

Some of the heaviest casualties were suffered by units that had been involved in the fighting since the *Blitzkrieg* – as mentioned earlier, No 32 Sqn was pulled out on 27 August, followed by Nos 56, 85, 151 and 615 Sqns by 6 September. Several days later the survivors of Nos 43, 111 and 601 Sqns also received orders to head north to No 13 Group. Twelve aces were amongst the Hurricane pilots killed (or fatally wounded – see next paragraph) during this phase of the battle – Sqn Ldr C W Williams of No 17 Sqn and Plt Offs H D Atkinson and J A L Philippart of No 213 Sqn on the 25th, Sqn Ldr J V C Badger of No 43 Sqn on the 30th, Flt Lt P S Weaver of No 56 Sqn on the 31st, Flt Sgt F G Berry of No 1 Sqn and Plt Off C A Woods-Scawen of No 43 Sqn on 1 September, Flg Off P P Woods-Scawen of No 85 Sqn and Sgt W L Dymond of No 111 Sqn on the 2nd, Flt Lt D C Bruce again of No 111 Sqn on the 4th, and Flt Lt W H Rhodes-Moorhouse and Flg Off C R Davis of No 601 two days later. A further nine aces were wounded.

The fact that these figures are roughly equal to those of the 8-19 August period (despite the fact that they cover an extra 48 hours of combat flying) reflects the waning number of experienced pilots remaining in the frontline. Indeed, as the previous listing shows, only Nos 43, 111, 213 and 601 Sqns suffered more than a single ace fatality

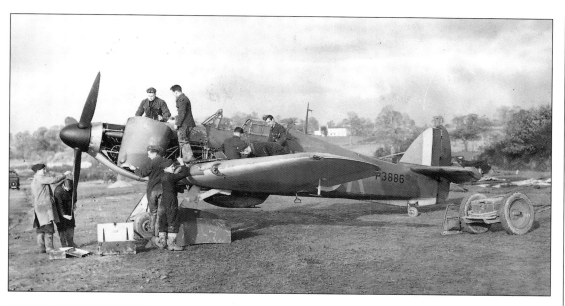

Veteran No 601 Sqn Hurricane I P3886 is seen being serviced on the perimeter dispersal at Exeter Airport in mid-September 1940. Note the aircraft's natural metal cowling over its reduction gear, which had been fitted in the wake of the engine failure suffered by the Hurricane on 26 July. Once repaired, this fighter enjoyed success whilst being flown by No 601 Sqn aces Sgt L N Guy (1/2 a Ju 88 on 15/8) and Flg Off C R Davis (1 and 1 shared Ju 87 and a Bf 109E on 18/8, followed by a Bf 110 probable on 31/8) – both pilots had been killed in action by the time this shot was taken (*via Jerry Scutts*)

Left

Up there with the likes of Carey, Crossley, Lacey and Frantisek was No 85 Sqn's leading ace, Sgt G 'Sammy' Allard, who was credited with 19 and 5 shared destroyed (at least 2 of which were unconfirmed) and 2 probables between 10 May and 1 September 1940. His score would have undoubtedly been much higher had his unit not been posted out of No 11 Group on 5 September (*via Phil Jarrett*)

Whilst Allard went north, his former squadron-mate Plt Off A G Lewis continued the fight with No 249 Sqn, adding a further 8 kills to his tally before being wounded in action on 28 September. He is seen here donning his parachute harness whilst still with No 85 Sqn at Castle Camps in July 1940 (*via A Thomas*)

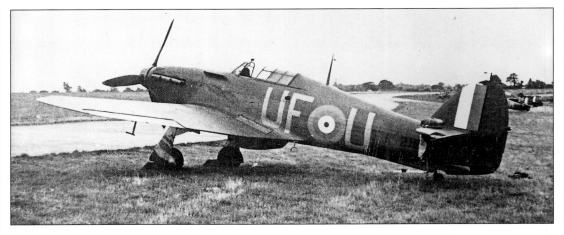

– the former unit actually lost three pilots as its battle-seasoned CO, Sqn Ldr 'Tubby' Badger (8 and 2 shared destroyed, 1 probable and 2 damaged), was so badly hurt when he was impaled on a tree after baling out of his stricken Hurricane on 30 August that he finally succumbed to his injuries on 30 June 1941.

The second No 43 Sqn pilot killed, Flg Off C A 'Tony' Woods-Scawen (7 destroyed, 1 unconfirmed destroyed, 4 probables and 1 damaged), who died on the afternoon of 2 September when he baled out of his blazing Hurricane (V7420) at too low an altitude – this was the seventh time he had vacated a stricken fighter in flight since June. Tragically, just 24 hours earlier his older brother, Plt Off P P 'Pat' Woods-Scawen (10 and 3 shared destroyed, 2 unconfirmed destroyed and 1 probable) had been posted missing after jumping out of his Hurricane (P3150) over Kenley whilst leading No 85 Sqn. His body was found four days later, the parachute still neatly packed on his back.

That 'Pat' Woods-Scawen was leading his unit into battle whilst still only a flying officer illustrates yet another problem facing Fighter Command in early September – the lack of suitably experienced squadron and flight commanders. Six squadron leaders and eight flight lieutenants were either killed or seriously wounded between 24 August and 6 September, and it not surprising to find that those units which suffered losses to senior pilots were withdrawn from the frontline soon afterwards – namely, No 43 Sqn (Sqn Ldr J V C Badger), No 56 Sqn (7-victory ace Flt Lt P C Weaver), No 85 Sqn (Sqn Ldr Peter Townsend wounded and Flt Lt H R Hamilton killed), No 111 Sqn (Flt Lt D C Bruce), No 151 Sqn (Sqn Ldr E B King) and No 615 Sqn (Flt Lt L M Gaunce).

Almost all squadrons were suffering heavy casualties during this phase of the battle, but there were insufficient reserves left to make wholesale changes. Indeed, those units drafted in as replacements for their combat-weary brethren often suffered a greater mortality rate than the squadrons they had relieved. New pilots fresh to the deadly skies of south-east England had no time in which to acclimitise themselves, the experiences of No 253 Sqn being typical of the fate which befell so many 'green' units in late August/early September.

Having lost eleven aircraft and five pilots in just six days over France

Gloster-built R4218 served with No 601 Sqn from 15 August until 7 October, when it was written off in a forced landing following combat over Portland. During this period the fighter was used predominantly by Australian-born ace Howard Mayers, who used it to claim two Do 17s and a Bf 110 destroyed, two Do 17s damaged and a half-share in a probable Bf 110. Indeed, it was Mayers who was at the controls of R4218 when it was hit in the glycol tank by enemy fire whilst engaging raiders sent to bomb the Westland aircraft factory at Yeovil on the afternoon of 7 October (via A Thomas)

Son of World War 1 VC winner Lt W B Rhodes-Moorhouse, Flt Lt 'Willie' Rhodes-Moorhouse DFC had made his own mark with No 601 Sqn by scoring 5 and 4 shared destroyed and 4 probables by the time he was killed in action over Tunbridge Wells on the morning of 6 September 1940 (via Norman Franks)

in May, the remnants of the squadron had been sent north to No 13 Group to reform. By the end of August it was deemed ready to be flung back into the fight from Kenley, and on the 29th the 18 'LD'-coded Hurricanes of No 253 Sqn duly relieved the 10 battle-scarred 'KW'-coded aircraft of No 615 Sqn – the latter unit, which had originally been part of the BEF, and seen continous action since 10 May, had lost six Hawker fighters in combat in the past five days, but fortunately with no loss of life. However, the same could not be said for No 253 Sqn by the end of their first day back in action, for the unit lost three pilots killed and a fourth (a flight commander) wounded, plus five aircraft written off and a further three damaged.

Things got no better on the 31st, as the unit's OC, Sqn Ldr H M Starr, was reportedly strafed in his parachute and killed (the second pilot from No 253 Sqn to suffer this fate in 48 hours) during a morning patrol, whilst his temporary replacement, Sqn Ldr T P Gleave, who had been serving as a supernumery with the unit until receiving a posting to his new squadron, was badly burned just hours later – the latter pilot had submitted claims for five Bf 109Es (of JG 27) destroyed in a single sortie the previous day, but only one confirmed and four probables had been credited to him. Postwar investigations by Gleave have found that JG 27 did indeed lose five aircraft over Kent on this day, although official Air Ministry records have never been duly altered.

A fifth pilot was killed on 1 September, and two more aircraft written off 24 hours later, but fortunately without loss of life on this occasion. Death returned to No 253 Sqn on the 4th and then again on the 6th, when ex-flight commander (and now acting OC) Flt Lt W P Cambridge was lost on a morning patrol. In just a week of fighting, the unit had seen both of its flight commanders and its squadron leader killed in action.

This shot of 'A' Flight, No 43 Sqn, was taken at Wick in the spring of 1940, and shows future Battle of Britain aces Flg Off 'Tony' Woods-Scawen (second from left) and Flt Lt Caesar Hull (centre) – both men were killed within days of each other during the first week of September 1940. The sergeant at the extreme right is Geoff Garton, who was sent as an attrition replacement to No 73 Sqn in France in late May 1940, and went on to claim a number of victories with the unit in France, England and North Africa. He finished the war with a score of 7 and 3 shared destroyed, 2 probables and 2 damaged. Like Woods-Scawen and Hull, the NCO pilot at the extreme left of this photo failed to see out the summer, James Buck being shot down (in P3531) when Bf 109Es of III./JG 27 bounced his section whilst it was patrolling between Selsey Bill and Bognor Regis on 19 July. The wounded pilot succeeded in baling out of his stricken fighter, but drowned before he could be rescued – the coastal rescue services' failure to locate Buck (who was considered to be a strong swimmer by his peers) drew strong criticism from his fellow pilots (*via Phil Jarrett*)

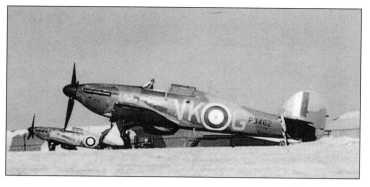

FOREIGN PILOTS

With reserves of pilots being rapidly eroded in an effort to stem the escalating casualty rate, Air Chief-Marshall Dowding was forced to draught all four of his recently-formed 'foreign' units into the frontline at this crucial stage in the battle. Two of these (Nos 302 and 303 Sqns) were manned by Polish pilots who had escaped firstly to France and then Britain following the invasion of their country almost a year before, a third unit (No 310 Sqn) was manned with Czech aviators who had followed a similar route into the RAF, whilst the fourth was No 1 Sqn of the Royal Canadian Air Force (RCAF). Nos 303 and 1 RCAF Sqns went 'straight in at the deep end' with No 11 Group at Northolt, whilst Nos 302 and 310 Sqns were sent to the No 12 Group sector station at Duxford.

For the RAF, the assimilation of an English-speaking unit manned entirely by Canadians (whose compatriots had been flying in Britain with the RAF since the mid-1930s) into a fighting force that relied heavily on voice communication for its success posed few problems. However, when it came to dealing with the Poles and Czechs – most of whom had only been in the country since June/July at the earliest – things got a lot more complicated. At first, communication problems had been overcome by the absorption of pilots into regular and auxiliary units, where the Czechs and Poles would follow the example of their squadron-mates in respect to flying procedures and battle tactics.

Despite being in action for longer than most Hurricane units during the summer of 1940, few photographs exist of No 238 Sqn pilots, or their aircraft. This rare shot shows two Hurricanes sitting at the unit's dispersal at Middle Wallop during No 238 Sqn's first spell at the Hampshire base in early August 1940. P3462/'VK-G' saw considerable action with the unit between June and October, and was used on the afternoon of 15 September by ace Plt Off C T Davis to claim a He 111 probable over Kenley – the fighter received superficial combat damage during this engagement (see profile 20 for more details) (*via Dr Alfred Price*)

As mentioned earlier in this chapter, virtually all of No 17 Sqn's Hurricanes boasted nose and door art during the second half of 1940. Perhaps the best example of this was the 'winged Popeye' motif which adorned N2359, the fighter serving with the unit between 6 June and 25 August 1940, when it was passed on to No 6 OTU. It is seen here being taxied out from the squadron dispersal at Debden by Plt Off L W Stevens (*via N Franks*)

Like No 238 Sqn, No 229 Sqn is also a unit that appears to have attracted little media attention during 1940, although this could be explained by the fact that it spent the first half of the Battle of Britain 'hidden away' at the No 12 Group airfield at Wittering. In mid-September the squadron 'came south' to Northolt, and it was from here that the pilot of P3039/'RE-D', future ace Plt Off V M M Ortmans, used the fighter to down a He 111, share in the damage of a second Heinkel, and also damage a Ju 88 (*via A Thomas*)

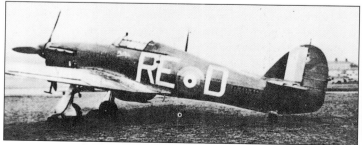

This fine official shot, taken at Northolt in September 1940, shows a number of the principal aces of No 303 'Polish' Sqn. From left to right; Plt Off M Feric (9 and 1 shared destroyed, 1 probable and 1 damaged); Flt Lt J A Kent (12 destroyed, 3 probables, 2 damaged and 1 destroyed on the ground); Flg Off B Grzeszczak (2 destroyed); unknown; Plt Off J E L Zumbach (12 and 1 shared, 5 probables and 1 damaged); Plt Off W Lokuciewski (9 and 1 shared destroyed and 4 probables); unknown; Flg Off Z K Henneberg (8 and 1 shared destroyed, 1 probable and 1 damaged); Plt Off J K M Daszewski (3 des-troyed and 2 probables); and Sgt E Szap-osznikow (8 and 1 shared destroyed and 1 damaged) (*via Jerry Scutts*)

V6665/'RF-J' was issued to No 303 Sqn in early September 1940, being adorned with a red stripe just forward of its fin soon after arriving at Northolt. It seems likely that this marking served to denote an aircraft flown by one of the unit's flight commanders – in this case Canadian ace, Flt Lt 'Johnny' Kent. Its career with No 303 Sqn was to be a short one, for V6665 was shot down over Kent by Bf 109Es on 27 September, carrying Sgt Tadeusz Andruskow to his death (*via Robert Gretzyngier*)

This worked well, and amongst the pilots to enjoy early successes were future Hurricane aces Plt Off K Pniak of No 32 Sqn, who scored his first kill on 12 August (to add to his two victories claimed whilst flying a PZL PXIc in Poland in September 1939 – his final score was 7 and 2 shared destroyed, 2 probables and 2 and 2 shared damaged), and Flg Off W Urbanowicz, whose two claims with Nos 601 and 145 Sqns on 8 and 12 August respectively preceded an impressive scoring run that saw him credited with 13 kills whilst serving as joint commander of No 303 Sqn with Hurricane ace Sqn Ldr R G Kellett (5 destroyed, 2 probables and 1 damaged).

Although initially only given the rank of flying officer, Witold Urbanowicz was a seasoned campaigner who had scored his first victo-ry (over a Soviet reconnaissance aircraft) as long ago as 1936. He had also been instrumental in securing the escape of a group of cadet pilots from Poland just before it was overrun, his charges reaching Britain via France.

Aside from Karol Pniak, whose scoring run was cut short on 24 August when he injured both a knee and an ankle on landing after baling out of a stricken Hurricane for the second time in just two hours (he was posted to No 257 Sqn upon his recovery the following month), two other Poles 'made ace' whilst flying exclusively with non-Polish Hurricane-equipped squadrons.

They were No 501 Sqn's Plt Off S Skalski (his 7 during the Battle of Britain came after he had claimed 4 and 1 shared destroyed in Poland in September 1939 – his final wartime tally was 18 and 3 shared destroyed, 2 probables and 5 damaged) and Sgt A Glowacki, whose five (three Bf 109Es and two Ju 88s) on 24 August made him the only Polish 'ace in a day' during the Battle of Britain – by war's end his score stood at 8 and 1 shared destroyed, 3 probables and 5 damaged. Plt Off W Witorzenc, who also flew with No 501 Sqn, came close with 4 and 1 shared during August/September, but he had to wait until September of the following year to finally claim his elusive fifth kill.

As more eastern Europeans arrived in Britain following the collapse of France, the RAF decided that special squadrons composed entirely of Polish and Czech speaking pilots would be a far more effective way of integrating these talented men into the mainstream force, so from late July onwards the majority of them were streamed into generic units. Throughout the Battle if Britain regular RAF officers filled the positions of squadron leader and flight commanders (and Intelligence Officer), although each of the senior men had a Polish or Czech equivalent.

One of the first flight commanders within No 303 Sqn was pre-war pilot Flt Lt 'Johnny' Kent, who had moved from Canada in early 1935 to join the RAF. Like his joint OCs, Sqn Ldrs Kellett and Urbanowicz, and fellow flight commander, Flt Lt A S Forbes (7 and 2 shared destroyed and 1 probable), Kent achieved ace status before the end of 1940, although his all important fifth kill came whilst he was commanding No 92 Sqn flying Spitfire Is in November.

In his excellent autobiography, *One of the few*, Kent explains some of the problems he initially encountered due to the language barrier, which slowed the Polish and Czechs units down in their efforts to be declared operationally ready;

'Although a knowledge of English was practically non-existent amongst the Poles, they all spoke French. Ronald Kellett also spoke

Plt Off Karol Pniak was one of the first Polish pilots to be posted into the frontline, joining No 32 Sqn at Biggin Hill on 8 August 1940. He had already encountered the Luftwaffe almost a year before whilst flying a PZL P.XIc with 142 *Eskadra* in the defence of his homeland – Pniak had joined the Polish Air Force as long ago as 1932. He was credited with a Do 17 and Ju 87 destroyed prior to fleeing Poland. Despite speaking little English, Pniak quickly let his flying skill 'do the talking' once operating with the RAF, downing four Bf 109Es (plus a fifth as a probable) by the end of August. He then joined No 257 Sqn following No 32 Sqn's withdrawal from No 11 Group, scoring his final victories with this unit on 11 November when he downed 1 and 1 shared Italian BR.20 bombers (*via Wojtek Matusiak*)

The highest scoring Polish pilot of the Battle of Britain was Flg Off Witold Urbanowicz who, like Pniak, had seen almost a decade's service with the Polish Air Force prior to joining the RAF in early 1940. He put his vast experience to good use in August/September, downing 15 German aircraft whilst flying with Nos 601, 145 and 303 Sqns. Urbanowicz's final wartime tally was 18 destroyed (possibly 20), 1 probable and 9 destroyed on the ground (*via Dr Jan P Koniarek*)

quite good French while Atholl Forbes was completely bi-lingual which helped enormously. Unfortunately my French was very poor and consequently I had to learn some Polish; this I did by taking one or two of the pilots out of the aircraft and pointing to it, saying "Aeroplane" slowly and distinctly. They got the idea and answered "Samolot" which I wrote down phonetically. I then went round the aircraft giving the English names for the various parts of, and getting the Polish in

return. Gradually I worked out a complete procedure in Polish and had it all written down phonetically on my knee pad and used it when giving instructions in the air. It worked very well and amused the Poles a lot.

'Because of our lack of knowledge of the Poles' experience and their general background we had to be very careful about their training, especially as regards R/T; we could not expect them to remember even what little English we were able to teach them during the excitement of combat. Whereas they could speak to one another, the Controller could neither understand them nor they him. It was necessary, therefore, to have at least one of the British pilots flying with them on all exercises and, later of course, in combat.'

The first kill to fall to the guns of No 303 Sqn was a Do 17Z, shot down on 30 August whilst the Poles were supposed to be conducting a training exercise intercepting Blenheims. When the enemy formation was sighted just to the north of London, the Hurricane pilots immediately formated with the vulnerable British bombers, but fortunately the escorting Messerschmitt fighters did not attack. 'Johnny' Kent details what happened next;

'The sight of these enemy machines was too much for Flg Off Paszkiewicz of "B" Flight and he broke formation and shot down a Dornier 17, following it right down to the ground to ensure that it crashed. This was the Squadron's first victory and the Poles were absolutely cock-a-hoop over it. Ronald Kellett was so pleased with the way they had behaved that he immediately asked for permission to declare the Squadron "Operational". This was granted and the squadron was placed on "Readiness" for the first time the following morning, 31st

No 501 Sqn was an early recipient of Polish pilots, no less than six of them arriving at Gravesend in early August as attrition replacements. Amongst this group were Sgt 'Toni' Glowacki (left) and Plt Off Stefan Witorzenc (right), both of whom went on to achieve ace status. Indeed, Glowacki, got 'five in a day' on 24 August (*via Wojtek Matusiak*)

Taken at the same time as the group photograph on page 91, this close-up view shows three of the leading pilots at No 303 Sqn during the Battle of Britain – Henneburg, Kent and Pisarek – who, between them, achieved 19 kills during a five-week period from 31 August to 5 October. Both Feric and Henneburg were killed later in the war whilst still flying with No 303 Sqn (*via Frank Mason*)

August, just a year after the German attack on their country.'

Flg Off L W Paszkiewicz went on to claim a further five victories before he was shot down and killed in Hurricane L1696 over Kent on the morning of 27 September. Ironically, in light of its later success in the final stages of the Battle of Britain, No 303 Sqn was the last of the four new units to gain a combat victory, fellow Polish-manned No 302 Sqn having scored its first kill (a Ju 88A of 8./KG 30) on 20 August, and the Czechs of No 310 Sqn two Do

17Zs and a Bf 110 six days later – the Messerschmitt fighter was credited to Flg Off E Fechtner, who had scored 4 destroyed, 1 probable and 1 damaged by the time he was killed in a flying accident on 29 October 1940.

No 1 Sqn RCAF was declared operational on 17 August and subsequently moved from Croydon to Northolt. The unit's veteran OC, Sqn Ldr E A McNab, had tasted victory some two days before whilst on detachment with fellow Croydon-based unit No 111 Sqn, downing a Do 17Z over the Channel coast. Despite having gleaned valuable operational experience during his brief time with 'Treble One', McNab was hardly prepared for the disastrous start to combat which befell his unit – on 24 August two sections intercepted a pair of Coastal Command Blenheim IVs of No 235 Sqn off Portsmouth and shot them down, believing them to be Ju 88s.

One of the pilots that claimed a shared kill in this fratricidal incident was future ace Flt Lt G R McGregor (5 destroyed, 2 probables and 5 damaged), who went on to even up the score two days later when the Canadians finally engaged the enemy. Three Do17s were destroyed, with Sqn Ldr McNab claiming one of the victories – he became the squadron's first ace on 27 September, and finished with a score of 4 and 1 shared destroyed, 1 probable and 3 damaged.

With the arrival of these new units, a number of battle-weary squadrons were sent north to rest and regroup. No 85 Sqn was one such unit, being removed from Croydon to Church Fenton in early September after losing eight experienced pilots killed or wounded in just five days – the squadron was so badly mauled that it was redesignated a Class C training unit, its experienced senior men being posted to other Class A or B units after a suitable period of rest. Plt Off 'Sammy' Allard was one of those pilots that thoroughly deserved a spell away from the action, for not only was he one of the few survivors of the unit's BEF campaign, he was also No 85 Sqn's leading scorer with at least 19 and 5 shared kills and 2 probables – 8 of these were credited to him between 24 August and 1 September. Having endured myriad combats in 1940, Allard was killed in a flying accident on 13 March 1941, having failed to add to his tally since September 1940.

Pilots and groundcrew study the tail of R4175/'RF-R' after Sgt Josef Frantisek had brought the fighter back to Northolt with combat damage on either 6 or 7 September. As the highest scoring ace of the Battle of Britain, Frantisek claimed seven victories with this fighter, but was duly killed in it on the morning of 8 October (via Robert Gretzyngier)

Few shots of Sgt Josef Frantisek serving with the RAF exist, this view showing him as a NCO in the Czech Air Force sometime prior to the commencement of World War 2 (via Robert Gretzyngier)

No 303 Sqn shared Northolt for much of the Battle of Britain with No 1 Sqn RCAF, the Canadian unit having moved in from Northolt after having been declared operational on 17 August. The unit was led throughout the summer by experienced pre-war RAF/RCAF pilot, Sqn Ldr E A McNab, who is seen here to the left of the suited Canadian High Commissioner, The Hon Vincent Massey. McNab scored 4 and 1 shared destroyed, 1 probable and 3 damaged during August/September, his first kill being achieved in a No 111 Sqn Hurricane whilst he was detached to the RAF unit to gain combat experience. He was one of only two pilots to 'make ace' with No 1 Sqn RCAF in 1940 . . . (via Frank Mason)

Another pilot whose successful run was brought to an abrupt halt when his unit was posted out of No 11 Group was Sgt H J L Hallowes of No 43 Sqn, who had increased his score to 16 and 2 shared destroyed, 2 probables and 2 damaged by 26 August – he had proven particularly adept at destroying Ju 87s, downing six during the final Stuka raids on the south coast on 16 and 18 August. Squadron-mate Plt Off H C Upton, who had also plundered the Stuka ranks by downing four on these dates to add to a pair he had been credited with on 8 August, was also sent north with the unit, having scored 10 and 1 shared destroyed and 1 probable between 12 July and 4 September.

Whilst other ex-BEF and AASF units were posted out of the front-line, No 501 Sqn remained in No 11 Group for the duration of the battle, and as a result it produced more Hurricane aces (11) than any other regular or auxiliary unit during this period, but at a price – some 43 Hurricanes were lost between 1 July and 31 October, 15 more than No 238 Sqn, who had the second-highest attrition tally.

No 501 Sqn engaged the enemy on a record 35 days during the Battle of Britain, followed again by No 238 Sqn with 24 days. Looking at these statistics, it is therefore unsurprising that the leading Hurricane ace by the end of the battle was a No 501 Sqn pilot – Sgt J H 'Ginger' Lacey, with 23 destroyed, 5 probables and 6 damaged. By 6 September he had raised his tally to 15, and whilst other equally successful Hurricane pilots were leaving the south-east, Lacey, and No 501 Sqn, remained steadfast.

. . . the second being Flg Off B D 'Dal' Russel. An original member of No 115 Auxiliary Sqn (as No 1 Sqn had been designated prior to its arrival in England in June 1940), he saw much action in August/ September, being credited with 2 and 4 shared destroyed, 2 probables and 3 damaged. Like his OC, Russel was awarded a DFC for his exploits towards the end of October 1940 (via Stephen Fochuk)

'Big Wings'

It was during this time of great crisis at the end of August that one of the Battle of Britain's most enduring tactical arguments arose. With the raids on sector airfields increasing in intensity, No 11 Group was having to rely more and more on support from neighbouring units within Nos 10 and 12 Groups to defend its bases whilst its own squadrons were engaged in intercepting incoming bomber formations.

Support from the former group to the west of the Home Counties was usually good, but the relationship between No 11 Group and their near-neighbours in No 12 Group was so poor that on 27 August AVM Park was forced to officially complain to his boss, Air Chief-Marshal Dowding. He stated plainly that his sector stations had been badly bombed because the latter group had not done what they had been asked to do – protect his airfields. The following quote by AVM Park clearly spells out his reasons for complaint;

'On a few dozen occasions when I had sent every available squadron of No 11 Group to engage the main enemy attack as far forward as possible, I called on No 12 Group to send a couple of squadrons to defend a fighter airfield or other vital targets which were threatened by outflanking and smaller bomber raids. Instead of sending two squadrons quickly to protect the vital target, No 12 Group delayed while they despatched a large wing of four or five squadrons, which wasted valuable time . . . Consequently, they invariably arrived too late to prevent the enemy bombing the target. On scores of days I called on No 10 Group on my right for a few squadrons to protect some vital target. Never on any occasion can I remember this Group failing to send its squadrons promptly to the place I requested, thus saving thousands of civilian lives and also the naval dockyards of Portsmouth, the port of Southampton and aircraft factories.'

As detailed above, the root cause of this friction was the belief by No 12 Group commander, AVM Trafford Leigh-Mallory, that his units were better employed hunting the enemy in larger formations ('Big Wings') of three to five squadron-strength, rather than waiting for the bombers to appear over the No 11 Group airfields. He believed that

Right
Although not technically part of any frontline squadron, Wg Cdr Victor Beamish was one of the most successful Hurricane pilots of 1940, claiming 5 destroyed, 9 and 1 shared probables and 4 damaged whilst serving as station commander at North Weald. Despite his senior position, Beamish would regularly join Nos 151 and 249 Sqns on interceptions during his time at the Essex airfield (via RAF Museum)

Still suffering from a foot wound inflicted by a Bf 110 over Tunbridge Wells on 31 August, Sqn Ldr Peter Townsend leans heavily on his walking stick at Church Fenton in mid-September. His is flanked on either side by the unit's sergeant pilots, three of whom had been posted into the squadron during Townsend's absence. They are, from left to right, E R Webster, G Goodman (two kills in 1940 – four in total), T C E Berkley (killed in action with the unit on the night of 13/14 June 1941), S Kita and K A Muchowski (both Polish), and K W Gray – the final three pilots had arrived at Castle Camps just prior to No 85 Sqn being posted north to No 13 Group (via Frank Mason)

No 17 Sqn pilots at Debden in July 1940. They are, from left to right; Sgt G A Steward (3 and 3 shared destroyed, 1 and 2 shared probables and 4 damaged – killed 23/10/41); Plt Off D H Wissler (killed 11/11/40); Plt Off J K Ross (2 and 3 shared destroyed and 2 probables – killed 6/1/42); Flg Off H A C Bird-Wilson (3 and 6 shared destroyed, 3 probables, 3 damaged and 1 destroyed on the ground); Sqn Ldr C W Williams (2 and 3 shared destroyed – killed 25/8/40); and Sgt D A Sewell (1 destroyed an 2 probables – killed 19/3/44) (*via Don Healey*)

R4224 was the short-lived mount of newly-arrived No 17 Sqn OC, Sqn Ldr A G Miller. He was forced to crash-land the fighter near North Weald on 3 September after being attacked by a Bf 110 (*via F Mason*)

the bombing of sector stations was of no consequence as long as sufficient quantities of enemy aircraft were shot down prior to them fleeing British skies. Leigh-Mallory's views were shared by both Deputy Chief of Air Staff, AVM Sholto Douglas, and legendary legless leader of the unofficially titled 'Duxford Wing', Sqn Ldr Douglas Bader, OC No 242 Sqn.

Despite his physical handicap, the latter pilot enjoyed great success whilst leading the wing, downing 11 aircraft to add to his Bf 109E kill claimed over Dunkirk during his brief spell on Spitfires whilst serving as a flight commander with No 222 Sqn. Indeed, the overall successes of the 'Big Wing' have remained controversial to this day, its opponents stating that on the few occasions the component units did manage to encounter the enemy in full combat strength, the level of over-claiming was so great that no true picture of their kills could be deduced. That said, the three Hurricane squadrons that usually comprised the 'Duxford Wing' (Nos 229, 242 and 310 Sqns) produced nine aces between them during the battle, the bulk of these (six) coming from the predominantly Canadian-manned No 242 Sqn.

Three of No 242 Sqn's leading aces pose for an official photograph beneath a suitably-marked Hurricane I at Coltishall in late September 1940. To the left is Flg Off G E Ball (6 and 1 shared destroyed and 3 damaged), in the middle squadron CO, Sqn Ldr D R S Bader (20 and 4 shared destroyed, 6 and 1 shared probables and 11 damaged), and on the right, Plt Off W L McKnight (17 and 2 shared destroyed and 3 unconfirmed destroyed – killed 12/1/41) (*via Frank Mason*)

The unit's top scorer, Flg Off W L McKnight, followed up his successes in France in May/June with a further 6 and 2 shared kills, which took his tally to 17 and 2 shared destroyed and 3 unconfirmed destroyed – he was subsequently killed in one of Fighter Command's first low-level 'Rhubarb' sorties over France on 12 January 1941 without having scored any further kills.

One of No 242 Sqn's aces in the summer of 1940 was not an RAF pilot at all, but rather a naval aviator seconded to the air force in June because of the shortage in pilots. Sub-Lt R J 'Dickie' Cork flew with the unit throughout the battle, being credited with 5 and 1 shared destroyed and three damaged – a score which resulted in him being awarded the DFC. He later rejoined the Fleet Air Arm and put his Hurricane experience to good use whilst flying from HMS *Indomitable* during the Operation *Pedestal* convoy to Malta in August 1942, claiming 4 and 1 shared destroyed, 1 probable and 1 damaged whilst flying Sea Hurricane Is with No 880 Sqn. Cork was subsequently killed in a flying accident in Ceylon on 14 April 1944.

Detractors of the 'Big Wing' were many, particularly within the hard-pressed squadrons of No 11 Group. One was No 601 flight commander and ace Flt Lt Sir Archibold Hope;

'The theory of the "Big Wing" was if you had a raid of say 50 '109s coming in with a lot of bombers below it, one of our squadrons of 12 aircraft couldn't do very much against them. You might shoot down four or five '109s. You might shoot down a couple of the bombers. But you couldn't really stop the raid. However – so the theory went – if you had 24 or more aircraft up there, you'd stand a better chance of stopping it. But Leigh-Mallory and Douglas Bader were absolutely wrong about the "Big Wing". Keith Park had no option. The way the Germans were coming in, he hadn't got time to form up "Big Wings". He hadn't got enough squadrons. He had to get his aircraft airborne as quickly as he damn well could, in such numbers as he could.'

Sqn Ldr Tom Gleave of No 253 Sqn was also scathing in his criticism;

'Douglas Bader was completely wrong on tactics at the time. He was very brave. But he'd been out of the air force for ten years. He lagged completely behind in modern concepts. All he could think of, as far as I could see, was the old First World War flying circuses, which had nothing to do with what we were up against in the Battle of Britain.'

LONDON'S BURNING

Just when it looked as if Fighter Command's defence of south-east England was coming apart at the seams through a combination of mounting casualties and damaged sector stations, the Luftwaffe's bombing strategy shifted its focus once again from RAF fighter stations to the sprawling conurbation of Greater London. This change of target came about by accident following a poorly executed night raid on industrial targets in Rochester and the oil tank farm at Thameshaven. Various postwar sources have reported that as few as two bombers overflew their targets and jettisoned their ordnance after being fired upon by AA batteries in central London. Although the resulting destruction was minimal (nine civilians were killed,. however, and a number of others injured), in the grander scheme of things, the raid so infuriated Prime Minister Winston Churchill that he ordered Bomber Command to carry out a series of reprisal attacks on Berlin over the following nights.

The direct result of these largely ineffective sorties was finally felt by No 11 Group on the afternoon of 7 September 1940, when *Reichsmarschall* Hermann Göring personally took charge of the assault on London. The awesome force sent across the Channel (348 bombers protected by 617 fighters) was the direct result of his pride having been dented by both the presence of British bombers over the German capital and the apparent lack of progress being made by the Luftwaffe in their efforts to crush the RAF in the prelude to invasion. Once spotted by radar and plotted on the sector control maps within the battered sector stations, Fighter Command braced itself for the onslaught by scrambling 11 units and bringing a further 10 to Readiness – there were no reserves left in No 11 Group.

One of the units thrust into action was No 303 Sqn, whose pilots engaged the huge formation as it approached the London docks. Future Polish ace Plt Off Jan Zumbach (12 and 2 shared destroyed, 5 probables and 1 damaged) scored his first kills during the combat;

'We were climbing at full speed when I saw a burst of ack-ack fire over London harbour and then, a little to the right, below us, a formation of German bombers escorted by a surprisingly large number of Me 109s. Coming from the south, the bombers approached the

Yet another of No 242 Sqn's Canadian aces was Flg Off H N Tamblyn, who scored 5 and 1 shared destroyed, 1 probable and 2 damaged prior to his death on 3 April 1941. A native of Saskatchewan, Tamblyn had scored his first kill (a Bf 109E) on 19 July in a Defiant I of No 141 Sqn – his aircraft was one of only two to survive out a formation of nine that was attacked by *Emils* off Folkstone. Although No 141 Sqn was posted north to Scotland to reform in the wake of this disastrous action, a number of its surviving pilots were instead sent to Hurricane and Spitfire squadrons – Tamblyn was posted to No 242 Sqn on 8 August. After surviving 1940, Hugh Tamblyn was lost whilst on a convoy patrol off Felixstowe on 3 April 1941, his Hurricane IIB (Z2692) being hit by return fire from a Do 17 that he had engaged. Although the Canadian pilot had safely baled out of his stricken fighter, he had died of exposure by the time a rescue launch found him (*via RAF Museum*)

Exhibiting a vast array of flying clothing, No 242 Sqn pilots pose in front of Sqn Ldr Bader's Hurricane I (note the aircraft's squadron leader's pennant beneath the cockpit) in late September 1940. The men are, from left to right; Plt Off D Crowley-Milling (4 and 1 shared destroyed, 2 probables and 1 and 1 shared damaged); Flg Off H N Tamblyn (5 and 1 shared destroyed, 1 probable and 2 damaged – killed 3/4/41); Flg Off P S Turner (10 and 1 shared destroyed, 3 unconfirmed destroyed, 1 probable and 8 damaged); on the wing, Sgt J E Savill (1 destroyed); Plt Off N N Campbell (1 and 2 shared destroyed – killed 17/10/40); Plt Off W L McKnight (17 and 2 shared destroyed and 3 unconfirmed destroyed – killed 12/1/41); Sqn Ldr D R S Bader (20 and 4 shared destroyed, 6 and 1 shared probables and 11 damaged); Flg Off G E Ball (6 and 1 shared destroyed and 3 damaged); Plt Off M G Homer (1 damaged – killed 27/9/40); and Plt Off M K Brown (killed 21/2 /41) (*via Stephen Fochuk*)

Thames to drop their bombs and then turn north. I thought we were going to rush at the enemy, but this was not so. It seemed that the squadron leader, a British officer, did not realise exactly which direction the bombers were taking. Then I heard someone shout in Polish, "Attack! Follow me!" It was Lt Paszkiewicz (who subsequently downed two Do 17Zs in this action – Ed.), a very experienced pilot, who shook his wings to show the others he was leaving the formation. He started to attack and was immediately followed by the other sections, and also by the leader, who now understood the manoeuvre.

'In front of me, two Dorniers were already on fire and parachutes were opening in the sky. The German bombers were approaching at tremendous speed. My leader was already firing. It was my turn. I pressed the button. Nothing happened. I swore violently. Already I had to move out. Tracer bullets were whizzing by on all sides and then I realised I had forgotten to realease the safety switch.

'Turning violently, crushed down by centrifugal force, bent in two, I found myself on the atil of a stream of bombers, with a Dornier 215 in front of me growing bigger and bigger in my sights, until it blotted out everything else. I saw the rear gunner aiming at me. I pressed the button and the rattle of my eight machine guns shook my plane. A long cloud of smoke came out of the Dornier. Another burst and it was ablaze. Over the radio, everyone was shouting, in English, in Polish.'

Zumbach was credited with two Do 17 kills on this sortie. Another pilot involved in this mid-afternoon clash was No 249 Sqn's 7-kill ace Sgt J M B Beard, who missed the first interception of the huge bomber formation because he was on a day's leave. However, having returned briefly to his North Weald base to see if a letter had arrived from his wife, Beard was duly scrambled on the squadron's second interception of the day.

His description of the action was included in *Their Finest Hour*, a volume chronicling Britons' in their first year of war (George Allen & Unwin Ltd, 1941 edition);

'My own Hurricane (N2440) was a nice old kite, though it had a habit of flying left wing low at the slightest provocation. But since it had already accounted for 14 German aircraft before I inherited it (an ex-No 56 Sqn machine which had been left behind for No 249 Sqn when the latter unit swapped bases with the former squadron on 1 September, N2440 had been used by No 56 Sqn's leading ace, Sgt F W 'Taffy' Higginson, to score 4 of his 12 kills, including his first 3 over France during the *Blitzkrieg*, and also by Flt Lt P S Weaver to down a Bf 110 and damage a second on *Adlertag* – Ed.), I thought it had some luck, and I was glad when I squeezed myself into the same old seat again and grabbed the "stick".

'We took off in two flights (six fighters), and as we started to gain height over the station we were told over the R/T to keep circling for a while until we were made up to a stronger force. That didn't take long, and soon there was a complete squadron (12 machines) including a couple of Spitfires which had wandered in from somewhere.

'Minutes went by. Green fields and roads were now beneath us. I scanned the sky and the horizon for the first glimpse of the Germans. A new vector came through on the R/T and we swung round with the sun behind us. Swift on the heels of this I heard "Yellow" Flight leader (Flt Lt D G Parnall, an RAF Volunteer Reserve pilot who had joined No 249 Sqn on its reformation in May 1940, and was shot down and killed just ten days after the action recounted here, having scored 1 and 4 shared destroyed, 2 probables and 1 damaged – Ed.) call through the earphones. I looked quickly towards "Yellow's" position and there *they* were!

Exhibiting greater uniformity in respect to their flying apparel when compared with their brethren at No 242 Sqn, pilots from No 249 Sqn stride towards the camera at North Weald in mid-September 1940. This shot was widely published during the war, and was also used on the cover of the official Air Ministry account of the Battle of Britain. The pilots are, from left to right; Plt Off P R F Burton (1 destroyed – killed 27/9/40); Flt Lt R A 'Butch' Barton (12 and 5 shared destroyed, 2 probables and 5 and 4 shared damaged); Plt Off A G Lewis (18 destroyed, 2 and 1 shared probables and 1 damaged); Plt Off J T Crossey (1 and 1 shared destroyed); Plt Off T F Neil (12 and 4 shared destroyed, 2 probables and 1 damaged); Plt Off H J S Beazley (2 and 2 shared destroyed, 1 probable and 1 damaged); Sqn Ldr J Grandy; Plt Off R G A Barclay (6 and 2 shared destroyed, 6 probables and 4 damaged – killed 17/7/42); and Flg Off K T Lofts (4 and 3 shared destroyed (plus 2 or 3 no details), 1 probable and 5 and 1 shared damaged) (*via Phil Jarrett*)

Plt Off Jan Zumbach poses with No 303 Sqn's Chief Mechanic, Wt Off Kazimierz Mozok, at the entrance to one of the unit's blast pens at Northolt during the height of the Battle of Britain. Polish, Czech and Canadian squadrons boasted foreign nationals in all trades (*via Dr Jan P Koniarek*)

The fabric-covered fuselage of Hurricane I V6684 serves as the perfect scoreboard for No 303 Sqn's burgeoning tally of victories towards the end of the Battle of Britain. No 303 Sqn claimed a total of 130 kills up to 31 October 1940, although the postwar analysis of Luftwaffe loss figures has since seen the tally revised down to 44 by many historians. This particular aircraft was one of the most successful Polish aircraft of the period, being credited with two Do 17Zs destroyed on 15 September (Urbanowicz), two Bf 109s, a He 111 and a Ju 88 on 26/27 September (Zumbach and Kent) and a Bf 110 on 5 October (Henneberg). After a long and distinguished career in Fighter Command, V6684 was used as a training aircraft by No 56 OTU until written off in a forced landing west of Arbroath, in Scotland, in August 1942 (*via Dr Jan P Koniarek*)

'It was really a terrific sight and quite beautiful. First they seemed just a cloud of light as the sun caught the many glistening chromium parts of their engines, their windshields and the spin of their airscrew discs. Then as our squadron hurtled nearer, the details stood out. I could see the bright yellow noses of Messerschmitt fighters sandwiching the bombers, and could even pick out some of the types. The sky seemed full of them, packed in layers thousands of feet deep. They came on steadily, wavering up and down along the horizon. "Oh, golly", I thought, "golly, golly . . ."

'And then any tension I had felt on the way suddenly left me. I was elated but very calm. I leaned over and switched on my reflector sight, flicked the catch on the guns button from "Safe" to "Fire", and lowered my seat till the circle and dot on the reflector sight shone darkly red in front of my eyes.

'The squadron leader's (Sqn Ldr J Grandy) voice came through the earphones giving tactical orders. We swung round in a great circle to attack on their beam – into the thick of them. Then, on order, down we went. I took my hand from the throttle lever so as to get both hands on the stick and my thumb played neatly across the gun button. You have to steady a fighter just as you have to steady a rifle before you fire it.

'My Merlin screamed as I went down in a steeply-banked dive on to the tail of a forward line of Heinkels. I knew the air was full of aircraft flinging themselves about in all directions but, hunched and snuggled down behind my sight, I was conscious only of the Heinkel I had picked out. As the angle of my dive increased, the enemy machine loomed larger in the sight field, heaved towards the red dot, and then he was there!

'I had an instant's flash of amazement at the Heinkel proceeding so regularly on its way with a fighter on its tail. "Why doesn't the fool move!" I thought, and actually caught myself flexing my muscles into the action I would have have taken had I been he.

'When he was square across the sight I pressed the button. There was a smooth trembling of my Hurricane as the eight-gun squirt shot out. I gave him a two-second burst and then another. Cordite fumes blew back into the cockpit making an acrid mixture with the smell of hot oil and the air compressors.

'I saw my first burst go in and just as I was on top of him and turning away I noticed a red glow inside the bomber. I turned tightly

Proudly wearing their DFC ribbons and RAF Volunteer Reserve (VR) pins, Plt Off 'Ginger' Neil and Flg Off George Barclay pose solemnly for an official photograph at North Weald in mid-November 1940. Upon discovering that he had been awarded the DFC, Barclay commented in his diary, 'I don't feel I deserve a medal, and I feel still less like the dashing type one imagines wins medals!' At the same time as Barclay received his award, he was also promoted to the rank of flying officer, whilst 'Ginger' Neil received a Bar to his DFC, having won the latter medal on 8 October 1940 (*via Frank Mason*)

Two sections of No 249 Sqn aircraft scramble from North Weald in early October 1940 – it is highly likely that 'GN-C' was being flown by George Barclay when this photograph was taken. The Hurricanes parked in the foreground are both devoid of the fuselage panelling which covers the compartment containing the radio, battery, oxygen on/off valve, parking gear and stowed starter handle (*via A Thomas*)

into position again and now saw several short tongues of flame lick out along the fuselage. Then he went down in a spin, blanketed with smoke and with pieces flying off.'

Despite his assertion that the He 111 went down almost certainly on fire, Sgt Beard was not even credited with a damaged on this date. He was scrambled for No 249 Sqn's third patrol of the day just after 4.00 pm, but just as he was about to inflict the *coup de grace* on a He 111 that he had already attacked, over docklands, his Hurricane (N2440 again) had its propellor blown off by AA fire aimed at the Heinkel formation. Beard quickly vacated his cherished fighter and landed in an allotment garden with a badly bruised shoulder, which he had hurt during the baling out process.

Sgt Beard was lucky to escape with his life on 7 September, for seven Hurricane pilots had been killed (including one from No 249 Sqn) and a further ten wounded during the day's action. Two of those to die were aces – Sqn Ldr C B Hull of No 43 Sqn (4 and 4 shared destroyed, 1 unconfirmed destroyed, 2 and 1 shared probable and 2 damaged) and No 73 Sqn's Flt Lt R E Lovett (3 destroyed, 1 probable and 1 and 1 shared damaged).

Thus, phase three of the Battle of Britain had begun, and although the death toll amongst non-combatants would, from this point on, far outstrip the casualty rate suffered by Fighter Command for the remainder of the daylight bombing campaign, the tide slowly began to turn back in favour of the defenders. Both fighter sector stations and radar sites that had been repeatedly bombed for over three weeks were now left alone by the Luftwaffe as Göring mistakenly ordered his *Luftflotten* to bomb London and other key cities in the south-east. With major conurbations now the primary targets, Fighter Command's sector controllers now knew where each raid was headed as it formed up over the French coast, and could thus better position their charges for effective interceptions, rather than scrambling fighters hastily from airfields that were under the threat of impending attack.

Between 7 September and 1 October Fighter Command and the Luftwaffe 'slugged it out' in the skies over Greater London, vast formations of German bombers, and escorting fighters, being opposed by varying numbers of Hurricane and Spitifre squadrons from all three groups in the south-east of England. During this time some 64 Hurricane pilots were killed and a further 71 injured. Just eight aces were amongst the former figure, which again reflects the fact that very few of the original high scorers from France and the early phases of the battle remained in the frontline well into September.

Of those that were still taking the fight to the Luftwaffe on a near-daily basis over the capital, several closed in on Sqn Ldr Crossley's record tally of 20 during the month of September – No 501 Sqn's 'Ginger' Lacey added a further 5 to his 15 victories scored up to the start of the bombing campaign on London, thus equalling the 'Red Knight's' tally, whilst Sqn Ldr G R Edge, formerly of No 605 Sqn but made OC of No 253 Sqn on 5 September, celebrated his return to action by downing 11 aircraft in just 8 days. His astounding run came to an end on 27 September when he was shot down (he claims by his Polish wingman) into the sea, although he was rescued having suffered

Right
New Zealander Plt Off I S Smith used this No 151 Sqn machine (V7434) to achieve ace status in the early evening of Wednesday, 2 October 1940, when he forced He 111H-5 Wk-Nr 3554 of 1./KG 53 to ditch into the surf off Chapel St Leonards, on the Lincolnshire coast. Having fought with the unit throughout July and August from North Weald, Smith went north to Digby with No 151 Sqn when it left the Essex fighter station on 1 September needing just half a kill to 'make ace'. He was frustrated in his efforts throughout September, but on 2 October was scrambled to intercept a solitary hostile contact performing a reconnanissance flight along the Lincolnshire coast. Locating the bomber in fading light, Smith made short work of the Heinkel, and returned to Digby an ace. He went on to score further victories with the unit in Defiant and Mosquito nightfighters in 1941/42, following No 151 Sqn's transition to the role of nocturnal hunters – his final tally was 8 destroyed, 2 probables and 4 damaged. V7434's career with No 151 Sqn was far shorter, however, as it was written off on the night of 26 October 1940 during practice night circuit training at Digby's satellite airfield at Coleby Grange. Its pilot, Kiwi Sgt D O Stanley, crashed soon after taking off, and was pulled from the wreckage with horrific burns – he died later that same night in Lincoln County Hospital. Soon after Stanley's crash, squadron-mate Sgt R Holder was also killed just minutes after taking off when he too flew into the ground barely 800 yards beyond the flaming wreckage of V7434 (*via A Thomas*)

Former No 56 Sqn flight commander E J 'Jumbo' Gracie (right) poses with a Wg Cdr R G Harman outside the gates of Buckingham Palace after receiving their DFCs from the King in early 1941. By now a squadron leader, Gracie had been awarded his medal for scoring 5 and 2 shared destroyed, 3 probables and 3 damaged during the summer of 1940. He went on to command Nos 23, 601 and 126 Sqns during 1941/42, adding several more victories to his tally in Malta. Gracie was finally killed in action on 15 February 1944

minor burns. Despite returning to command No 605 Sqn later that year, Edge failed to add any further kills to his tally – his final score is estimated to be about 20, of which 1 or 2 were shared destroyed, plus 3 or more probables and at least 7 damaged.

No 303 Sqn's Czech sensation, Sgt Josef Frantisek, was undoubtedly *the* Hurricane pilot of this month, however, for his tally of 17 kills between 2 and 30 September made him the highest scoring Fighter Command pilot of the actual Battle of Britain period. Frantisek's OC, Sqn Ldr W Urbanowicz, also enjoyed great success during the large-scale aerial clashes over the south-east, downing 13 (he claimed 15) aircraft to add to his solitary scores with Nos 601 and 145 Sqns, and his sole Polish Air Force kill of 1936.

As mentioned earlier in this chapter, No 242 Sqn's Canadian ace Flg Off 'Willie' McKnight claimed three kills during limited opportunities presented to him as part of the Duxford 'Big WIng', taking his score to 17 and 1 shared by the end of September. A second pilot to finish with 17 was No 605 Sqn flight commander, Flt Lt A A McKellar, who was credited with 8 kills during this month alone – half of these were scored in a single day (9 September). He would go one better on 7 October when he was credited with five Bf 109Es destroyed and a sixth damaged. Three of McKellar's kills came after encountering some 50 to 60 *Emils* in the Sevenoaks area of west Kent, his typically matter-of-fact combat report for this action reading as follows;

SERGT JOZEF FRANTISEK

RAF artist Cuthbert Orde was kept incredibly busy throughout the summer of 1940 producing charcoal sketches of pilots and aircrew, his volume of work being quite outstanding. Along with his contemporary, Eric Kennington, Orde produced a moving record of the 'face' of Fighter Command during the Battle of Britain. He visited Northolt on 19 September, and whilst at the Middlesex fighter station, Orde sketched No 303 Sqn's Sgt Josef Frantisek, as well as a number of other pilots – note the Polish *Virtuti Militari*, 5th Class, medal sketched in below his wings. At the time the Czech ace was in the middle of his incredible scoring run, having downed a Bf 109E just 24 hours before – his 12th kill that month. A further five victories and a solitary probable would come his way before the end of September (*via Frank Mason*)

'I attacked the Number One and saw a bomb being dropped from this machine. I fired and pieces fell off his wing and dense white smoke and vapour came from him and he went into a violent outside spin. In my mirror I could see another '109 coming to attack me and therefore turned sharply right and found myself just below and behind another '109. I opened fire and saw my De Wilde (explosive ammunition) hitting his machine. It burst into flames and went down inverted east of Biggin Hill. As I again had a '109 on my tail I spiralled down to 15,000 ft and by this time there appeared to be '109s straggling all over the sky. I followed one, pulled my boost control and made up on him. I gave a burst from dead astern and at once his radiator appeared to be hit as dense white vapour came back at me and my windscreen fogged up. This speedily cleared and I gave another burst and this machine burst into flames and fell into a wood with a quarry near it, west of Maidstone.'

No less than 11 of McKellar's 17 victories were against *Emils*, although it would seem that II./JG 27 *experten*, and Battle of Britain Knight's Cross winner, Hauptmann Wolfgang Lippert (see *Osprey Aircraft of the Aces 11 - Bf 109D/E Aces 1939-41* for further details), gave the Messerschmitt fighter the final word for he is credited with having sent the Scottish ace crashing to his death in Kent on 1 November 1940. As the top scoring Auxiliary Air Force pilot of the Battle of Britain, McKellar was awarded the DSO, DFC and Bar, although he was unable to collect any of his decorations prior to his death due to his unit being almost in action in September/October.

'Archie' McKellar's 'five in a day' was a stunning example of how effective the venerable Hurricane I could be against the *Emil* even this late in the conflict, and it came close to equalling the best single-day haul by a Fighter Command pilot during the Battle of Britain. However, he fell just one short of South African ace Plt Off A G Lewis, who had been the first RAF pilot to down five Bf 109Es in a day when he had achieved instant 'acedom' near Lille airfield on 19 May whilst serving with No 85 Sqn. Lewis went one better on 27 September when, during the course of four sorties with No 249 Sqn, he destroyed three Bf 109Es, two Bf 110s and a Ju 88 – he was also credited with a third Bf 110 as a probable and a fourth *Emil* damaged. This stunning success took his tally to 18 destroyed, 2 and 1 shared probables and 1 damaged.

However, the very next day Lewis was shot down by Bf 109Es again over Kent, and although he successfully baled out of his stricken Hurricane (V6617), he was so badly burnt that he was not fit to return to flying until May 1941 – Lewis failed to add any further victories to his score.

THE BATTLE IS WON

Although Fighter Command had suffered heavy losses during the month of September, their opponents had endured nothing short of a major haemorrhaging of experienced fighter and bomber crews. On 15 September alone (a date which for the past 57 years has been celebrated as Battle of Britain Day by the British public), the Luftwaffe had 36 bombers and 23 fighters shot down by Hurricane and Spitfire squadrons, resulting in some 163 flying personnel being either killed or captured. It was the massive casualty rate on this day which finally convinced Adolf Hitler that to proceed with the invasion of Britain whilst Fighter Command was still obviously far from beaten would result in huge losses to the *Wehrmacht*. Operation *Sealion* was duly abandoned.

Several large raids were, however, flown later in September and during the first week of October, but as the days became shorter, the Luftwaffe turned its attention more to the night *Blitz* of London and other major cities on the eastern side of England. With the medium bombers finding sanctuary under the cover of darkness, the main combatants encountered by Fighter Command in October and November were small formations of Bf 109E-7 fighter-bombers equipped with a single bomb, which they would drop, often at random, from high altitude (28,000 ft+) over London and the south-east. Although Spitfire squadrons could just about reach such rarefied heights at a push, Hurricane units were usually left wallowing around at about 25,000 ft, hoping that the *Emils* would come down to their altitude and tangle with them before fleeing back across the Channel.

Many pilots found these new German *Jabo* tactics very frustrating, but for Plt Off K W Mackenzie of No 501 Sqn, the challenge was irresistible – he scored 8 and 3 shared destroyed and 2 and 1 shared damaged between 4 October and 15 November. He explains this phase of the battle in his autobiography, *Hurricane Combat* (*William Kimber*, 1987);

'October had been no less a strain than the previous heavy bomber daylight raids with fighter escort. In fact October had been a very telling period, due to the high altitude of the operations and the greatly increased speed and mobility of the large Bf 109 fighter-bomber and fighter sweeps no longer tied to the relatively slow pace of the heavy bombers. The vigilance and operational activity had been greater and essential to survive or attack the enemy. The total volume of sorties and operational flying had been increased by the necessity to keep standing patrols over Kent and the continuous workload was telling on pilots, operations staffs and the controllers, without whom we could not have succeeded in intercepting raids. The groundcrews and supporting staffs worked round the clock to give us the aircraft and weapons with untiring vigour and cheerfulness. It had been a wonderful team effort.'

MacKenzie's squadron-mate, Sgt J H 'Ginger' Lacey, also enjoyed success during this month of intense fighter-v-fighter action, downing three Bf 109Es to take his final score on Hurricanes to 23. This made him joint top scorer for the RAF at the time, a position he held with Spitfire pilot Flg Off E S Lock, formerly of No 41 Sqn, who ended 1940 in hospital

Flt Lt A W A 'Alfie' Bayne was an experienced pre-war fighter pilot who had seen several years of service with No 54 Sqn prior to being posted as a flight commander to No 17 Sqn on 7 June 1940. One of a number of pilots drafted into the unit to help it return to full strength following losses suffered over the Dunkirk beaches (No 17 Sqn had lost five experienced pilots, including its OC), Bayne enjoyed success through to late November – his score at the end of 1940 stood at 6 and 4 shared destroyed, 1 and 4 shared probables and 2 damaged. He later added 1 destroyed and 1 probable whilst OC No 136 Sqn in the Far East in 1943 (*via N Franks*)

By the autumn of 1940 No 79 Sqn ace Plt Off Don Stones had adorned 'his' Hurricane with 11 'Jerry' (chamber pots!) symbols to denote his successes over both France and England. The fighter is seen at Pembrey in November 1940 (*via N Franks*)

recovering from serious wounds suffered in action on 17 November (see *Osprey Aircraft of the Aces 12 - Spitfire Mk I/II Aces 1939-41* for further details).

Despite the absence of huge formations of bombers darkening the skies over England during daylight hours in October and November, Fighter Command had still suffered heavy casualties – predominantly to marauding Bf 109 *Gruppen*. Some 94 Hurricane pilots were killed (including 10 aces) and a further 42 injured to all causes between 1 October and 31 December. The first ace to die during this period was none other than Sgt Josef Frantisek of No 303 Sqn who, having survived the fiercest of aerial clashes the previous month and emerged as the leading scorer of the Battle of Britain, was inexplicably killed in a landing accident whilst nearing Northolt at the end of a fruitless patrol on the morning of 8 October. His flight commander, Flt Lt 'Johnny' Kent, was at a loss to explain what had happened to the talented Czech pilot;

'On the 8th October, the squadron was ordered off and was given the usual vectoring around, but nothing was seen or encountered. Before long the squadron was recalled to base. As we approached Northolt, we closed up into a tight formation of four vics of three in line astern from which we normally did a break over the airfield and put the sections into echelon prior to landing. On this occasion we were just over the Staines Reservoirs when Frantisek, who was in the rear section, pulled out and flew alongside the squadron. Someone called him on the R/T and told him to get back into formation at which he turned slowly away to the east and disappeared. Some time later we heard that he had crashed near Sutton and was dead when the rescuers got to the wreckage. He was seen approaching an open space

No 257 Sqn pilots 'ham it up' for the Air Ministry photographer at Martlesham Heath following their successes against the Italian Air Force on Armistice Day 1940 – an event dubbed the 'Spaghetti Party', by its RAF participants. The seasoned combat veterans of Nos 46 and 257 Sqns made short work of the BR 20 bombers, and escorting CR 42 biplane fighters, sent to attack a convoy off Lowestoft, claiming 9 bombers destroyed and 1 damaged, and 4 fighters destroyed, 3 probably destroyed and 1 damaged – only 2 Hurricanes were damaged in return. In reality, however, the Italians had 'only' lost 3 bombers and 3 fighters, one of the BR 20s landing not far from Martlesham Heath in Tangham Forest. Upon learning this, No 257 Sqn sent a 'raiding' party to the crash site and liberated the national insignia, a bayonet sheath and a steel helmet for its dispersal hut. The latter item is seen here on Polish ace Plt Off K Pniak's head (he claimed 1 and 1 shared BR 20s destroyed). Squatting alongside him is Canadian ace Flt Lt H P 'Cowboy' Blatchford, who also claimed 1 and 1 shared BR 20s destroyed, plus 2 CR 42s damaged. Standing between the two aces is Sqn Ldr Bob Tuck (*via Jerry Scutts*)

apparently trying to make a forced-landing when suddenly his aircraft flicked on to its back and dived into the ground. We never did find out why this happened as we had not been in action and there were no bullet holes in either him or the aeroplane (R4175). It was not only a very great loss, it was a very worrying one.'

Frantisek was not the only ace to be killed without any direct involvement by the Luftwaffe, for two others were lost in collisions whilst on patrol – fellow Czech, Flg Off E Fechtner, of No 310 Sqn on 29 October and Flg Off D T Jay (7 and 1 shared destroyed, 1 shared probable and 1 damaged) of No 87 Sqn five days earlier, the latter pilot having hit the tail of a Hurricane being flown by Australian ace, Plt Off J R Cock (10 and 1 shared destroyed, 1 unconfirmed destroyed, 4 probables and 5 damaged), who managed to land his damaged fighter. A further two pilots were lost in bad weather in late December, Sgt H N Howes (11 and 1 shared destroyed, 2 probables and 5 damaged) of No 85 Sqn on the 22nd and No 17 Sqn's Plt Off D C Leary (5 and 3 shared destroyed, 3 and 1 shared probable and 1 and 1 shared damaged) six days later.

As the days grew shorter and the incursions by the Luftwaffe became fewer and fewer, at last Fighter Command could begin to take stock of what it had achieved in 1940. The German invasion threat had been thwarted, at least until the spring, and in the intervening months many new squadrons would be formed and the lessons learned over the south-east put into practice. Many new pilots were already undergoing training to help restore established units to full strength, or help form new squadrons.

For the Hurricane, its finest moment in the Western European theatre at least had passed, for it was already obvious to senior RAF commanders that the Hawker fighter was barely a match for the *Emil*, particularly at the altitudes at which fighter combat was now taking place. The Spitfire had plenty of development potential left in it, but the Hurricane, because of the nature of its construction, had not. Although the latter type would remain in the frontline with Fighter Command well into 1941 (and serve as a night intruder/fighter-bomber on the Channel front until early 1943), its greatest contributions to the routing of the Axis alliance post-1940 would now take place overseas.

Two of the unsung heroes of 1940 stand proudly in front of their charge, Hawker-built P3395, parked in the No 1 Sqn dispersal area in late October. This aircraft was the personal mount of Flt Lt A V Clowes, who had his groundcrew paint a wasp below the exhaust stacks on either side of the Hurricane. Stripes were then added to the tail of the insect to denote each of Clowes' kills – his final tally was 9 and 1 shared destroyed, 1 shared unconfirmed destroyed, 3 probables and 2 damaged (see profile 2 for more details) (*via RAF Museum*)

MALTA AND NORTH AFRICA

Whilst literally hundreds of Hurricanes formed the backbone of Fighter Command as the RAF struggled to defend Britain during the summer of 1940, some 2500 miles south-east of England, a fraction of this number were taking the fight to the might of the Italian Air Force over the desert scrub of Libya and Egypt and the cool blue waters of the Mediterranean. Indeed, the losses suffered by No 11 Group on 18 or 31 August in respect to Hurricanes written off easily exceeded the number of Hawker fighters available to the Desert Air Force throughout 1940!

Despite their paucity in numbers, the motley collection of Hurricanes achieved successes which belied their numerical strength, with the exploits of No 33 Sqn in Libya and Egypt being particularly praiseworthy. Although it could be argued that fighting Italian aircraft of the calibre of the CR 42 and SM 79 was hardly the same as engaging Bf 109Es and Ju 88s, when the former types always outnumbered the intercepting Hurricanes by at least five-to-one, the achievements of the Desert Air Force pilots take on due importance.

When Italy declared war on Britain and France on 10 June 1940, the RAF's fighter force in North Africa consisted of three squadrons

Early-build Hurricane I (Trop) L1669 was the sole example of its type in North Africa during the first months of war. It had been sent to Khartoum to carry out tropical trials, and once these had ended, the fighter was left for the pilots of No 80 Sqn to fly at Helwan alongside their Gladiators. Devoid of guns, the aircraft's only useful role once the Italians entered the war in North Africa in June 1940 was for it to act as a decoy in order to try and convince the enemy that Hurricanes were present in numbers in the Middle East. The originator of this spoof tactic was Air Officer Commanding No 202 Group in Egypt, Air Commodore Raymond Collishaw – the Hurricane was duly dubbed 'Collie's Battleship' from that point onwards
(*via Frank Mason*)

(Nos 33, 80 and 112) of Gladiators based in eastern Egypt in defence of the Suez Canal and the port of Alexandria as part of No 202 Group. A sole Hurricane (L1669) could also be found on the strength of No 80 Sqn, this aircraft having been left behind at Helwan after the completion of tropical trials in order to allow the Gladiator pilots to gain familiarity on the monoplane type. Despite it having no armament, the aircraft (dubbed 'Collie's Battleship' after Desert Air Force OC and World War 1 ace, Air Commodore Raymond Collishaw) performed outstanding service as a decoy, being moved from base to base within Egypt in order to convince Italian reconnaissance flights that Hurricanes were in-theatre in some strength.

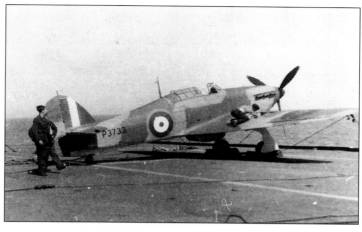

Hurricane I P3733 is prepared for launch from HMS *Argus* during Operation *Hurry*, performed on 2 August 1940. This machine was the newest of 12 Hurricanes despatched to Malta from Scotland aboard the Royal Navy carrier, RAF pilots flying the final 380 miles to the island. P3733 survived on Malta firstly with No 418 Flt and then No 261 Sqn until 12 February 1941, when it was one of two aircraft bounced by Bf 109Es of 7./JG 26 – its pilot, Plt Off D J Thacker, managed to bale out of the stricken fighter despite being wounded in the attack. These victories were the first claimed by *Emils* over Malta, and they ushered in a new phase in the Mediterranean air war that would see the RAF fighter pilots battling for their lives in distinctively inferior equipment to that flown by their *Jagdwaffe* opponents (*via A Thomas*)

With the invasion of Libya by the Italian army following soon after the declaration of war, a handful of Hurricanes were swiftly flown out to Egypt via France and Malta, but these aircraft could not be used in battle until tropical air filters had been fitted to them – this supply route was soon lost following the capitulation of France in late June. The Hurricane had enjoyed its first success in combat when future ace, Flg Off P G Wykeham-Barnes (14 and 3 shared destroyed, 1 probable and 2 and 2 shared damaged), used No 80 Sqn's sole forward-deployed Hurricane (P2639) to down two CR 42s of 4° *Stormo* over the Libyan coast on the morning of 19 June. He would destroy a further five aircraft (plus four more in Gladiators) before the end of 1940.

If RAF fighter assets were thin on the ground in North Africa, they were virtually non-existant on the now strategically important Mediterranean island of Malta. Four hastily assembled ex-Fleet Air Arm Sea Gladiators initially formed the island's sole defence, being organised as the Hal Far Fighter Flight. On 21 June the weary biplane fighters were joined by eight Hurricanes ferried out from Britain via France, these aircraft having initially been earmarked for the Desert Air Force (three were later flown on to Africa for use by No 202 Group). The Hurricane scored its first kill on the morning of 3 July when future ace Flg Off J L Waters (4 – possibly 5 or 6 – and 1 damaged) destroyed a SM 79 bomber of 36° *Stormo* off the Maltese coast. However, just as the British pilot was about to recover back at Hal Far his aircraft was bounced and badly shot up by CR 42s of 4° *Stormo*, forcing him to crash land – the Italians recorded their first fighter victory over Malta as having been against a Spitfire!

Further successes fell to the guns of the surviving Hurricanes throughout the rest of July, with future aces Flg Off F F Taylor (7 destroyed, 2 probables and 1 damaged – killed over Malta on 26 February 1941), Flg Off W J Woods (6 and 1 shared destroyed, 1 unconfirmed destroyed, 2 probables and 1 damaged – killed over Greece on 20 April 1941) and Flt Lt G Burges (7 destroyed, 2 proba-

The Desert Air Force's first
Hurricane ace gingerly climbs down
from his fighter at Sidi Haneish in
late October 1940. Flg Off J H
Lapsley proved a revelation in the
Hawker fighter during the second
half of 1940, claiming 11 kills
between 17 August and 19
December. A vastly experienced pre-
war pilot, Lapsley had flown the
Gladiator with No 80 Sqn since early
1938, having moved out to Egypt
with the unit in April of that year –
prior to joining the squadron he had
spent time flying Gauntlets with No
32 Sqn at Biggin Hill. One of the first
pilots assigned to No 80 Sqn's
newly-formed Hurricane flight in
August 1940, Lapsley had duly
transferred to No 274 Sqn when it
grew out of the latter outfit later
that same month (*via Aeroplane*)

bles and 7 damaged) all scoring their premier victories. Indeed, the latter was so successful in the numerous combats over Malta that he was awarded the island's first DFC in late July, the medal's citation crediting him with three kills and three probables.

Despite helping to destroy some 14 Italian aircraft in the six weeks since hostilities had commenced, the Hurricane element of the Fighter Flight had been effectively grounded by the beginning of August due to a chronic shortage of spare parts. However, help was at hand for on the 2nd of the month 12 Hawker fighters of the specially formed No 418 Flt were flown in from the aircraft carrier HMS *Argus* as part of Operation *Hurry*. Crewed by ex-Fighter Command pilots (who were unaware of the fact that they were to stay on Malta and fight the Italians until they actually arrived on the island itself!) drawn from a variety of Spitfire and Hurricane units, the dozen aircraft were pooled with the surviving fighters to form No 261 Sqn – the first new unit established in the Mediterranean since the start of the war. With Malta now possessing an adequate force to protect it against Italian aggression, RAF attentions turned once again to North Africa, where the handful of Hurricanes in-theatre continued to be used in ones and twos alongside the more abundant Gladiator I/IIs of Nos 33 and 80 Sqns.

The former type's destructive potential against Italian bombers, in particular, was graphically shown on 17 August when a lone Hawker fighter from No 80 Sqn engaged SM 79s for the first time as they attempted to attack Royal Navy vessels off Alexandria. The Hurricane was flown by future ace Flg Off J H Lapsley (11 destroyed), an experienced pre-war fighter pilot who proceeded to down three of the Savoia Marchetti bombers in quick succession.

Buoyed by this success, and the promise of more Hawker fighters from England (30+ aircraft were shipped out again aboard the venerable carrier *Argus* in early September), Desert Air Force formed No 274 Sqn on 19 August through the combination of the single Hurricane flights within Nos 33 and 80 Sqns. Sqn Ldr P H Dunn (6 and 3 shared destroyed, 2 probables and 1 and 1 shared damaged), who was formerly OC of No 80 Sqn, was placed in charge of the unit, and he took combat veterans Flg Offs Lapsley and Wykeham-Barnes with him.

INVASION

On 13 September the Italian army advanced eastward across the Libyan border into Egypt, its commanding officer, Marshal Graziani, using his superior force of tanks and artillery to capture great tracts of formerly Allied territory. As a prelude to this action, SM 79s had been sent to bomb the Allied coastal stronghold at

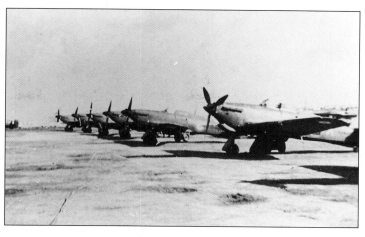

Sidi Barrani on 10 September. The RAF fighters based at the nearby airstrip scrambled to defend the town, and in the ensuing melee, Flg Off Lapsley downed a further two bombers to make him the first Hurricane ace of North Africa – he scored his sixth kill (another SM 79) over the front five days later. At about this time No 33 Sqn also began transitioning from Gladiators to Hurricanes thanks to the arrival of the *Argus* aircraft, although this process was not completed until the opening of the Trans-African ferry route from West Africa across the Sahara to Khartoum, and then due north to Cairo, in late September.

On Malta, No 418 Flt had recorded its first success during a night interception on 13 August, an SM 79 of 36° *Stormo* being downed through the aid of searchlights and radar. That the Italian bombers were now performing nocturnal raids speaks volumes about the psychological effect that a handful of Hurricanes had had on the attackers. Three days later No 261 Sqn was officially formed, and on 24 August Flg Off F F Taylor of Hal Far Fighter Flight fame scored the unit's first kill (and his second) when he shot down a CR 42 of 23° *Gruppo*. A further four claims against the Fiat biplane fighter were recorded on 5 September when CR 42s escorted the first Italian-manned Ju 87Bs to be seen over Malta. Two of the fighters were credited to Kiwi pilot, Sgt R J Hyde (5 destroyed, 1 probable and 1 damaged), who had flown one of the dozen Hurricanes to Malta the previous month.

The Italians maintained their sporadic cycle of bombing raids on Malta through to the end of the year, attacking both during daylight hours and at night. Throughout this period No 261 Sqn's main adversaries were CR 42s and MC 200s sent to escort the bombers, and by 31 December the Hurricane pilots had claimed ten of the former and six of the latter type shot down. Added to this tally were 13 SM 79s and 2 Ju 87s, with a further 11 undisclosed types as probables. Only two pilots had achieved 'ace' status during this period, however, Flg Off W J Woods downing three kills in Hurricanes by 17 September to add to his double score attained whilst flying Gladiators three months earlier (he was duly awarded the DFC for his exploits in December), and Flg Off Waters, who had achieved an identical kill split by 2 November. Finishing just one short was Flg Off F F Taylor, who was actually the highest scoring Hurricane pilot on Malta at the time for all

Although not the best quality, this rare shot of No 261 Sqn's Hurricanes lined up at Luqa in late November 1940 is worthy of inclusion on two counts. Firstly, its shows a number of fighters freshly flown in from *Argus* just days before, and secondly, the Hurricane closest to the camera is Mk I (Trop) V7474, which was used by at least two aces during its time on Mal ta. The fighter had indeed been flown onto the island as the lead aircraft of a six-Hurricane flight despatched from *Argus* on 17 November. Its pilot on this occasion was ex-BEF Battle pilot, and future ace, James MacLachlan, who would later lose an arm in combat over Malta in February 1941 – but not before he had been credited with eight kills and a probable. Fitted with an artificial limb, he returned to action in November of the same year, adding a further 8 destroyed, 1 shared and 3 damaged to his score before being lost in action over Dieppe in July 1943. Returning to V7474, this aircraft was also used by Fred Robertson to damage a CR 42 on 23 November 1940 and destroy a Ju 87 from StG 1 (plus claim a second as a probable) on 19 January 1941. V7474 was shot down by a Bf 109E of 7./JG 26 on 26 February 1941, its pilot, Battle of Britain veteran Plt Off C E Langdon from New Zealand, being killed – see profile 27 for more details (*via A Thomas*)

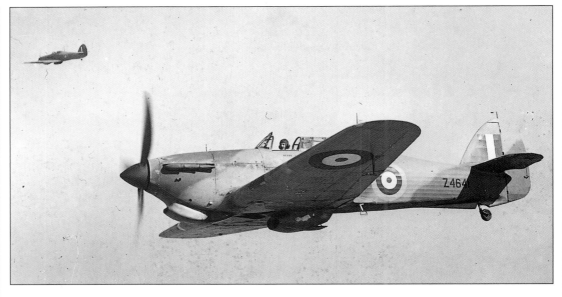

Devoid of any distinguishing markings, save its serial, a late-build Mk I (Trop) conducts a training sortie with its section mate near the Egyptian coast in late 1940. The Hurricane's 'glasshouse' did little to help stop the heat build up in the cockpit even when aloft, so many pilots chose to fly with the canopy slid back and locked in the open position (*via Norman Franks*)

Canadian V C 'Woody' Woodward was another pre-war pilot who quickly made his mark in combat against the Italians in North Africa in 1940, and then the Germans in Greece the following year. Flying firstly Gladiators and then Hurricanes with No 33 Sqn, he scored 18 and 4 shared destroyed, 2 unconfirmed destroyed, 3 probables and 11 damaged between 14 June 1940 and 12 July 1941 (*via Stephen Fochuk*)

four of his kills had been scored whilst flying the Hawker fighter – he would achieve ace status on 9 January 1941.

DESERT BATTLES

With the Italians pushing steadily eastward into Egypt, No 33 Sqn was thrust into the fray with its new Hurricanes on the last day of October. A large formation of SM 79s and CR 42s was engaged over Mersa Matruh, and in the ensuing battle, future aces Flg Offs P R St Quintin (9 destroyed and 1 – possibly 4 – probables) and F Holman (6 and 1 shared destroyed – killed in action on 19 April 1941) each claimed their first kills. No further victories were attained by the Hurricane units until the Allies commenced their counter-offensive into Libya on 9 December (codenamed Operation *Compass*). In the meantime, the Desert Air Force's ranks had been further bolstered with the arrival of No 73 Sqn from Britain, although this veteran unit had lost six precious Hurricanes during the first leg of its ferry flight from Takoradi, in West Africa, when they ran out of fuel. As a result of this calamitous start to its North African campaign, only a section of No 73 Sqn was available for the Libyan campaign, and this duly operated as part of No 274 Sqn.

On the opening day of Operation *Compass*, No 33 Sqn drew first blood when it shot down three CR 42s whilst ground-strafing in support of General Wavell's troops. Two of the fighters fell to Canadian pilot Flg Off V C Woodward (18 and 4 shared destroyed, 2 unconfirmed destroyed, 3 probables and 11 damaged), who had already achieved ace status flying Gladiators in the skirmishes of June and July. Relishing the opportunity to tackle the Italian biplane fighters in the superior Hurricane, 'Woody' went on to claim a further three CR 42s destroyed, one probable and two damaged, plus a pair of SM 79s also damaged, by year end.

Other aces to claim kills on 9 December included Sqn Ldr Dunn, Flg Offs Wykeham-Barnes and Lapsley, Plt Off E M Mason (15 and 2 shared destroyed, 3 and 3 shared damaged and 1 and 13

shared damaged on the ground – he was killed in action on 15 February 1942), Flt Sgt T C Morris (3 and 2 shared destroyed and 3 shared damaged) and Plt Off T L Patterson (7 destroyed, 1 probable, 1 damaged and possibly 1 destroyed by collision – he was lost in action on 25 April 1941).

Both Nos 33 and 274 Sqns continued to see much action over the few days as the Allied army pushed further into Italian territory. On 11 December, pre-war fighter pilot, Flg Off C H 'Deadstick' Dyson, set an RAF record that would last through to the end of the war when he destroyed seven Italian aircraft in a single sortie – six CR 42s and an SM 79. His feat is detailed in the following extract from Christopher Shores' and Hans Ring's excellent treatise *Fighters Over The Desert* (Neville Spearman, 1969);

'FO C H "Deadstick" Dyson, DFC, did not return from a lone patrol; six days later he returned safely to the unit with an amazing story. He claimed to have shot down no less than six CR 42s and probably a seventh. This claim was at first treated with some scepticism, but his claim was more than confirmed by the Army, which had witnessed the whole fight. Coming out of a cloud bank, Dyson found himself directly behind a formation of CR 42s escorting an SM 79 over the British lines. He fired two bursts at two vics, each of three fighters, all six starting to burn and fall. He was then attacked by others, and forced down near Sollum after claiming the probable from among his attackers. Unseen to him, one of the falling CR 42s crashed into the SM 79, bringing this down too.'

No 73 Sqn got its first kill on

No 73 Sqn was the first fighter outfit sent from the UK to North Africa following the Battle of Britain, the unit embarking aboard the carrier HMS *Furious* with 34 new tropicalised Hurricane Is for the trip to West Africa in November 1940. Upon arriving at its destination, the unit off-loaded the aircraft and flew them across the breadth of Africa along the Takoradi route to Heliopolis. Once in Egypt, No 73 Sqn's groundcrews (who had sailed through the Mediterranean directly to Heliopolis) took two to three weeks to prepare the Hurricanes for combat – the unit 'moved up the blue' to the frontline during the last week of December 1940. Exactly a year before, No 73 Sqn pilots and groundcrew had been fighting the cold at Rouvres during one of the bitterest winters ever experienced in northern Europe!
(*via Norman Franks*)

14 December when Flt Lt J D Smith (7 and 1 shared destroyed, 1 probable and 2 damaged – he was killed in action on 14 April 1941) destroyed an SM 79 to add to his previous successes during the Battles of France and Britain – he would down a further two bombers over the next four days. By 31 December some eight pilots had achieved ace status with the Hurricane in North Africa, No 274 Sqn's Flt Lt J H Lapsley leading the list with 11 kills. Although No 274 Sqn had produced more aces (six), No 33 Sqn had scored the highest number of victories during the Libyan offensive, its pilots being credited with 36 confirmed kills, 10 probables and 11 damaged by month's end.

Operation *Compass* had proven to be a resounding success, with just 60 RAF fighters (Hurricanes made up roughly half of this figure) soundly defeating the Italian force, which comprised 140 bombers and 191 fighters and tactical support aircraft. Indeed, the Allies had so effectively routed their opponents both on the ground and in the air that by the New Year the Italians were in danger of being kicked out of North Africa altogether. However, in mid-January the Germans arrived in Tripoli, and the Hurricane's unrivalled supremacy over the battlefield was soon under threat . . .

An example of a typical desert landing ground somewhere along the Egyptian coastline in December 1940. The Desert Air Force utilised literally dozens of these barren sites throughout the war in North Africa, the Hurricane's wide-splayed undercarriage proving capable of tackling the roughest of 'runways'. Note how virtually all the fighters have been parked into wind to facilitate a rapid scramble should the alarm bell toll – shades of France during the previous spring
(*via Norman Franks*)

APPENDICES

1

Hurricane Mk I L1679 of No 1 Sqn, flown by Flg Off Paul Richey, Vassincourt, late 1939

This aircraft was the regular mount of Flg Off Paul Richey throughout most of the 'Phoney War', although it was not amongst the original 16 Hurricanes flown from Tangmere to Octeville on the morning of 7 September 1939 – Richey had flown the metal-winged L1971 across the Channel on this occasion. By contrast, L1679 was a fabric-winged, two-bladed (note its insignia red airscrew tip) Hurricane that formed part of the first batch of 14 Mk Is delivered to No 1 Sqn at Tangmere from the Hawker factory at Kingston in October 1938. The precise date of its transfer to France is unknown, but Richey used the fighter to claim a third of kill against a Do 17Z of 7./KG 3 on the opening day of the *Blitzkrieg*, and then got an unconfirmed victory against a second Dornier bomber (a Do 17P from 3.(F)/10) with it the following day. However, at the end of the latter combat he was forced to recover at a bombed-out French airfield due to a shortage of fuel, and during his landing roll he swerved to miss a crater and dug L1679's port wing in. The aircraft was abandoned there, and three days later a party of No 1 Sqn riggers returned to patch the aircraft up. However, within minutes of their arrival the airfield was attacked, and the forlorn Hurricane (plus the 15 French Potez Po 63s based at the site) was summarily strafed for two-and-a-half hours by marauding Do 17s. Paul Richey described how he felt upon hearing the news in *Fighter Pilot* – 'poor old "G" was sieved with bullets. I can only hope she burned before the Huns laid their rude hands on her'.

2

Hurricane Mk I P3395 of No 1 Sqn, flown by Flt Lt A V Clowes, Collyweston, early November 1940

This Hurricane was issued to No 1 Sqn upon the unit's return from France in mid-June, and served throughout the Battle principally as 'Darkie' Clowes' 'Yellow 1'. One of only two pilots to fly with the unit throughout the 'Phoney War', the *Blitzkrieg* and the Battle of Britain (15-kill Canadian ace Flt Lt 'Hilly' Brown was the other), Clowes had been promoted from sergeant pilot to flight lieutenant by November 1940. Commensurate with his progress through the ranks was the accumulation of a score of 9 and 1 shared destroyed, 1 shared unconfirmed destroyed, 3 probables and 2 damaged – of this total, 1 (Bf 110) and 1 shared confirmed (Do 17), 3 probables (2 Do17s and a Bf 110) and 2 damaged (a Bf 110 and a He 111) were claimed whilst flying P3395. For every kill he scored, Clowes instructed his groundcrew to add a yellow stripe to the wasp motif painted below both the port and starboard exhaust stubs – the same shade of roundel yellow was used by No 1 Sqn to mark the Rotol prop spinners on each of its Hurricanes. This weary veteran was passed to No 55 Operational Training Unit (OTU) on 8 November 1940, were it stayed until being issued to No 5 Flying Training School (FTS) sometime in 1941. The Hurricane was written off whilst still with this unit when its trainee pilot landed P3395 at Ternhill on 24 March 1942 without first extending its undercarriage, causing the

fighter to slew off the grass strip and hit a gun position on the edge of the runway.

3

Hurricane Mk I P3878 of No 17 Sqn, flown by Plt Off H A C Bird-Wilson, Debden, 24 September 1940

This Hawker-built Mk I was issued to No 17 Sqn at Debden on 1 July 1940 fresh from the factory, and went on to see much action from the Essex base predominantly with Harold 'Birdy' Bird-Wilson at the controls. However, on the morning of Tuesday, 24 September, the aircraft's brief contribution to the defence of Britain came to an end, courtesy of JG 26's *Geschwaderkommodore*, Major Adolf Galland. Bird-Wilson was badly burned during his efforts to bale out of the stricken fighter, keeping him off operational flying for six months. After the war he commented, 'I was Galland's 40th victim. So I was the sucker that got him his Knight's Cross of the Iron Cross with Oak leaves!'

4

Hurricane Mk I P3144 of No 32 Sqn, flown by Sqn Ldr J Worrall and Flt Lt M N Crossley, Biggin Hill/Hawkinge, mid-July 1940

Like the aircraft featured in the previous profile, this Hurricane was delivered to No 11 Group directly from the Hawker production line, being received by No 32 Sqn at its Biggin Hill base on 12 July 1940. It lasted just seven days in the frontline, however, being shot down over Dover on the afternoon of 19 July by an Unteroffizier Mayer, who was flying a Bf 109E of III./JG 51. The Hurricane's pilot, Flt Sgt Guy Turner, baled out with severe burns – he later became one of Dr Archibald McIndoe's 'Guinea Pigs', returning to flying almost two years later. During P3144's brief stay with No 32 Sqn (the aircraft had accumulated just 8 hrs and 15 mins flying time when it was lost in combat), the Hurricane was flown by both the unit OC, Sqn Ldr 'Baron' Worrall, and leading ace, Flt Lt Mike 'Red Knight' Crossley, although neither claimed any victories with it.

5

Hurricane Mk I P2921 of No 32 Sqn, flown by Flt Lt P M Brothers, Biggin Hill/Hawkinge, July 1940

Unlike P3144, this Hurricane enjoyed a long life both in the frontline and in secondary training establishments, before eventually being passed on to the Fleet Air Arm (FAA). Issued to No 15 MU on 30 May 1940, it was one of three Hawker fighters sent to No 32 Sqn on 11 June as attrition replacements for the trio of aircraft lost by the unit in combat during a patrol over Le Tréport 48 hours earlier. As the newest of the three Hurricanes to arrive at Biggin Hill, P2921 was immediately 'acquired' by 'B' Flight commander, 'Pete' Brothers. Convinced that speed was the key to success in air combat, Brothers had his rigger delete the drag-inducing external rear-view mirror atop the windscreen and fit a curved car mirror (bought locally from Halfords in Bromley) inside the cockpit instead! He also instructed the airman to file down the aircraft's wing rivets in order to further reduce the level of drag – Brothers would often lend his rigger a hand between sorties completing this task. The end result was the fastest Hurricane on the squadron by at least 5 mph, according to its pilot. Brothers further

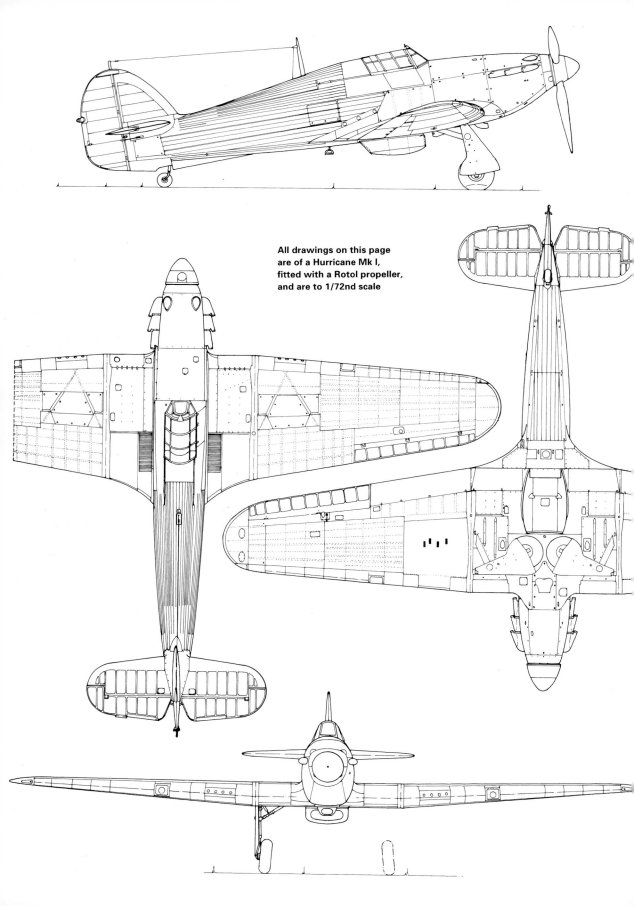

All drawings on this page
are of a Hurricane Mk I,
fitted with a Rotol propeller,
and are to 1/72nd scale

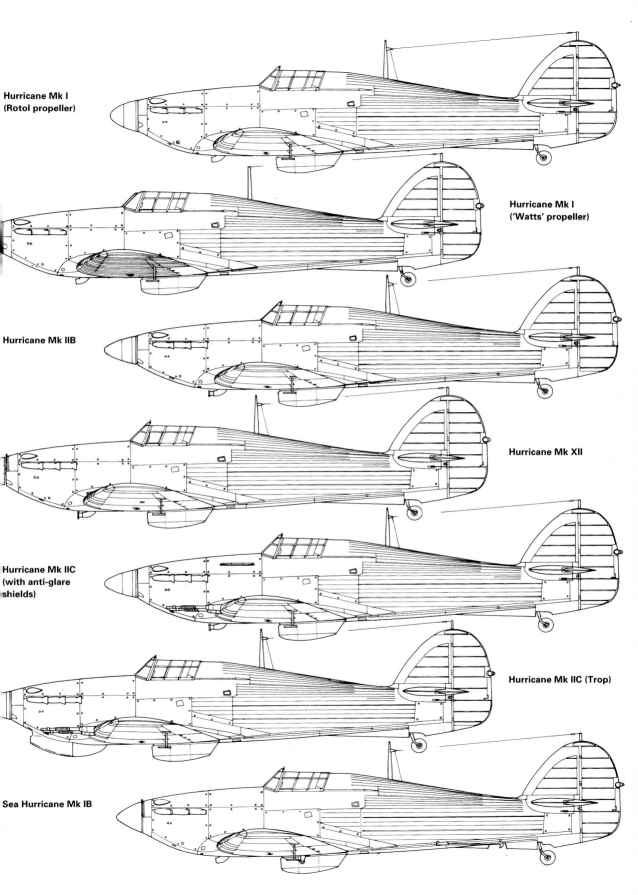

Hurricane Mk I
(Rotol propeller)

Hurricane Mk I
('Watts' propeller)

Hurricane Mk IIB

Hurricane Mk XII

Hurricane Mk IIC
(with anti-glare
shields)

Hurricane Mk IIC (Trop)

Sea Hurricane Mk IB

personalised 'his' fighter by having a 'Blue Peter' flag painted below the cockpit (on the port side only) – note, too, the 40-in code letters on this machine (and on the previous profile), which were the largest employed by any Fighter Command squadron in 1940. Astoundingly, official Air Ministry Orders (AMO) at the time (which stemmed from 27 April 1939) stipulated that squadron codes – dubbed 'Munich Codes' after the crisis of the previous year – should be 48 inches high and stroked 6 inches in width, although the lack of space on the fuselage of a Hurricane or a Spitfire meant that units usually applied 30-in high lettering instead. Brothers flew P2921 throughout July/August 1940, during which time he was credited with destroying eight German aircraft (six Bf 109Es, a Bf 110 and a Do 17). The fighter remained with No 32 Sqn until 21 February 1941, when it was transferred to the newly-formed No 315 'Polish' Sqn at Speke, near Liverpool. Five months later it was passed onto No 245 Sqn in Ireland, before finally being sent to a maintenance unit the following August. Issued to the Fleet Air Arm on the last day of October 1941, P2921 was converted into a Sea Hurricane Mk IA later that same year and assigned to the Merchant Ship Fighter Unit for deployment aboard a CAM (catapult aircraft merchantman) ship. According to its service card, the fighter sailed as far afield as Ceylon, where it was damaged in September 1942, but the aircraft was soon repaired and returned to Yeovilton. P2921 was last noted at St Mawgan in September 1943, but its final fate is unknown.

6

Hurricane Mk I (Trop) P3729 of No 33 Sqn, flown by Flg Off V C Woodward, Fuka, Egypt, October 1940

Shipped out to Takoradi, on the Gold Coast (now Ghana), as part of the second delivery of 36 Hurricanes made to the Desert Air Force, this brand new aircraft was uncrated, reassembled and then despatched on the arduous 3697-mile overland trans-African ferry route to Abu Sueir, on the banks of the Suez Canal, in late September 1940. Like a number of the other 'tropicalised' Mk Is sent to North Africa at this time, P3729 was issued to No 33 Sqn, who had been able to start their conversion from the Gladiator to the Hawker fighter following the arrival of the Hurricanes. As part of the transition from biplanes to monoplanes, Canadian Gladiator ace 'Woody' Woodward collected this aircraft from Abu Sueir on 5 October and flew north-west to No 33 Sqn's new base at Fuka, near the Egyptian coast – it is likely that he saw action in the fighter during Operation *Compass*. During the December battles, Woodward downed five CR 42s and claimed a sixth as a probable, as well as damaging a further three aircraft. P3729 survived the fighting of late 1940/early 1941 to be passed firstly to No 238 Sqn and then No 274 Sqn. On 15 July 1941, the aircraft's combat career came to an abrupt end when it was shot down by a Bf 109E of 7./JG 26 off Tobruk whilst defending an Allied shipping convoy from marauding Stukas of II./StG 2. It is likely that its pilot on this fateful sortie was a Plt Off Lauder, who was on secondment from No 229 Sqn.

7

Hurricane Mk I P2970 of No 56 Sqn, flown by Plt Off A G Page, Rochford, 12 August 1940

This aircraft was delivered to No 56 Sqn 24 hours after the unit had returned to their 'Phoney War' base at North Weald on 5 June 1940, following just six days of rest at the No 12 Group air station at Digby in the wake of the squadron's evacuation from France. It soon became the regular mount of squadron 'new boy', Plt Off Geoffrey Page, who had arrived at the Essex base after spending several weeks flying Spitfires on Channel patrols with No 66 Sqn from Coltishall – despite the influx of several new pilots, No 56 Sqn was still four short of its full establishment of 26 by 1 July. Page was assigned to 'A' Flight, and enjoyed his first success on 13 July when he was credited with the destruction of a 'He 113' (actually a Bf 109E of 4./JG 51) off Calais whilst flying P2970. He was awarded a third of a kill against a Ju 88 of 4.(F)/122 south-west of Clacton a week later, the destruction of the recce bomber being shared with fellow No 56 Sqn aces Flt Lt E J 'Jumbo' Gracie and Flg Off P S Weaver. On this occasion P2970 was superficially damaged by return fire from the stricken Ju 88. On 25 July, whilst flying from Rochford, Page and P2970 scored their third victory when they were credited with the destruction of a II./LG 1 Ju 87B, which was attacking a coastal convoy off Dover. *LITTLE WILLIE*, as Page had by now nicknamed his well-weathered Mk I, was finally lost during the early-evening interception of a force of 27 Do 17Zs (and 40+ escorting Bf 109Es) over the Channel as they headed for Manston. Page was caught in the defensive cross-fire of the tight Dornier formation as his flight engaged the enemy from close quarters. P2970 was hit in the fuel tank ahead of the cockpit and this immediately burst into flames, forcing Page to take to his parachute – but not before his hands and face had been so badly burnt that he would spend the next two years in hospital recovering. Showing both exceptional determination and considerable courage, Page eventually returned to the frontline and finished the war with a score of 10 and 5 shared destroyed and 3 damaged.

8

Hurricane Mk I R2689 of No 56 Sqn, flown by Flt Lt E J Gracie, North Weald, 30 August 1940

One of three factory-fresh Mk Is delivered to No 56 Sqn on 28 July 1940, this aircraft eventually became the regular mount of 'B' Flight Commander, Flt Lt E J 'Jumbo' Gracie – his nickname stemmed from his portly figure and distinctive waddling stride! Despite appearances, Gracie quickly proved to be both a skilled leader and a crack shot, and by the end of August he had downed 3 and 1 shared destroyed, 1 probable and 3 damaged in R2689. These successes combined with his 2 and 1 shared destroyed and 1 probable, scored flying other No 56 Sqn Hurricanes in July, to make him an ace. Late in the afternoon of 30 August, Gracie was scrambled with 11 other No 56 Sqn pilots from North Weald to engage a large raid heading for their Essex home. The force, comprising 60 He 111H-2s from II./KG 1 and I. and II./KG 53 and escorting Bf 110s from ZG 26, flew past the No 11 Group fighter station, however, and bombed the Vauxhall works at Luton and the Handley Page factory at Radlett instead. Harassed all the way by numerous Spitfire and Hurricane units, the German raiders were badly mauled, with Gracie claiming one He 111 destroyed and a second damaged before exhausting his ammunition. However,

R2689 had itself been mortally hit during the fierce fighting, and when its engine seized during Gracie's return flight to North Weald, he was forced to hastily land in a field near Halstead – the aircraft was burnt out in the subsequent crash, and although its pilot appeared to escape unscathed, it was discovered 48 hours later that he had actually broken his neck! Like Page's Hurricane, R2689 had a sky spinner, which was an unofficial modification to the standard scheme adopted by a small number of units during the summer of 1940. Even more unique are the twin horizontal sky bars applied over the fin flash, which almost certainly served to denote the flight commander's aircraft.

9
Hurricane Mk I (serial unknown) of No 73 Sqn, flown by Flg Off E J Kain, Rouvres, France, early spring 1940

The exact identity of this two-bladed aircraft remains a mystery, as all No 73 Sqn 'Phoney War' Hurricane Is had had their serials obliterated by the spring of 1940 for security reasons. 'Cobber' Kain used at least four P-coded Mk Is during his time with the squadron, reputedly favouring this letter in deference to his Irish fitter, who had been with him since his pre-war days with the unit at Digby – the British press succeeded in annoying Kain when it was intimated in an interview conducted with him in late March 1940 that his aircraft was named in honour of a girlfriend back in New Zealand. A fourth PADDY was also flown by Kain towards the end of his stay in France, although the suggestion that he was at the controls of this machine when he was killed in a flying accident over Echemines airfield on 7 June 1940 is almost certainly erroneous – recent research by historian Don Minterne indicates that the ace was flying L1826 (coded TP-B or TP-R), a war-weary 'two-blader' that Kain was returning to England for an overhaul, after which he was due to go on leave before becoming an instructor.

10
Hurricane Mk I P2569 of No 73 Sqn, flown by Flt Lt R E Lovett, Rouvres, France, 19 April 1940

Although wearing an identical scheme to Kain's Mk I, this aircraft was fitted with a de Havilland three-bladed variable pitch propeller, which gave the fighter a significant performance advantage during take-off over Hurricanes fitted with the Airscrew Company's wooden 'Watts prop'. P2569 was amongst the first of its type built by contractors Glosters in late 1939, the fighter being supplied straight from the factory to No 73 Sqn early in the new year. Once in France, it was regularly flown by 'A' Flight commander, Flt Lt Reg 'Unlucky' Lovett, who had earned his nickname due to a series of unfortunate events which included the shooting down in error of a French Potez Po 637 west of Verdun on 21 December 1939, and the infliction of serious burns to his hands on the opening day of the *Blitzkrieg* after being shot down by return fire from a Do 17 – Lovett was so badly burned in the latter action that he had to force land his Hurricane (P2804/E) because he feared that he would be unable to pull the parachute ripcord. Extricated from the wreckage of his fighter by local farmers, Lovett was lucky to survive – he was sent back to England to recuperate. P2569 was flown by Lovett on 19 April 1940 for a series of official RAF photographs taken from the back of a commandeered

Battle by a photographer known as Mr 'Glorious' Devon during a sortie from Reims. Two sections (six aircraft) of No 73 Sqn fighters were involved, and the subsequent images have since been seen in innumerable publications. It is likely that Lovett was at the controls of this aircraft some 48 hours later when No 73 Sqn was credited with the destruction of six Messerschmitt fighters, plus a further four as probables – Lovett claimed a Bf 110 of I./ZG 1 destroyed. Awarded a DFC whilst recovering from his burns, Reg Lovett returned to No 73 Sqn in late July 1940, but was killed in action over Essex on 7 September, by which time his score stood at 3 destroyed, 1 probable and 1 and 1 shared damaged. P2569 was one of seven Hurricanes officially recorded as having been 'Lost in France – May 1940' with No 73 Sqn, its ultimate fate remaining unknown to this day – the Hurricane was probably abandoned due to unserviceability during the BEF's retreat to the Channel coast

11
Hurricane Mk I (serial unknown) of No 85 Sqn, flown by Flt Lt R H A Lee, Lille/Seclin, France, 6 December 1939

This early-build Mk I, with its wooden 'Watts prop', was the regular mount of No 85 Sqn's 'B' Flight commander, Flt Lt 'Dickie' Lee, during the 'Phoney War'. A Cranwell graduate who had flown with this unit since 1938, Lee had the honour of scoring No 85 Sqn's first kill of the conflict – He 111 Wk-Nr 1567 of Stab./KG 4, shot down during a recce mission off the Boulogne coast on 21 November 1939. Lee was awarded a DFC for the action, which was flown almost certainly in the fighter depicted in this profile. Like other French-based Hurricanes of the period, this machine is devoid of its serial, although it does wear No 85 Sqn's famous hexagonal marking on its tail (this version of the decoration – the base resting on a point, rather than a horizontal surface – signified aircraft of 'B' Flight) and a non-standard white airscrew tip. The hexagon appears to have been uniformly applied to all No 85 Sqn aircraft either immediately before the unit moved to France in September 1939, or soon after their arrival on the continent. 'VY-R' was inspected by His Majesty King George VI, the Duke of Gloucester and the Commander-in-Chief of the BEF, Viscount Lord Gort, at Lille/Seclin on 6 December 1939 as part of an Air Component 'show of force' which also included Hurricanes from No 87 Sqn, Gladiators from No 615 Sqn and Blenheim IVs from Nos 53 and 59 Sqns.

12
Hurricane Mk I P3854 of No 85 Sqn, flown by Sqn Ldr P W Townsend, Church Fenton, September 1940

This Hawker-built aircraft was issued to Peter Townsend upon his return to No 85 Sqn in mid-September 1940 following the healing of his wounded left foot, which had been struck by the nose cap of a cannon shell during an aerial engagement with Bf 109s and Bf 110s on 31 August over Tunbridge Wells. He had destroyed a Bf 109E, and claimed a second as a probable, prior to being shot down (in P3166) by a *Zerstörer*. Whilst convalescing in Croydon General Hospital, Townsend saw the survivors of his unit posted north to No 12 Group for a period of well-earned rest, No 85 Sqn having been one of the first outfits to receive a Class C classification by Air Chief-Marshal

Dowding, which earmarked it for immediate withdrawal from the frontline. The unit had effectively been left 'leaderless' through the wounding of its OC, the death of both flight commanders in action at the end of August and the loss of 'stand-in' OC, Flg Off Patrick Woods-Scawen, just 24 hours after Townsend himself had been injured. This aircraft wears the squadron's hexagon badge below the cockpit, the marking having been 'ousted' from its previous position on the fin by an RAF flash – the latter first started appearing on Fighter Command aircraft in the wake of an AMO issued on 1 May 1940. Initially sent to No 7 OTU upon its delivery to the RAF, P3854 flew with No 257 Sqn following its spell with No 85 Sqn. It was finally written off during a bombing raid on Sutton Bridge on 2 May 1941 whilst on the strength of No 56 OTU.

13

Hurricane Mk I P2923 of No 85 Sqn, flown by Flg Off A G Lewis, Castle Camps, June 1940

P2923 was one of more than a dozen Hurricanes delivered to No 85 Sqn in late May/early June to replace those left behind in France following the unit's hasty evacuation from Boulogne to Debden on 20 May – in the ten days of *Blitzkrieg*, the unit had lost twenty-four Hurricanes in action, bringing just three machines back from the continent. However, it had exacted a heavy toll on the Luftwaffe, its pilots being credited with 90 confirmed kills. One of its more successful members was South African Albert Lewis, whose seven-kill tally in France included five Bf 109Es downed on 19 May. Awarded a DFC for his exploits the following month, Lewis adopted P2923 soon after it arrived at Castle Camps on 11 June. Note the high and wavy demarcation line between the sky undersides and the camouflage upper surfaces forward of the wing leading edge, as well as the two grey stripes (in the same shade as the squadron codes) on the Rotol prop spinner. This fighter was lost on the afternoon of 18 August whilst being flown by fellow No 85 Sqn ace (and Lewis' close friend) 'Dickie' Lee – the latter was last seen by his OC, Peter Townsend, chasing a trio of Bf 109Es out to sea some ten miles off the Essex coast. No traces of either P2923 or Flt Lt Lee were ever found.

14

Hurricane Mk I L1630 of No 87 Sqn, flown by Plt Off W D David, Lille/Seclin, May 1940

Part of the original batch of 20 two-bladed Hurricane Is delivered to No 87 Sqn at Debden between July and September 1938 as replacements for the unit's Gladiator Is, this fabric-winged machine was sent to the continent (along with the rest of the squadron) just 24 hours after Britain declared war on Germany. Having survived eight months of relative inactivity in northern France, L1630 enjoyed ten days of near-constant fighting during the *Blitzkrieg* before finally being abandoned by No 87 Sqn (almost certainly at Merville) during the unit's retreat to the Channel coast. It was flown almost exclusively throughout this period by pre-war pilot Dennis David, who seemed to find the reduced performance of the fighter due to its original 'Watts prop' of little consequence in combat. Indeed, he was credited with 7 and 2 shared destroyed (plus an eighth solitary kill in 'two-blader' L1870), three unconfirmed and 2 damaged whilst

flying L1630 between 10 and 19 May. Like the Hurricane of No 85 Sqn's 'Dickie' Lee, this machine also participated in the Lille/Seclin inspection held on 6 December 1939, although photographs taken at the time indicate that it was then devoid of the squadron standard (a serpent) on its fin. Prior to the German invasion, the aircraft had had a crowned red lion on a yellow crest painted onto its starboard cockpit door, and as Plt Off David scored more victories, so small skulls (five in total) were added above the artwork. An enterprising No 87 Sqn rigger unhinged the door soon after L1630 was abandoned in France and brought it back to England with him for eventual presentation to the unit. Donated to the Air Historical Branch in the early 1960s following the disbandment of No 87 Sqn, the door went on display at the RAF Hendon Museum in the 1970s. In 1996 now Grp Capt Dennis David (retired) arranged for the historic relic to be exhibited on a long-term loan basis at the Shoreham Aircraft Museum in Kent.

15

Hurricane Mk I P2798 of No 87 Sqn, flown by Flt Lt I R Gleed, Exeter, August 1940

Yet another 'LK-A', and like L1630, this machine also exacted a heavy toll on the Luftwaffe in 1940 – it seems likely that No 87 Sqn had *two* identically coded Hurricanes on strength for at least 72 hours in mid-May 1940. Built by Gloster under licence at the end of March 1940, P2798 was issued to No 20 MU on 5 April for final airframe outfitting and flight testing, before being sent to No 87 Sqn at Lille/Seclin in mid-May as an attrition replacement – the unit had lost ten Hurricanes in the first six days of the *Blitzkrieg*. Its arrival in France coincided with the posting of experienced pre-war pilot Flt Lt 'Widge' Gleed to the embattled unit as a replacement for 'A' Flight commander, Canadian Flg Off J A Campbell. The latter had been shot down and killed by 2./JG 27 Bf 109Es over Maastricht whilst trying to defend No 2 Group Blenheim IVs sent to bomb the Dutch bridges spanning the Maas. Gleed made an immediate impression with P2798 (it remained devoid of its serial for much of 1940), which had been decorated with Disney's 'Figaro' on its starboard door' and had its prop spinner painted red – the latter signified a flight commander's aircraft – prior to his arrival. He downed two Bf 109Es on 18 May, followed by a further trio of kills (plus a shared victory and a probable) 24 hours later. Finally, just prior to the unit retreating to England, he shared in the destruction of a Ju 88. Gleed continued to use this machine throughout the Battle of Britain, claiming a further four kills, two probables and a damaged with it between 15 August and 30 September. P2798 remained his personal mount after he was promoted to command No 87 Sqn in December 1940, and it enjoyed further successes over France with Gleed in March and May 1941. He finally replaced P2798 with a Mk II in August 1941, although the veteran Hurricane remained with the unit until abandoned in flight by its pilot following an engine failure during a night sortie over Gloucestershire on 23 October 1941.

16

Hurricane Mk I P3394 of No 87 Sqn, flown by Plt Off J R Cock, Hullavington, 26 July 1940

One of five Hurricanes issued to No 87 Sqn at Church Fenton on 28 May 1940 as part of the unit's restoration to operational strength, P3394 was used by Australian Battle of France ace 'Johnny' Cock to score his sixth kill on the night of 26 July. In one of the first successful nocturnal interceptions performed by No 10 Group, Cock took off from Hullavington (a satellite field north of Bath used as a base from which to fly night patrols over Bristol) and headed for Bristol. He soon sighted a He 111H-4 of 1./KG 4 (which had just finished sowing mines in the Bristol Channel), and with the bomber coned in the glare of the city's searchlights, he proceeded to fire into the belly of the bomber. Cock succeeded in knocking out the Heinkel's starboard engine before he lost sight of his quarry, but the bomber had been mortally hit, and it crashed near Honiton. Of the five-man crew, only pilot Unteroffizier Georg Strickstrock survived;

'We were flying high, having dropped two magnetic mines near Barry Docks and were on our way home. I can remember a sudden thud and I lost power completely – the 'plane went out of control within a very short while. The only other thing I could remember was parachuting to earth.'

This was Cock's only success with P3394, although the fighter was later used by Flt Sgt I J Badger (3 destroyed, 4 probables and 6 damaged) to score a probable kill against a Ju 88 and damage a Bf 109E during a fierce battle off Portland on 25 August. Having survived the Battle of Britain, the Hurricane was eventually issued to the Merchant Ship Fighter Unit, before ending up with No 59 OTU. On 8 September 1943 P3394 was finally lost when it suffered engine failure whilst in flight off the Northumberland coast.

17

Hurricane Mk I L2001 of No 111 Sqn, flown by Flg Off H M Ferriss, Wick, February 1940

Originally built in early 1938 and delivered to No 56 Sqn at North Weald in May of the same year, this aircraft had its wooden propeller replaced with a de Havilland variable pitch 'three-blader' sometime in 1939. The fighter was then issued to No 111 Sqn, who used it throughout the winter months of 1939-40 to patrol the Scottish coast in defence of naval installations at Scapa Flow. L2001 was regularly flown during this period by future ace Henry Ferriss, who scored his first kills off the Orkneys in early April 1940. In mid-May the unit was split by flights at Northolt and despatched to France, 'A' Flight forming a composite unit with 'B' Flight of No 253 Sqn at Lille/Marcq, whilst 'B' Flight joined forces with No 253 Sqn's 'A' Flight at Vitry. Ferriss, who was part of No 111 Sqn's 'A' Flight, was quickly thrust into action, being credited with the destruction of four Messerschmitt fighters on the 18th. The following day he was set upon by a formation of Bf 110s whilst flying L2001, and although the Merlin engine in his fighter was 'running rough', Ferriss not only succeeded in out-manoeuvring his attackers, but he also reported damaging one of the Messerschmitts prior to escaping. No 111 Sqn pulled out of France on 21 May, but returned to patrolling French skies some ten days later when the unit commenced flying over the Dunkirk beaches as part of Operation Dynamo – Ferriss scored a further three kills during this period, but none were achieved with L2001. Having survived the chaos and carnage of both the Blitzkrieg and the Dunkirk evacuation, this pre-war veteran was lost on 19 June 1940 when its engine inexplicably cut soon after taking off on a routine training sortie from Hatfield. Unable to stop the fighter from stalling, its pilot, a Sgt Pascoe, was killed when L2001 dived into the ground.

18

Hurricane Mk I P3221 of No 145 Sqn, flown by Flt Lt A H Boyd, Westhampnett, August 1940

Equipped with what is believed to be one of the first 'blown' canopies fitted to a Hurricane serving in the frontline, this Gloster-built Mk I was modified at squadron level sometime after being issued to No 145 Sqn on 22 July 1940. Where the 'blistered' hood was manufactured remains a mystery, and although there appears to be no official report as to how effective the modification was, the exploits of P3221's regular pilot, 'B' Flight commander Adrian 'Ginger' Boyd, speak for themselves – five aircraft confirmed destroyed and a sixth damaged on 8 August, a further damaged claim on 26/27 August, a shared kill on 12 October and yet another victory three days later. Although it cannot be confirmed if Boyd used this machine on any of these sorties, it appears that he valued the improved visibility offered by the new canopy so much that he had a new one fabricated and fitted to P3321 after the original (on P3736) was damaged by stray rounds fired by an over-eager Spitfire pilot during an engagement off the Isle of Wight on 12 August. No 145 Sqn lost 26 Hurricanes in 18 days of combat during the Battle of Britain, but P3321 survived with the unit until the latter received Spitfire IIAs in February 1941. Even then it refused to be relegated to second-line duties, being issued to No 1 (RCAF) Sqn (re-numbered No 401 Sqn in March 1941) at Digby, where the fighter wore the codes 'YO-Q' and was fitted with a conventional framed canopy. With the arrival of Hurricane IIAs in May, this battle-weary veteran was finally 'retired' into Training Command, being sent to No 56 OTU – it lasted just days in its new role, however, as it was written off in a crash on the 15th of the month.

19

Hurricane Mk I P3039 of No 229 Sqn, flown by Plt Off V M M Ortmans, Northolt, September/October 1940

On 12 July 1940 four brand new Gloster-built Hurricane Is were delivered to No 229 Sqn at Wittering, three of which had consecutive serials – P3037, P3038 and P3039. Of this latter trio, only P3039 would survive the Battle of Britain, enjoying some success with Belgian pilot 'Vicky' Ortmans at the controls. Like several other Belgian aces, London-born Ortmans had escaped to Britain, via Gibraltar, following the withdrawal of his unit (Fairey Fox-equipped 7/III/3) from Belgium into France on 18 May 1940. Commissioned as a pilot officer in the RAF within weeks of his arrival, Ortmans was sent firstly to No 7 OTU at Hawarden in July and then to No 229 Sqn at the completion of his conversion on to the Hurricane in early August. Initially flying from the No 12 Group fighter station at Wittering, Ortmans started his career as a fighter pilot rather inauspiciously when his Hurricane was hit by return fire from a Do 17 on 30 August, forcing him to hastily crash-land. However, he soon exacted his revenge, and by the end of October had claimed 2 and 1 shared destroyed, 1 probable and 1 and 1 shared damaged.

Of these successes, one victory (a He 111 on 27/9) and one and one shared damaged (a Ju 88 on 18/10 and a He 111 on 27/9 respectively) were scored whilst flying his personally-marked P3039. Ortmans finished the war with a score of 5 and 2 shared destroyed, 1 probable, 5 and 2 shared damaged (plus 2 destroyed and 1 probable unconfirmed), whilst his aircraft was eventually passed on to No 312 'Czech' Sqn in November 1940. It remained on strength until the unit re-equipped with Mk IIs in the spring of 1941, after which it was relegated to training duties firstly with No 56 OTU, and then No 55. P3039 was finally written off whilst flying with the latter unit when it spun into the ground near Edderside, in Cumberland, on 27 May 1943.

20

Hurricane Mk I P3462 of No 238 Sqn, flown by Plt Off C T Davis, Middle Wallop, September 1940

Initially issued with Spitfires upon its reformation at Tangmere in May 1940, No 238 Sqn switched to Hurricanes the following month. Amongst the first Hawker fighters to wear the unit's 'VK' codes was this recently-built aircraft, which arrived on 12 June. The unit then moved north-west to the still incomplete No 10 Group sector station at Middle Wallop. At about this time Welshman Charles Davis joined No 238 Sqn, the young 'Cranwellian' having had his course drastically shortened in order to hasten his arrival in the frontline. This truncating of his training seemed to have no adverse effects on the 20-year-old pilot, who proceeded to score 4 and 6 shared destroyed, 1 probable and 1 and 1 shared damaged between 13 July and 21 September. During this period Davis twice returned to base with battle-damaged aircraft, the second time (15 September) whilst at the controls of P3462 – he claimed a He 111 probable south of London on this date. Both Davis and P3462 survived the Battle of Britain, although the former was killed on 26 March 1941 when he flew into a hill in cloud near Winchester whilst still serving with No 238 Sqn. P3462 saw further flying with No 43 Sqn, Nos 55 and 59 OTUs and No 5 (Pilots) Advanced Flying Unit, before finally being Struck off Charge on 23 September 1944.

21

Hurricane Mk I V7467 of No 242 Sqn, flown by Sqn Ldr D R S Bader, Coltishall, September 1940

Despite seeing much action at the head of firstly No 242 Sqn and then the Duxford 'Big Wing', the charismatic Douglas Bader used only three Hurricanes throughout the Battle of Britain. P3061 was his first mount, which had arrived at No 242 Sqn's Coltishall base at about the same time as Bader. He proceeded to destroy six aircraft with this Hurricane before it was severely damaged during the first 'Big Wing' operation on 7 September. Bader then flew an anonymous Mk I for just a few days, claiming one kill and two damaged with it on 9 September, before finally settling on recently-delivered V7467 (issued to the unit on 11/9). The latter fighter was swiftly adorned with his rank pennant and the unofficial No 242 Sqn motif below the exhaust stubs. Bader continued his scoring run with the new Hurricane, claiming a further 4 destroyed, 1 probable and 2 damaged by the end of September. Following his 'purple patch' in September, no further claims were made by Bader with the Hawker fighter,

although he continued to fly V7467 until he left No 242 Sqn in March 1941. Always maintained in immaculate condition, this machine was passed on to No 111 Sqn soon after Bader's departure, who in turn handed the fighter over to No 59 OTU. It was whilst flying in the training role that V7467 was lost near Dumfries on 1 September 1941.

22

Hurricane Mk I P2961 of No 242 Sqn, flown by Flg Off W L McKnight, Coltishall, December 1940

Despite being issued to No 242 Sqn on 2 June 1940, and fighting with the unit both in France in support of the Brittany evacuation and during the entire Battle of Britain campaign, P2961 seems to have had a rather unremarkable summer and autumn. Its pilot by December was leading Canadian ace 'Willie' McKnight, who had scored 17 and 2 shared destroyed and 3 unconfirmed destroyed since May – squadron records fail to indicate whether he scored any of these kills in this aircraft. Like other No 242 Sqn machines, it wore the 'booted Hitler' motif on its nose, as well as an anatomically impressive half skeleton and sickle artwork on both sides of the fuselage. Having studied medicine in Canada prior to joining the RAF in 1939, McKnight used his knowledge of human biology to advise the 'squadron artist' during the application of his personal marking. Aside from the individual motifs, P2961 also wears the very latest Fighter Command scheme introduced on 27 November 1940 – standard brown/green camouflage, sky undersides, propeller spinner and fuselage 'fighter band', and an all-black port wing (washable paint used for ease of removal). McKnight was killed on 12 January 1941 when P2961 was bounced by Bf 109Es near Calais during one of the first low-level 'Rhubarb' sorties (known at the time as 'Mosquito" raids) flown by the RAF – fellow No 242 Sqn ace, Canadian Plt Off J B Latta (7 and 1 shared destroyed), was also killed performing a 'Rhubarb' on this day.

23

Hurricane Mk I W9145 of No 245 Sqn, flown by Sqn Ldr J W C Simpson, Aldergrove, December 1940

A veteran of combat off northern Scotland and the French coast, John Simpson had 'made ace' by 7 June 1940 whilst serving as a flight commander with No 43 Sqn. His run of success finally came to an end on 19 July when he baled out of his blazing fighter (P3140) off Selsey Bill after being attacked by a Bf 109E from III./JG 27. Already wounded in the ankle by a machine gun round, Simpson suffered a broken collar-bone in a particularly heavy landing which involved the roof of a house, a garden fence and a cucumber frame! The injuries he sustained kept him off flying until the autumn. He added a further probable to his tally with No 43 Sqn on 30 November, and was then promptly posted to Northern Ireland to take command of No 245 Sqn. Once at Aldergrove he chose Gloster-built W9145 as his personal mount, having his jester marking and scoreboard painted onto the aircraft's cockpit door. Although Simpson scored a further three kills whilst with No 245 Sqn, these were all claimed using W9200. After serving in Northern Ireland, W9145 was passed firstly to No 5 FTS, then back into the frontline with No 87 Sqn, before being issued to No 1449 Flt. From there it went to No 318 Sqn, who in turn passed it to No 59 OTU, where it was written off in an aerial collision with Canadian Car & Foundry-built Mk I T9532 near Dunbar on 6 September 1943.

24

Hurricane Mk I P3870 of No 249 Sqn, flown by Plt Off R G A Barclay, Church Fenton, July 1940

'Cranwellian' George Barclay was one of three pilots sent to No 249 Sqn on 23 June 1940, having volunteered to move from the School of Army Co-operation to Fighter Command earlier that same month. His 'lightning' conversion course at No 5 OTU had seen him make the transition from flying a Lysander to a Spitfires after just ten hours of 'stick time'. However, Barclay's rapid mastery of the RAF's premier fighter proved to be of minimal value, for when he arrived at his new posting, he found that the unit was equipped with Hurricanes – a type that he had *never* flown! Fortunately for him, No 249 Sqn was still in the process of completing their operational flying training (the unit had only be reformed on 16 May), and Barclay was able to familiarise himself with the Hawker fighter whilst performing his duties as part of 'A' Flight. His mount for much of this time was P3870, which had arrived at the unit's Church Fenton base on 13 July. This machine would subsequently fight throughout the Battle of Britain, firstly with No 249 Sqn (although Barclay scored no kills with it) and then No 56 Sqn – it suffered a forced landing at Warmwell whilst serving with the latter unit after being hit by return fire from a 'Do 215' (almost certainly a He 111 of KG 55) over Portland on 30 September. Quickly repaired, P3870 remained with No 56 Sqn until 2 December 1940 when it was placed in storage, before eventually being transferred to the FAA in April 1941 for conversion by General Aircraft Ltd into a Sea Hurricane Mk IA.

25

Hurricane Mk I V6555 of No 257 Sqn, flown by Sqn Ldr R R S Tuck, North Weald, October 1940

Another Battle of Britain veteran that ended its days as a Sea Hurricane Mk IA, V6555 was flown by no less an ace than Bob Tuck, who 'acquired' the aircraft soon after he arrived at Martlesham Heath to take charge of No 257 Sqn. In order to raise the morale of his new command, he had his groundcrew decorate the fighter (which had arrived on the squadron just days before Tuck) with a scoreboard denoting his combat successes, and this was fastidiously kept up to date as Tuck claimed a further four kills by the end of the Battle. He also had a cigar chewing, stick waving, Churchill caricature added to the port side of the fuselage beneath the ever increasing row of swastikas. This aircraft suffered minor battle damage in October 1940, and was eventually replaced (possibly by V6962) later that same month. V6555 then saw brief use with No 73 Sqn, before being passed to the FAA in February 1942 after a long spell in storage.

26

Hurricane Mk I (Trop) P3731 of No 261 Sqn, flown by Sgt F N Robertson, Luqa, Malta, December 1940

This aircraft was amongst the first batch of 12 Hurricanes flown to Malta from the carrier HMS *Argus* as part of Operation *Hurry* on 2 August 1940. Initially part of No 418 Flt, P3731 became a No 261 Sqn machine when the former

unit was redesignated on 16 August. During its lengthy spell on the island, the Hurricane was regularly flown by ex-Spitfire pilot Fred Robertson, who had also been sent to Malta as part of *Hurry* – his arrival on the island had been a less than auspicious one, however, as he had crashed his valuable fighter (N2700) on approach to Luqa when it ran out of fuel. Despite this chequered start, Robertson soon proved his worth as a fighter pilot, claiming 10 destroyed, 3 probables and 7 damaged between 20 August 1940 and 23 March 1941 – he had earlier scored 1 and 1 shared whilst flying with No 66 Sqn over the Channel. Robertson enjoyed success with P3731 on two occasions, downing a 30° *Gruppo* SM 79 at night on 18/19 December, followed by a CR 42 (plus a second as a probable) from 23° *Gruppo CT* on 19 January 1941. Malta's top scorer for the first year of the war, Robertson was duly awarded a DFM and finally sent back to England in April 1941. He returned to operations flying nightfighters in 1942, but was killed in a mid-air collision on 31 August 1943 without having added to his tally. P3731 left Malta soon after Robertson, being passed to newly-formed No 127 Sqn, who duly took it into action against Vichy French forces over Syria in June/July 1941. Having previously fought the Italians and the Germans with some degree of success, P3731 was finally shot down by a Dewoitine D.520 over Deir-es-Zor (on the banks of the Euphrates River) on 3 July 1941.

27

Hurricane Mk I (Trop) V7474 of No 261 Sqn, flown by Flt Lt J A F MacLachlan and Sgt F N Robertson, Ta Kali, Malta, November 1940

With few fighters on Malta during the final months of 1940, it was inevitable that the same Hurricanes would frequently appear in the log books of No 261 Sqn's future aces, V7474 being one such machine – see page 113 for further details.

28

Hurricane Mk I (Trop) P2544 of No 274 Sqn, possibly flown by Flg Off E M Mason, Amiriya, Egypt, November 1940

P2544 was one of the first Mk Is delivered to No 274 Sqn in the autumn of 1940, and like most other 'tropicalised' Hurricanes sent to Malta or North Africa at around this time, it was camouflaged in dark earth and middle stone upper surfaces and azure blue undersides. When photographed at Amiriya soon after its delivery, the aircraft was adorned with No 274 Sqn's 'YK' code only, although at some point later in its career the letter 'T' was added to complete the unit markings. Passed to No 71 OTU in the spring of 1941, P2544 was so badly damaged in a forced landing at Ismailia following an engine failure on 6 June 1941 that it served out the rest of its RAF career as an instructional airframe.

29

Hurricane Mk I P3931 of No 302 'Polish' Sqn, flown by Flg Off W S Król, Northolt, 15 October 1940

An experienced pilot who had scored kills (2 and 1 shared destroyed and 1 probable) with both his native Polish Air Force in September 1939 and then the French *Armée de l'Air* (3 shared kills according to French records) between April and June 1940, Król made his way to England, via North Africa, in July. He joined No 302 'Polish' Sqn the following month, and went into action with the unit towards the end of the Battle of Britain. Król's solitary kill during this period was scored in P3931 over Hawkinge, the Pole being credited with the destruction of a Bf 109E. This aircraft was written off just three days later when it was one of five No 302 Sqn Hurricanes that crashed on, or around, Kempton Park racecourse after their pilots became lost in foggy weather whilst attempting to return to Northolt at the end of an uneventful patrol. Four of the men were killed in this tragic accident, including P3931's pilot, Englishman Plt Off P E G Carter, who attempted to bale out at just 50 ft. Unlike his aircraft, Król survived the Battle, and went on to score a further 5 and 1 shared kills, flying firstly Hurricane Mk IIs, then Spitfire Mk Vs and IXs. He ended the war as Wing Leader of the Coltishall Wing.

30

Hurricane Mk I P3975 of No 303 'Polish' Sqn, flown by Sgt J Frantisek, Northolt, September 1940

One of the last Hurricanes built by Hawkers as part of their third production batch of Mk Is, this machine enjoyed great success with No 303 Sqn following its move from No 257 Sqn to the Polish-manned unit on 10 August. The first two kills credited to the aircraft (both Bf 109Es) on 2 and 3 September also happened to be Sgt Josef Frantisek's first victories of the campaign – by the end of the month the Czech pilot's score would stand at 17 destroyed and 1 probable. Four days after Frantisek achieved his second kill with P3975, future Polish ace Plt Off Witold 'Tolo' Lokuciewski (9 and 1 shared destroyed and 3 damaged) claimed a Do 17Z destroyed and a second bomber as a probable whilst flying this aircraft over Essex. Frantisek was at the controls of P3975 once again on 9 September when he used it to down a 7./JG 27 Bf 109E-4 (Wk-Nr 1617) over Horsham and a He 111H-2 (Wk-Nr 5548) from III./KG 53 over Beachy Head. However, within minutes of attaining his seventh kill, the Czech was forced to crash land P3975 after being shot up by a second *Emil*. The Hurricane was back in the air just eight days later, however, Sgt Miroslaw Wojciechowski (4 and 1 shared destroyed) destroying a 9./JG 53 Bf 109E-1 (Wk-Nr 3177) with it over the Thames. Having survived countless combat sorties in 1940, P3975 was eventually passed to the FAA in March 1941.

31

Hurricane Mk I R4175 of No 303 'Polish' Sqn, flown by Sgt J Frantisek, Northolt, September 1940

As Josef Frantisek was only a sergeant pilot, he was not considered to be senior enough to have his own assigned Hurricane. However, he seems to have had a definite affinity with this Gloster-built Mk I, which eventually resulted in their joint demise in an unexplained crash in Surrey at the end of a routine patrol on the morning of 8 October 1940. Prior to his death, Frantisek had scored no less than seven kills with R4175 – a Bf 109E and a Ju 88 on 6 September, another Bf 109E 24 hours later, two He 111s on the 26th of the month, and finally a Bf 110 and a He 111 the following day. Struck by enemy fire on two occasions during the deadly aerial battles of early September, the Hurricane returning to Northolt on consecutive days (6th and 7th) with damage inflicted in pursuing Bf 109Es over East Kent.

32

Hurricane Mk I P3901 of No 303 'Polish' Sqn, flown by Flg Off W Urbanowicz, Northolt, September 1940

It is unlikely that any single Hurricane serving with No 303 Sqn in the latter half of 1940 was flown by more current, or future, aces than P3901. Some nine pilots who achieved five or more kills flew combat patrols in this aircraft, with Flg Off Witold Urbanowicz and Sgt Stanislaw Karubin actually downing German aircraft with it. The former pilot destroyed a He 111 on 26 September, followed by a Bf 109E and a Bf 110C (from 15./LG 1) the next morning and two Ju 88As (from 5./KG 77) that same afternoon. The final day of September saw Urbanowicz claim a pair of Bf 109E-1s (from II./JG 53 and 4./JG 54) over Bexhill, P3901 enjoying further success five days later when yet another *Emil* (from 1./JG 3) fell to its guns near Rochester, the aircraft being flown on this occasion by Stanislaw Karubin (7 kills – this was his last victory). P3901 had seen brief service with No 615 Sqn prior to being issued to No 303 Sqn in mid-September, the fighter then remaining with the Poles until 3 January 1941, when it was left behind at Leconfield for the newly-arrived No 253 Sqn – the latter unit had been relieved by No 303 Sqn within No 11 Group. Eventually passed to No 55 OTU, P3901 was lost on 28 April 1943 when it flew into a hill in Cumberland.

33

Hurricane Mk I P3120 of No 303 'Polish' Sqn, flown by Flg Off Z K Henneberg, Northolt, September 1940

This aircraft was one of several No 303 Sqn Hurricanes to be adorned with a non-standard red fuselage band just forward of the tail during September/October 1940. It is believed that this marking was used by the unit to denote aircraft flown by the senior squadron and flight commanders, such a practice having been employed by Polish Air Force units during the 1930s. As a 'marked' aircraft, P3120 (an ex-No 302 Sqn machine) was flown by senior men of the calibre of Sqn Ldr Ronald Kellett, Flt Lts 'Johnny' Kent and Zdzislaw Henneberg, and Flg Offs Wojciech Januszewicz and Witold Urbanowicz. Indeed, two of its three recorded kills were achieved by 'A' Flight commander Henneberg (8 and 1 shared destroyed, 1 probable and 1 damaged), who claimed a Do 17Z and a Bf109E on 15 September south of London. It tasted further success 11 days later when Plt Off Bohdan Grzeszczak used it to down a He 111 over Portsmouth, but the Luftwaffe's bomber force got its revenge on 6 October when a lone Ju 88 attacked Northolt airfield and destroyed P3120 with two well placed bombs. The aircraft was being taxied back to its dispersal point at the time by Sgt Antoni Siudak (2 and 2 shared destroyed), who was killed instantly by the exploding ordnance.

34

Hurricane Mk I V6665 of No 303 'Polish' Sqn, flown by Flt Lt J A Kent, Northolt, September 1940

This aircraft was one of five Hurricanes delivered to No 303 Sqn on 7 September as attrition replacements to make good the unit's early losses during their first week of sustained combat. Soon after its arrival, V6665 received a red tail stripe to signify its allocation to flight commander, Canadian 'Johnny' Kent. The latter was flying the aircraft on 9 September when he downed his first kill, Bf 110C Wk-Nr

3108 from III./ZG 76, which had been preceded just minutes earlier by a probable victory over a Ju 88. V6665 tasted success again on 26 September when Sgt Tadeusz Andruszko destroyed a He 111 near Portsmouth. However, barely 24 hours later the same pilot/aircraft combination was downed by Bf 109Es whilst attempting to intercept a bombing raid over Kent, Andruszko being killed in this action.

35
Hurricane Mk I P3700 of No 303 'Polish' Sqn, flown by Plt Off M Feric, Northolt, September 1940

This ex-No 238 Sqn machine was shot down by Bf 109Es over Beachy Head on the afternoon of 9 September, its pilot, Flt Sgt K Wünsche (4 and 3 shared destroyed and 1 probable), baling out with slight burns. Having been on the squadron since 8 August, P3700 was flown by at least three aces (Zumbach, Henneberg and Feric) during its short spell at Northolt, with 'Ox' Feric actually using it to shoot down a Bf 109E over Sevenoaks on 6 September. A number of No 303 Sqn aircraft wore the distinctive unit badge featured on 'RF-E', which was comprised of US 'stars and stripes' with a Polish peasant's hat and scythes superimposed over the top. Originally devised in 1920 by an American volunteer unit that had participated in the Polish-Bolshevik war of that year, the badge was far more prevalent on No 303 Sqn Hurricanes in 1940 than the Polish Air Force insignia.

36
Hurricane Mk I V7503 of No 303 'Polish' Sqn, flown by Flg Off M Pisarek, Leconfield, November 1940

Yet another aircraft passed to No 253 Sqn in the first week of January 1941 at Leconfield, this Hawker-built fighter had been delivered fresh from the factory to Northolt on 27 September. Flown by Marian Pisarek (11 and 1 shared destroyed, 1 probable and 1 damaged), the fighter helped its pilot gain ace status on 7 October when he downed a Bf 109E over south London. He had also used V7503 to score his fourth kill (a Bf 110) 48 hours earlier, Pisarek claiming a second Zerstörer damaged in the same engagement over Rochester. It was one of the first Polish aircraft at Leconfield to receive a sky spinner and fighter band in late November following the Air Ministry edict issued on the 27th of that month, although for some reason it seems to have missed out on having its port wing repainted black as per the same instruction. V7503 was eventually issued to the FAA in February 1942 for conversion into a Sea Hurricane.

37
Hurricane Mk I L1926 of No 312 'Czech' Sqn, flown by Plt Off A Vasatko, Speke, October 1940

One of the oldest Mk Is still in frontline service by the autumn of 1940, fabric-winged L1926 had originally been issued to No 3 Sqn at Kenley as long ago as April 1939. Part of the first batch of nine Hurricanes (all elderly L-prefixed aircraft) delivered to the newly-formed No 312 Sqn at Duxford on the last day of August 1940, this aircraft was used by Czech Armée de l'Air veteran Alois Vasatko (4 and 10 shared destroyed, 2 and 2 shared probables and 1 damaged) to score his sole kill of the Battle of Britain. Having been credited with 3 and 9 shared victories flying Curtiss H-75As with GCI/5, Vastako's first score with the RAF was also a shared claim split between the three pilots of 'Yellow' Section (one of whom was ex-No 616 Sqn Spitfire I ace, Flt Lt D E Gillam). Their victim was 2./KGr 806 Ju 88A-1 Wk-Nr 4068, which was shot down whilst attempting to bomb Liverpool docks. Promoted to command the Exeter Wing by mid-1942, Vasatko was killed on 23 June that same year when his Spitfire Mk VB collided with a Fw 190 over the West Country. L1926 had its operational status reduced to that of a maintenance airframe following a landing accident on 15 April 1941 whilst serving with No 55 OTU.

38
Hurricane Mk I P3059 of No 501 Sqn, flown by Plt Off K N T Lee, Gravesend, 18 August 1940

This aircraft was the last of four No 501 Sqn Mk Is shot down in just two minutes over Canterbury on the afternoon of 18 August by the Staffelkapitan of 9./JG 26, Oberleutnant Gerhard Schöpfel. This haul brought the experten's tally to 12, and he would ultimately survive the war with a score of 40 kills. His description of the action was as follows;

'Suddenly I noticed a Staffel of Hurricanes underneath me. They were using the English tactics of the period, flying in close formation of threes, climbing in a wide spiral.'

Having despatched both the 'weavers' (one of whom was future 14-kill ace Sgt D A S McKay) above the RAF formation and then the rearmost aircraft in the trailing 'vic', he lined up his fourth victim in his reflector sight – P3059, flown by Battle of France ace, 'Hawkeye' Lee;

'The Englishmen continued on, having noticed nothing. So I pulled in behind the fourth machine and took care of him also.'

Wounded in the leg, and with his Hurricane on fire, Lee rolled the stricken fighter onto its back and baled out at 17,000 ft. Due to the rarefied height of his egress (and fully aware of reports of German pilots shooting at men in parachutes), Lee chose to free-fall down to 6000 ft before finally deploying his parachute.

39
Hurricane Mk I V6799 of No 501 Sqn, flown by Plt Off K W Mackenzie, Gravesend, 18 August 1940

One of the RAF's most successful Hurricane pilots in the autumn of 1940, Ken Mackenzie scored 8 and 3 shared destroyed and 2 and 1 damaged in October/November with No 501 Sqn following his move to the unit from No 43 Sqn on 28 September – he had been with the latter outfit for just a week. V6799 arrived at Kenley 24 hours after Mackenzie, the Irishman using the fighter to destroy a Bf 109E on 5 October, followed by a shared and a solitary kill over two Emils two days later. The second of these victories was only achieved after he had rammed the port tailplane of the Bf 109E with his starboard wing tip at low altitude over the Channel following the exhaustion of his ammunition. Having seen his quarry plunge into the water, Mackenzie fled back towards the English coast, but was bounced by two more Emils. With his aircraft shot up, and missing a 4-ft chunk of its wingtip, Mackenzie somehow managed to pull off a forced landing in a field near Folkestone without causing too much further damage to V6799. Once repaired, the fighter spent the rest of its career with secondline training units until it was struck off charge in November 1944.

40

Hurricane Mk I (serial unknown) of No 601 Sqn, flown by Flg Off W H Rhodes-Moorhouse, Tangmere, July 1940

When featured in a sequence of photographs taken by Charles E Brown during a visit to No 601 Sqn at Tangmere in early July 1940, this aircraft had only the L-prefix of its serial visible on its rear fuselage. The elderly fighter also lacked roundels with yellow surrounds, fin stripes, sky only undersides and larger codes (as ordered by the Air Ministry on 6 June 1940). The Hurricane was in the throes of being prepared for a flight by 'Willie' Rhodes-Moorhouse when 'shot' by Brown, the pre-war pilot going on to score 5 and 4 shared destroyed and 4 probables before being killed in action over Tunbridge Wells on 6 September.

41

Hurricane Mk I P3308 of No 605 Sqn, flown by Acting Sqn Ldr A A McKellar, Croydon, October 1940

Despite being only 5 ft 3 in tall and of slight stature, 'Archie' McKellar was nevertheless a fearless pilot who had been credited with 17 and 3 shared destroyed (including five Bf 109Es in a day on 7 October), 5 probables and 3 damaged by the time of his death in combat on 1 November 1940. No fewer than 13.5 kills, 4 probables and 1 damaged were claimed by the Scot in this very aircraft between 15 August and 7 October – note his personal marking beneath the cockpit. Issued to No 605 Sqn on 11 June 1940, this aircraft had been slightly damaged on 15 August when McKellar took part in the interception of *Luflotte 5*'s attempted raid on airfields within No 13 Group. Once repaired, it remained with the unit until passed to No 312 Sqn on 4 January 1941, the Czechs' in turn sending P3308 to No 55 OTU by the spring. Boasting the highest tally of kills scored by any Hurricane during the Battle of Britain period, P3308 was written off in a landing accident in County Durham on 30 April 1941.

42

Hurricane Mk I R4194 of No 615 Sqn, flown by Flg Off A Eyre, Kenley, August 1940

Another successful Hurricane, Gloster-built R4194 was used by pre-war No 615 Sqn pilot Tony Eyre to claim 4 kills, 2 probables and 1 damaged between 20 and 28 August, thus taking his final tally to 8 and 2 shared destroyed, 2 unconfirmed destroyed, 2 probables and 6 damaged. He failed to add to his score before being shot down and captured whilst leading the North Weald Wing in March 1942. R4194's entire frontline career was spent with No 615 Sqn, the aircraft surviving for four months with the unit during the summer/autumn of 1940, before being passed on to No 9 FTS on 7 December. It was struck off charge just over a year later on 22 December 1941.

FIGURE PLATES

1

No 274 Sqn's black-bearded Flg Off Ernest 'Imshi' Mason is seen in his weathered pre-war white flying overall, the latter complete with a No 80 Sqn patch (his previous unit) sewn onto its left breast pocket. Beneath his overall he is wearing a ribbed off-white roll-neck sweater, and on his head is a Type B flying helmet. Attached to his head-gear is a Type D oxygen mask, whilst Mason's goggles are pre-war Mk IIs. His unpainted life jacket is a 1932 Pattern issue, whilst on his feet he is wearing virtually 'suedeless' desert shoes.

2

The unmistakable figure of No 242 Sqn's Sqn Ldr Douglas Bader in September 1940. He is wearing a spotless 1930 Pattern Sidcot flying suit over similarly impeccable officer's Battle Dress. Bader's steel-capped shoes have also been vigorously polished, and only the addition of a blue and white spotted silk scarf (worn to prevent the pilot from suffering a chafed neck whilst continually scanning the skies during combat) adds a personal touch to the charismatic squadron leader's flying clothing.

3

Canadian Flg Off V C 'Woody' Woodward, depicted here as he appeared in December 1940 whilst serving with No 33 Sqn in Egypt, is wearing an RAF pattern khaki drill shirt and shorts, with matching stockings. His shoes are of the suede desert type, whilst his head-gear comprises a Type B helmet, Type D oxygen mask and Mk II goggles. Woodward is depicted in the process of strapping on his 'seat type' parachute.

4

Flg Off E J 'Cobber' Kain of No 73 Sqn is clothed in standard RAF officer's service dress (note the ribbon for his DFC beneath his wings and the lack of a waist belt), but the tall Kiwi ace had dispensed with his bright pale blue shirt in favour of a white sweater in an attempt to protect his neck – the colour of the sweater matched his thick white socks, worn beneath his 1936 Pattern flying boots. A rather laid back character, Kain often wore two tunic buttons undone in order to expose his lucky charm – a green jade tiki (a Maori god) – which was affixed to a chain around his neck, along with his service identity discs. He is carrying a helmet and gas respirator case over his right shoulder.

5

No 501 Sqn's Sgt J H 'Ginger' Lacey is seen holding his bulky 'seat type' parachute and gauntlet-style flying gloves between sorties at Bétheniville, in France, in mid-May 1940. Wearing airman's service dress, again with the top button on his tunic undone, Lacey has retained the standard shirt and tie as befits an NCO. His boots are also 1936 Pattern, and note the R/T lead and plug and oxygen tube draped over his right shoulder.

6

Flg Off Zdzislaw Henneberg, 'A' Flight commander of No 303 'Polish' Sqn in September 1940, is wearing the grey Battle Dress adopted by Polish pilots whilst serving with the RAF. Similar in cut to the RAF Battle Dress, the uniform was finished off with standard British flying equipment like the 1938 Pattern Irvin flying jacket, 1932 Pattern life jacket, leather flying gloves and Type B helmet. Finally, Henneberg is wearing steel-capped lace-up shoes again of standard RAF regulation issue

INDEX

References to illustrations are shown in **bold**. Colour Plates are prefixed 'pl.' and Figure Plates 'fig.pl.', with page and caption locators in brackets.